Fellow Creatures

Christine M. Korsgaard presents a compelling new view of humans' moral relationships to the other animals. She defends the claim that we are obligated to treat all sentient beings as what Kant called "ends-in-themselves." Drawing on a theory of the good derived from Aristotle, she offers an explanation of why animals are the sorts of beings for whom things can be good or bad. She then turns to Kant's argument for the value of humanity to show that rationality commits us to claiming the standing of ends-in-ourselves, in two senses. Kant argued that as autonomous beings, we claim to be ends-in-ourselves when we claim the standing to make laws for ourselves and each other. Korsgaard argues that as beings who have a good, we also claim to be ends-in-ourselves when we take the things that are good for us to be good absolutely and so worthy of pursuit. The first claim commits us to joining with other autonomous beings in relations of moral reciprocity. The second claim commits us to treating the good of every sentient creature as something of absolute importance.

Korsgaard argues that human beings are not more important than the other animals, that our moral nature does not make us superior to the other animals, and that our unique capacities do not make us better off than the other animals. She criticizes the "marginal cases" argument and advances a new view of moral standing as attaching to the atemporal subjects of lives. She criticizes Kant's own view that our duties to animals are indirect, and offers a non-utilitarian account of the relation between pleasure and the good. She also addresses a number of directly practical questions: whether we have the right to eat animals, experiment on them, make them work for us and fight in our wars, and keep them as pets; and how to understand the wrong that we do when we cause a species to go extinct.

Christine M. Korsgaard is Arthur Kingsley Porter Professor of Philosophy at Harvard University, where she has taught since 1991. She is a fellow of the American Academy of Arts and Sciences, and a Corresponding Fellow of the British Academy. Before coming to teach at Harvard she held positions at Yale University, the University of California at Santa Barbara, and the University of Chicago, and visiting positions at Berkeley and UCLA. She is the author of *The Sources of Normativity* (Cambridge University Press, 1996), *Creating the Kingdom of Ends* (Cambridge University Press, 1996), *The Constitution of Agency: Essays on Practical Reason and Moral Psychology* (Oxford University Press, 2008), and *Self-Constitution: Agency, Identity, and Integrity* (Oxford University Press, 2009).

UEHIRO SERIES IN PRACTICAL ETHICS

General Editor: Julian Savulescu, University of Oxford

Fellow Creatures

Our Obligations to the Other Animals

Christine M. Korsgaard

OXFORD

UNIVERSITY PRESS

OXFORD
UNIVERSITY PRESS

Great Clarendon Street, Oxford, OX2 6DP,
United Kingdom

Oxford University Press is a department of the University of Oxford.
It furthers the University's objective of excellence in research, scholarship,
and education by publishing worldwide. Oxford is a registered trade mark of
Oxford University Press in the UK and in certain other countries

First Edition published in 2018
First published in paperback 2020

Published in the United States of America by Oxford University Press
198 Madison Avenue, New York, NY 10016, United States of America

British Library Cataloguing in Publication Data
Data available

Library of Congress Cataloging in Publication Data
Data available

ISBN 978-0-19-875385-8 (Hbk.)
ISBN 978-0-19-885487-6 (Pbk.)

For:
Alexandria
Pepper
Lucy
Diotima
and
Cleo

Contents

Part III. Consequences

Preface

In this book I defend the claim that we human beings are obligated to treat all sentient animals, that is, all animals who have subjective experiences that are pleasant or painful, as what Kant called "ends in themselves," at least in one sense of that notion. I also try to say something about what those obligations are, for like most people who write about this subject, I think that the way human beings now treat the other animals is a moral atrocity of enormous proportions. But the book is also about some of the philosophical perplexities that I now think make this subject fascinating. When I became a vegetarian many years ago, it was for moral reasons, but they did not strike me as being philosophically interesting enough to write about. I thought it was obvious that you need a good reason to kill an animal, and that since we do not need to eat meat, we do not have one. In a way, the central issue still seems almost that simple to me. As I will argue, we take the things that are *good for us* to be *good absolutely*, both in the sense that we take them to be worthy of pursuit and in the sense that we take them to be the legitimate basis for making claims on other people. When we come to understand why we do that, we see that we are committed to the view that every creature for whom things can be good or bad has moral claims on us.

My argument is framed by two philosophical commitments: to the basic correctness of Kant's account of why we have obligations, and to a particular theory, derived from Aristotle, about why some things are good and some bad—that is, why there is such a thing as good and bad at all. The elements of my own view can be found in Chapter 2, where I spell out the theory of the good in question, and in Chapter 8, where I explain why I think Kant's argument for the Formula of Humanity supports the moral claims of animals. While it is a familiar point in the animal ethics literature that you can believe animals have moral claims or rights without believing they have the same moral claims or rights as people, I also believe that the *basis* of our obligations to animals is not exactly the same as the basis of our obligations to other people. I reject Kant's view that our duties to animals are "indirect," that is, owed to ourselves rather than to the animals. But I think there is something right about his view that our moral obligations to the other animals arise from something about our relations to ourselves, while our obligations to other people arise from the relations of reciprocity in which we stand with them. There are two different though related senses of being an "end in oneself," two different senses in which a creature can be a source of laws or claims for us. I explain all this in Chapter 8.

Along the way to explaining my position, I raise questions about how human beings are different from the other animals, whether human beings are more important than the other animals, and whether we are in any sense superior to the other animals. I ask what it means to have moral standing and what sort of thing can have it, and how exactly pleasure and pain are related to things being good or bad. Although I end up agreeing with the utilitarians about which creatures have moral standing, my views on the two issues I just mentioned are very different from theirs, as I explain in Chapter 5 and Chapter 9, respectively. In the last three chapters of the book, I turn to straightforward ethical questions. I ask whether those who champion the moral claims of animals are committed to the idea that we should try to put an end to predation, as people often claim. I offer an account of how we should understand the wrong we do when a species goes extinct because of human activity. I explain what my view implies about familiar issues such as eating animals, the use of working animals and animals in the military, the use of animals in research experiments, and whether we should keep pets.[1]

It is one of the perennial problems of trying to write about philosophy that you are haunted by the idea that your reader will not really understand anything you say until after she has understood everything you say. Although the other chapters in this book of course draw on the ideas presented in Chapters 2 and 8, I have tried to write the other chapters of the book so that, as far as possible, they can be read as independent treatments of their various topics. An exception is Chapters 10 and 11, since one of the questions in Chapter 10—whether it would be a good idea to eliminate predation if we could—cannot be answered until the question of Chapter 11—how we are to understand what is bad about a species going extinct—is resolved.

By the time you reach a certain age in philosophy, the burden of your intellectual debts is so heavy that you cannot face writing acknowledgments without a profound sense of inadequacy. What I say here will necessarily be

---

[1] Some people think that the use of the term "pet" is demeaning, and prefer to say "companion animals." I think it is demeaning to call a person a "pet" if that is taken to imply a pampered and dependent favorite. People are not supposed to be pampered and dependent, or to benefit from favoritism. But I do not think it is demeaning to call an animal companion a "pet" if the animal is in fact a pampered and dependent favorite. There is nothing wrong with a domestic animal being pampered and dependent. However, many animal companions are not, or not just, pampered and dependent favorites, since they have work to perform in their households. Seeing-eye dogs and guard dogs are obvious examples. So I regard "companion animal" as a wider term, and use both expressions in this book.

selective, probably arbitrarily so. I first tried to write about how you could make a Kantian case for duties to animals when I was invited to give the Tanner Lecture at Michigan in 2004. Some of the research for the book was done under the auspices of a Mellon Distinguished Achievement Award that I held from 2006 to 2009. I am profoundly grateful to the Mellon Foundation for providing the time. I produced a somewhat distant ancestor of the present book in a series of lectures I called "Moral Animals," delivered as the David Ross Boyd lectures at the University of Oklahoma in 2007. The present book most immediately comes out of the Uehiro Lectures I delivered at Oxford in 2014. I would like to thank those institutions for the opportunities they provided me, and the audiences of those lectures, as well as the many other audiences on whom I have tried out my views on animals and my more recent views on the good. In 2011, Dale Jamieson organized a workshop on my views on animals, where I got useful feedback from Beatrice Longuenesse, Peter Singer, and Jeremy Waldron. In 2015, Andy Reath organized an enormously helpful workshop on part of the manuscript of this book with his colleagues at Riverside. Andy also provided me with extremely helpful written commentary and encouragement. Peter Godfrey-Smith helped me with the sections in which I talk about what a species is. Michael Kessler served as a very able research assistant when I first began to look into this area. Byron Davies skillfully proofread the manuscript. Aleksy Tarasenko-Struc both helped with the proofreading and provided useful written comments. I would also like to thank the students who took my course "Animals and Ethics" in 2015 and 2016. For personal discussions of my views about animals, I would particularly like to thank Melissa Barry, Charlotte Brown, Andy Reath, Tamar Schapiro, and Jonathan Vogel. I will restrain my desire to personally thank all of the pets I've ever had, and all of the sparrows and squirrels who have dined at my feeder over the years, for sharing my life and for making me think. Instead I will settle for dedicating this book to just a few of them, the cats who have been the home companions of my adult life.

Christine M. Korsgaard

August 2017

PART I

Human Beings and the Other Animals

1

Are People More Important than the Other Animals?

We are all of us born in moral stupidity, taking the world as an udder to feed our supreme selves: Dorothea had early begun to emerge from that stupidity, but yet it had been easier to her to imagine how she would devote herself to Mr. Casaubon, and become wise and strong in his strength and wisdom, than to conceive with that distinctness which is no longer reflection but feeling—an idea wrought back to the directness of sense, like the solidity of objects—that he had an equivalent center of self, whence the lights and shadows must always fall with a certain difference.

George Eliot, *Middlemarch*, p. 211

1.1 Introduction

1.1.1 We share the world with fellow creatures.

But I can't just say that, can I? For "we" is a word fraught with assumptions, about who's us and who's them and what the implications of the difference might be. By "we" I mean "we human beings" here, as philosophers usually do. But the fact that I'm using "we" in this way has more to do with who I'm addressing—we human beings, who can have obligations, and can read books that raise questions about what those obligations might be—than about who I'm speaking for. For there might be a "we" that includes all of the animals, and speaks of, and acknowledges, a fate that we share, and I could have been using that "we." That word "share" also embodies some assumptions. You don't share your secret with an eavesdropper, or your house with an intruder, or your land with a colonial oppressor, although in all of these cases he has it and you have it too. "Share" suggests something more, that you have something together, that you both have it legitimately, that you have a common right to it. "Creatures" is the word I am going to use when I want to talk about both human beings and the other animals. I could just say "animals," since we human beings are also animals, but "human" and "animal" are so often used in contrast that that might be confusing.

Etymologically, "creature" suggests a created being, and that might in turn suggest a being created by someone, say by a god. But the implication I want is not that one, but one traditionally associated with it, especially when "creature" is used in conjunction with "fellow." It is the implication that we are related in something like the way that children of the same family are, just as we would be if we were all children of the same parental god. So almost everything I'd like to convince you of is already contained in that opening sentence. If you didn't balk at the sentence before I pointed all this out, perhaps I've got a chance.

1.1.2 We share the world with fellow creatures.

That is to say, we share the world with other living beings who are, to varying degrees, sentient, intelligent, and self-aware. These other creatures find themselves, as we find ourselves, thrown into the world and faced with basic tasks of living: feeding themselves, raising children, and dealing with all the difficulties and dangers that arise from doing these things in a world where others, with competing interests, are trying to do them too. We eat these fellow creatures, raise them for that purpose in factory farms, force them to work for us and live with us, do experiments on them, make products out of them, decide where they may live, kill them when they interfere with our projects, and kill or injure or control them for various forms of entertainment and sport. These practices raise some obvious moral questions. In this book I will address these questions: questions about whether we have any moral obligations to the other animals, what they are, and what the grounds for them are.

1.1.3 These are questions about which philosophers over the centuries have had astonishingly little to say, and that is a fact that is itself of philosophical interest. Until Peter Singer published *Animal Liberation* in 1975, philosophical treatments of what we owe to the other animals were few and far between. This is especially surprising because the question how we should treat the other animals is in one important way different from some of the other practical questions that philosophers discuss nowadays. Many of the moral problems that we talk about in philosophy are intended to illustrate the general features of ethical theories, and do not come up much in everyday life. Others have more practical urgency, but are faced mainly by public officials or medical doctors. At critical moments of your life, you may face the question whether to have an abortion, or to terminate the medical care of a dying loved one. But few of us, as individuals, will ever have to decide whether to torture a terrorist who knows the location of a ticking bomb—although we may have to vote on laws that concern that question. And I am willing to bet that no one reading this book will ever have to decide whether to push a fat man into the path of a runaway trolley which is barreling towards five innocent people tied up on the track.[1] But we all make decisions about how to treat the other animals many times every day, when we decide what to eat, what to wear, what medications to take, and what products to use on our bodies, in our homes, and in our gardens. The kinds of decisions that depend on what you think about the issues I treat in this book are decisions you are going to make today.

1.1.4 But it's not just their moral urgency that makes it puzzling that philosophers should have had so little to say about these questions. It is also that thinking about the other animals, and how we are related to them, and whether we may kill them, eat them, or experiment on them, takes us right into the existential heart of philosophy. You cannot raise these questions without also taking on questions like these: how and why does death matter? How and why do we, that is, we human beings, matter? Are human beings really just unusually intelligent animals, or is there something distinctively different about us, and if there is, how should that affect the way we treat the other animals? What does it mean to be human? Can it really be true, as people sometimes claim, that human beings are somehow just more important than the other animals? Does that claim even make sense? Thinking about how we stand with respect to our fellow creatures is a way of thinking about the questions that draw most of us into philosophy in the first place, and that make philosophy itself such an essential part of being human.

1.2 Reasons to Treat People and Animals Differently

1.2.1 In this chapter I want to start by questioning a view that I think that many people hold—the view that human beings are just more important than the other animals.

Most people agree that we have some obligations to the other animals—that we ought to treat them, as we like to say, as "humanely" as possible. In fact, in the philosophical literature, skinning a cat, or setting her on fire as a juvenile prank, is one of the standard examples of *obvious* wrongdoing. Like torturing babies,

---

[1] This is one instance of a category of cases used to test people's moral intuitions that have come to be called trolley problems. They are cases in which an agent must decide how to respond to a situation in which a runaway trolley is barreling down a track on which a number of people are tied up, and the protagonist may redirect it to another track where others are tied up, or take other morally questionable measures to stop it. These problems are much discussed in moral philosophy, and also used in empirical research in moral psychology. The original example came from Philippa Foot in "The Problem of Abortion and the Doctrine of Double Effect." In the case I am referring to, the only way to stop the trolley is to push a fat man onto the track in front of it. This example was offered by Judith Jarvis Thomson in "The Trolley Problem."

another philosophical favorite, it is the kind of example we use when we are looking for something morally uncontroversial, so that disputes about the example will not get in the way of the point. But at the same time, human beings have traditionally counted nearly *any* reason we might have for hurting or killing animals, short of malicious enjoyment, as outweighing any claims of the animals themselves. We kill non-human animals, and sometimes inflict pain on them, because we want to eat them, because we can make useful products out of them, because we can learn from experimenting on them, and because they interfere with agriculture or gardening or in other ways are pests. We also kill them, and sometimes inflict pain and injury on them, simply for sport—in hunting, dogfighting, horseracing, and so on. So many people seem to believe that animals matter morally, but matter so little that we need never be seriously inconvenienced by the fact. What could justify this? I think that many people assume that animals are simply less important than people, and therefore that what happens to them matters less.

That's the view that I want to discuss. I think it is wrong. But the problem is not exactly that it is substantively false—that, by contrast, animals are just as important and valuable as people. The problem is rather that it makes (almost) no sense at all.

1.2.2 Before I explain why, I want to talk about what makes the idea tempting. Let's think about how the differences between people and the other animals might affect the way we ought to treat them. Philosophers nowadays characteristically raise the question whether we have duties to animals by asking whether animals have "moral standing."[2] Having moral standing is usually thought of as having some property that makes you an appropriate object of direct or intrinsic moral concern. Among the popular choices for the property that confers moral standing are sentience, consciousness, rationality, self-consciousness, personhood, being the subject of a life, and having interests, leaving aside for now the question whether some of those properties are the same or coincide. So one way in which we might think that differences between human beings and animals matter is this: we might believe that humans have a property that confers moral standing on us, while the other animals lack that property. In that case, we would have no obligations to the other animals at all.

1.2.3 Another way the differences might matter, however, is simply in determining the content of our obligations. Within the human moral community, we owe

---

[2] In 5.2–5.4, I will discuss this notion in more detail.

different things to different people simply because of differences in their natures, or because of other facts about them: we owe gentler treatment to the fragile, or more protection to the vulnerable, or more guidance through the bureaucracy to the illiterate, say. It is obvious that even if animals have moral standing, there will be differences in the ways we treat people and animals that are based on differences of these kinds. For example, in liberal societies human beings have a whole range of rights—to freedom of speech and of conscience and of assembly, for example—that are designed to protect our autonomy and our right to live in accordance with our own values. We need not concern ourselves with securing these kinds of rights for the other animals, who live in accordance with their natures, not in accordance with their values, and so lack the kind of autonomy that is protected by such rights.

Some of the most urgent questions about how we may treat animals involve differences of this kind. For example, many people believe that it does not matter to a non-human animal in the way it does to a human being how long she lives, or, at any given moment, whether her life continues. They agree that it matters to an animal that her life should be pleasant and comfortable for as long as it does last and that she should not suffer pain or fear or unnecessary constraint.[3] But they think it does not matter to an animal how long she lives or whether her life should continue from this moment.[4] In that case, our only concern about killing her should be whether it is done humanely. But continuing to live does matter to human beings, who have projects to carry out, relationships we want to maintain, loved ones we want to stay with, and various milestones we hope to meet. For myself, I think that in many cases the continuation of life might matter *more* to a human being than to another animal, for reasons of this kind.[5] But I think that the absence of those reasons does not mean that a longer life is not better for an animal than a short one, provided it is otherwise good. Obviously, this is an important question, because it bears on the issue whether or not killing animals when they are still young enough to make for good eating can be made morally acceptable by treating them humanely during their lives and then killing them in a merciful way (12.3.4). So even if animals have "moral standing," the differences between people and animals can lead to important differences in what counts as treating them acceptably or not.

---

[3] We will look at an argument along these lines from Peter Singer later on, at 9.2.3 and again at 12.3.4.

[4] These somewhat awkward formulations reflect the fact that there is philosophical disagreement about whether we should assess the value of length of life from an atemporal perspective or from a temporal point of view within the life.

[5] But see 4.3.6–4.3.8 for some qualms about this.

1.2.4 I have just described two very different ideas: the idea that there is a difference in moral standing between people and animals and the idea that we have different kinds of duties to people and animals because of differences in their natures or other facts about them. I think, however, that many people tend to run these two different ideas together, and to conclude that animals have moral standing but have less of it than people—that animals are, in some general sense, less important than people. That's a confusion. Suppose you do believe that it is all right to kill an animal so long as you do it humanely. If the reason you believe that is that you think that an ongoing life is not important to the animal in the way it would be to a person, your view does not and need not involve the idea that the animal is less important or has a lesser standing than the person. We might even argue that you are treating the person and the animal "equally" insofar as you accord to each what you suppose is important to her. This is an important part of Peter Singer's point in *Animal Liberation* when he declares that all animals, humans included, are "equal."[6]

1.2.5 Here is another thought that it is important to distinguish from the thought that moral standing comes in degrees. I mentioned cases in which we treat people differently because of differences in their natures, or because of other facts about them, such as being unusually vulnerable or unable to read. Perhaps more often, however, when we treat different people differently, it is because of the special relationships in which we stand to them. Most of us believe that we owe different things to friends or family than to strangers, or to our fellow citizens than to people in other countries, say. We sometimes describe these differences by saying, for instance, that our friends and family are more important to us than strangers are. Exactly how to understand this sort of partiality, and when and why we are permitted to act on it, is a contested question in moral philosophy. But although there is room for argument about this, most of us think that exercising this kind of partiality in certain well-defined circumstances is perfectly compatible with regarding all people as having equal moral standing. To say that someone is more important to you is not to say that he is more important or valuable absolutely. People who think their own children or their own nation or the members of their own racial or ethnic group are absolutely more important than others—not just more important to them, but more important period—commit what most of us regard as some of the very gravest wrongs.

---

[6] Singer, *Animal Liberation*, p. 1. But see 4.3.6–4.3.7.

Could this kind of partiality be at work in our dealings with animals? I suppose there might be circumstances in which a sense of solidarity with our own kind might reasonably enter into moral deliberation.[7] Epidemiological emergencies, or rats and mice invading our granaries, come to mind as possible examples. Suppose a certain species of animal is infecting human beings with some dangerous form of influenza, or that rats are breeding rapidly in our barns, and we decide to kill large numbers of them to defend ourselves. We might do this for the reasons I mentioned before—because we think the continuation of their lives is less important to them than the continuation of our lives is to us, and it's a case in which, regrettably, we have to choose. But we might also do it with some sense that in situations where the issue is one of self-defense in an emergency, we may legitimately prefer our own species, just as we may legitimately prefer our own families in emergencies of various kinds. I am not necessarily advocating that position. I am not very confident about these particular examples. I mention them only to point out that if we did legitimately prefer human beings to the other animals for reasons of solidarity or partiality in situations of this kind, it would not necessarily imply that we think human beings are more important than animals—it would only imply that this is one of the situations in which we think we are allowed to prefer those who are more important *to us*.

So we should not confuse either the thought that we owe different things to animals than to people, or the thought that sometimes we may legitimately exercise a partiality to our own species, with the thought that human beings are more important than animals generally. Those are all different ideas.

1.3 Tethered Values

1.3.1 I've been trying to explain how we might arrive at the mistaken idea that human beings are more important than animals, but I have not yet said why I think the idea is mistaken.[8] I believe that nothing can be important without being important to someone—to some creature, some person or animal. If that is right, we need to be more specific about what exactly the claim of superior human importance is supposed to be. To whom are human beings supposed to be more important? To the universe? To God? To ourselves? Obviously, as individuals we may be more important to ourselves than other people are, just as our families may be more important to us than strangers, and in certain circumstances, the

---

[7] For a defense of the appeal to human partiality in this context, see Bernard Williams, "The Human Prejudice."

[8] Some of the material in this section is also appearing in "Animal Selves and the Good."

fate of human beings may be more important to us than the fate of the members of some other species. But as I have just been suggesting, the fact that something is more important to us justifies only a limited form of partiality in certain well-defined circumstances.

But the more general point is that if everything that is important must be important to someone, to some creature, then there is no place we can stand from which we can coherently ask which creatures, or which kinds of creatures, are more important absolutely. Things are important to creatures; the creatures themselves do not stand in some absolute rank ordering of importance.

Or rather, there is *almost* no place we can stand to make this sort of judgment, as I will now explain.

1.3.2 There are two slightly different inferences you might draw from the point I just made, and it is important to distinguish between them and draw the right one. You might think what I have just said implies the view that all importance is, in a certain popular sense of the term, relative. Then you will think what I am saying is that there are things that are important to me and things that are important to you but there is nothing that is quite simply and absolutely important. But actually what I have in mind is a different view, which I will call the view that all importance is tethered. In particular, it is tethered to the creature to whom the thing in question is important, and it cannot be cut loose from that creature without ceasing to be important at all. Although the view that importance is tethered denies that there is such a thing as free-floating import-ance, it doesn't have to imply that nothing is important absolutely. This is because it still might make perfectly good sense to say that there are things that are important-to us all—to everyone for whom things can be important. In fact, if you think about it, you will see that this is what we want from a notion of absolute importance and nothing more: that it is something important to anyone to whom things can be important. There's no real difference between being absolute, and being relative to everyone. So there is logical space for these theses:

The Absolute Importance of Importance-To: It is absolutely important, import-ant to us all, that every sentient creature get the good things it is important-to her to get and avoid the bad things that it is important-to her to avoid.

Or to put the same point another way:

The Absolute Goodness of Goodness-For: It is absolutely good, good-for us all, that every sentient creature get the things that are good-for her, and avoid the things that are bad-for her.

1.3.3 Of course, there is a complication that arises from the view that all value is tethered, about how we could establish these theses. We cannot move from the claim that something is good-for you to the claim that it is good absolutely, by invoking the premise that it is good absolutely, in an untethered way, that all sentient creatures should get what is good-for them. Instead we have to arrive at the conclusion that what is good-for you is good absolutely by showing that it is, in a certain way, good-for everyone, or from everyone's point of view, that all sentient creatures get what is good for them.

We'll be coming back later to the question whether and how that could be true (8.4.5, 8.8.3, 12.1.1). But—this is the problem I mentioned at the end of 1.3.2—the logical opening for *The Absolute Goodness of Goodness-For* also leaves a *logical* opening for the view that human welfare is more important absolutely than that of the other animals. It is just that *what* we would have to show is that even from the point of view *of the other animals*, what is good-for human beings matters *more* than what is good-for those other animals themselves. We would have to show that human good is what is best-for them, or from their point of view. It is hard to imagine anything that could make that even remotely plausible except some sort of teleological view, according to which human good is the purpose of the world towards which all things in some way strive. And of course that is no accident. The view that human beings are more important than the other animals wears its religious heritage on its sleeve.

Does it make any difference if there is a deity and human beings are more important to that deity than the other animals are? In general, the fact that I am more important to some third party—say, my mother—than other people are does not make my value any more absolute. Whatever value that gives me is still tethered to her point of view, which may not be shared by others. This is part of the problem with the teleological argument I have just gestured at, if we suppose that argument to be supported by religious considerations. Even if a deity created the animals for our use, or to play some other auxiliary role in a drama of which human beings are the protagonists, there is nothing, absent further argument, to say that this fact should be important from the point of view of the animals themselves. If there were an Evil Demon instead of a god, who created human beings to serve as food for crocodiles, that would not make being eaten by a crocodile a good thing for you, or from your point of view. So in the absence of some further argument, I cannot see that it would make a difference. If value is tethered to the point of view of someone who can value things, being valued by a deity could only give us a tethered value.[9, 10]

Of course, those who hold that human beings are more important absolutely can deny that they hold the implausible view that human beings and the human good are more important than the other animals even from the point of view of the other animals themselves. They can do this by denying that importance and goodness are tethered. Then they can suppose that human beings can be more important than the other animals, without being more important to anyone in particular. The belief in untethered importance puts human beings in a position to imagine we can make claims about our own superior value that do not in fact make any sense outside of an antiquated teleological conception of the world.

1.4 Why Tethered Values and Superior Importance Are (Almost) Incompatible

1.4.1 There is another way in which we might be tempted to think that the superior importance of human beings is compatible with a tethered conception of importance and value. J. M. Coetzee, in *The Lives of Animals*, conjures up (without endorsement) an imaginary philosopher, Thomas O'Hearne, who says, "It is licit to kill animals...because their lives are not as important to them as ours are to us."[11] One difficulty with this remark is that it is ambiguous, in a way that talk of the "value of life" tends to be ambiguous. When we talk about someone's "life" we may simply mean their duration through time, or we may mean something more like the totality of their endeavors and experiences. If O'Hearne is using "life" in the first sense, to mean one's duration through time, he is voicing a view that I mentioned earlier—the view that it is only the immediate or local quality of life and not its duration or continuance that matters to the other animals, so that it does not matter if we kill them so long as we do it humanely. But if he means something like "the totality of one's endeavors and experiences," then O'Hearne is saying something much more radical: that things in general just

---

[9] When I first advanced these ideas in the form of the David Ross Boyd Lectures in 2007, Linda Zagzebski asked me if I thought it would make any difference if human beings were more important to God than the other animals are. This discussion is prompted by that question. But of course the ultimate conclusion I would draw from the discussions in this book is not that it does not matter if we were created by a god for some sort of purpose, but that no morally good God would create sentient beings just to be means to someone else's ends.

[10] In "The Human Prejudice," Bernard Williams ascribes to the Renaissance Humanists the view that "If man's fate is a very special concern to God, there is nothing more absolute than that: it is a central concern, period" (p. 136).

[11] Coetzee, *The Lives of Animals*, p. 64.

matter more to people than they do to the other animals. Perhaps he thinks that there is some metric along which we can compare how important everything is to you to how important everything in another animal's life is to her. Then if your life is more important to you measured by that metric, it somehow follows that it is more important absolutely—more important in some way that makes everything that happens to you more important, so that the other animal's interests may always be sacrificed to yours. Does that idea make any sense?

First ask yourself by what metric we might measure how important your life is to you, and compare it to how important some other animal's life is to her. Would you be willing to chew your leg off to save yourself if you got caught in a trap? How much pain are you prepared to endure in order to go on living? How likely are you to commit suicide because you are sick of yourself and your life? How likely is your dog to do that? Or pressing in the other direction, what sorts of things are you prepared to die for because they are *more* important to you than your own life? For human beings, especially good human beings, think that many things, such as justice and the welfare of others, and perhaps the continuing existence of our species (3.4, 11.2.2, 11.9.3), can be worth dying for, while for the other animals, their own lives and perhaps those of their offspring are pretty much all that there is.

Now you may want to protest that this last thought suggests that I am missing the point O'Hearne is making. For you may wish to say that the fact that we human beings value many things in life more than our own pleasant experiences while the other animals do not is *exactly* what shows that there is a sense in which everything is more important to us than it is to the other animals. We treasure ourselves as a species more, we value ourselves more, we have more meaning in our own eyes than the other animals do. The other animals just have a pleasant time or not, while for us human beings, existence is fraught with meaning and value.

1.4.2 One response to this would be to point out that our tendency to think this may just be another instance of the egocentric predicament, that is, of our inability to empathize sufficiently with others and to grasp that the subjectivity of others is just as real as our own. In *Middlemarch*, George Eliot tells the story of Dorothea, an idealistic young woman hungry to do some good in the world, who marries Mr. Casaubon, an older man whom she conceives to be a scholar engaged in a great work. Describing a moment when Dorothea has seriously misunderstood Casaubon's feelings, Eliot writes:

We are all of us born in moral stupidity, taking the world as an udder to feed our supreme selves: Dorothea had early begun to emerge from that stupidity, but yet it had been easier to her to imagine how she would devote herself to Mr. Casaubon, and become wise and strong in his strength and wisdom, than to conceive with that distinctness which is no longer reflection but feeling—an idea wrought back to the directness of sense, like the solidity of objects—that he had an equivalent center of self, whence the lights and shadows must always fall with a certain difference.[12]

Eliot describes the moment when Dorothea realizes this as one of moral revelation, a moment in which Dorothea first grasps the fact that "there is as great a need on his side as on her own" and in this way acquires "a new motive." Eliot here reminds us how hard it is to keep in view—not just to tell yourself, but to feel with "the directness of sense"—that even other *people*'s lives are as just as important, just as real and vivid, just as fraught with meaning and value, to them as yours is to you.

It is the perpetual temptation, especially of the safe and the privileged, to harbor the thought that those less fortunate than ourselves are also simpler beings to whom misfortune probably does not matter as much, or in the same vivid way, as it would if the same things were happening to us. It is particularly easy to harbor such thoughts if the unfortunate ones are illiterate or inarticulate or unsophisticated, and if they are in some other way alien, like being of another race. It is easy to assume, without realizing you are assuming it, that having to work 14-hour days or losing yet another child to malaria, or even dying young, cannot really matter to the kind of people to whom these things routinely happen quite as much as it would matter to you if you were in their place. It is therefore all too easy to be insufficiently struck with the hardness or tragedy of their experience. How much harder, then, must it be to wrap our minds around the ways in which creatures of a different species, whose minds are in some ways deeply alien to our own, might experience their own fates and their own existence, and how important they might be to themselves, from the point of view of what Eliot calls their own "centers of self."

For all that, I think there is something right about the claim that we human beings matter to ourselves, and value ourselves, in a way that is *different* from the way the other animals do, as I will soon explain. But this does not have the implication that what happens to us matters *more* than what happens to our fellow creatures. In fact, if importance and value are tethered, then even if it did make sense to say that we matter more to ourselves than the other animals do to themselves, this would not mean that we mattered more absolutely. The fact that we matter more to ourselves, if it were a fact, need not be important to the other animals at all.

---

[12] Eliot, *Middlemarch*, p. 211.

I have claimed that everything that is important must be important to some creature—that goodness is "tethered" to the creatures for whom it is good. In this chapter I have discussed the implications of that claim, but I have not yet explained why I think it is true. In Chapter 2, I will present an account of the good from which it follows that value is tethered. But before I go on, I want to make sure that my message is clear. I have not exactly been arguing that animals are just as important as people.[13] I have been arguing that the comparison is nearly incoherent. If everything that is important is important to someone—to some person or animal—there is no place to stand and make a comparative judgment, or at least one with any plausibility, about the comparative importance of people and animals themselves.

---

[13] Earlier I endorsed Peter Singer's claim that you can treat people and animals differently without treating them "unequally." The remark I just made may seem incompatible with that. In 4.3.7–4.3.8, I explain what I think is a little off about the idea that all creatures are "equally" important.

2

Animal Selves and the Good

Presumably, however, to say that happiness is the chief good seems a platitude, and a clearer account of what it is is still desired. This might perhaps be given, if we could first ascertain the function of man. For just as for a flute-player, a sculptor, or an artist, and, in general, for all things that have a function or activity, the good and the "well" is thought to reside in the function, so would it seem to be for man, if he has a function.

Aristotle, *Nicomachean Ethics*[1]

2.1 The Origin of the Good

2.1.1 In Chapter 1, I argued that people are not more important than animals— not exactly because animals are just as important as people, but because the comparison does not make much sense.[2] People and animals are the beings to whom things are important, and all importance must remain tethered to them. Everything that is important is important-*to* someone. To put it another way, everything that is good or bad must be good- or bad-*for* someone. We may, of course, be important-to ourselves, and our own existence, among other things, may be a great good-for us. But the other animals may also be important-to themselves, in their way, and their own existence may also be a great good-for them. In fact, I am about to argue that this is so: conscious existence is in itself a good for people and animals alike.

2.1.2 Let's start with a fundamental question. Why is anything important or valuable at all? Why is there such a thing as value? In arguing that the importance of something is always tethered to some creature, I have already given you a clue to what I think the answer is. I think that there are things that matter because there are entities to whom things matter: entities for whom things can be good or

---

[1] Aristotle, *Nicomachean Ethics* 1.7 1097b21–7. References to Aristotle's works are given by the standard Bekker page, column, and line numbers.

[2] Parts of this chapter have previously appeared in Korsgaard, "On Having a Good," and are appearing in "Animal Selves and the Good."

bad, in the sense that might matter morally. What are these entities? The answer, I am about to argue, is basically *animals, creatures*, including ourselves. This remark, as we will see, is almost *true by definition*. For there is a very tight connection between the concept of an animal, at least on one philosophical conception of what an animal is, and the concept of a being for whom things can be good or bad—a being who, as I like to put it, has a good.

2.1.3 I said a moment ago that animals, almost by definition, have a good *in the sense that might matter morally*. This qualification is necessary because we use the word "good" in two different ways, each associated with its own sense of "good-for." First, "good" is our most general term of positive evaluation, a term we apply to nearly every kind of thing, or at least every kind of thing for which we have any use, or with which we interact. Think of the wide variety of things we evaluate as good or bad: cars, houses, machines and instruments, dogs and cats, food, weather, days, prose, pictures, movies; people considered as occupying roles or having jobs such as mother, teacher, son, president, friend, carpenter; and people considered just as people, among many other things. All of these things may be evaluated as good or bad. I am going to call that the *evaluative*, or, for reasons I will explain later, the *functional* sense of good. I call "good" in the second sense in which we use the term the *final* sense of good, borrowing one familiar translation of the Greek word *telos*, meaning a goal or an end. We call something "good" in the final sense when we consider it worth having, realizing, or bringing about for its own sake. We suppose that something we call "the good," or in our own case "the human good," is the end or aim of all our strivings, or at any rate the crown of their success, the *summum bonum*, a state of affairs that is desirable or valuable or worth achieving for its own sake. Final goods are the ends of action, and the conditions that result from the successful pursuit of those ends.

Ask yourself, why do we use the same word, "good," both as our most general term of positive evaluation, and to designate the ends of action and the conditions that result from their successful pursuit? What do the two uses have in common? I think most people think that the answer to this question is obvious, that in both cases we are using the term evaluatively. That is, they think that when we use the word "good" to refer to a final good, that is just a special case of the evaluative good—one in which what we are evaluating is a person's ends or his or her life as a whole.

That seems reasonable, but there is a puzzle about how exactly we are supposed to go about evaluating lives and ends. As Plato and Aristotle pointed out long ago, evaluation is usually related to the purpose, role, or function of the entity that is judged good or bad: an entity is good in the evaluative sense when it has the properties that enable it to serve its function—either its usual or natural function or one we have assigned to it for some specific purpose.[3] A good knife is sharp, because the function of knives is cutting; a good teacher is clear, because the function of a teacher is to help her students to understand the material; a good car handles easily, gets good gas mileage, and goes fast, because the function of a car is to get people quickly and safely to destinations they cannot easily reach on foot. These things are evaluated as good because they have the properties that enable them to perform their functions well. But what is the function of an end or a life? Ends and lives do not have functions. In fact, to say something is an end and not a means is precisely to say that we do *not* value it merely because of some other purpose that it serves. But then how are we evaluating it when we say that it is good—to what evaluative standard are we appealing?

2.1.4 One thing that seems clear is that when we say that a life is good, in the sense we want now—the sense that allows us to say that it is good-*for* the creature, or important-*to* the creature, whose life it is—we are looking for a standard that makes it good from the point of view of that creature. A life could be good from some other point of view, like that of the farmer who values his cow, but that does not give us the sense that supports the idea that the life is good-for the cow. This point turns out to be the key to solving our problem—I mean the problem of how we evaluate ends and lives—although it will take me a little while to explain why.

First, notice that evaluative or functional sense of good, the sense in which a good knife is sharp and a good car handles well, also supports the notion of "good-for" in a particular way. If a thing is good when it has the properties that enable it to perform its function well, then the conditions and actions that tend to give rise to those properties, or enable the thing to maintain them, count as good-for it. In this sense, which I am going to call "the functional sense of good-for," it might be good-for your knife to get sharpened regularly, and bad-for your knife to be used on material that tends to dull its blade. A whetstone is good-for your knife, too. A certain kind of gasoline might be good-for your car, and it might be bad-for the car to leave it sitting idle too long. When we use the concept of good-for in this way, we refer to activities or conditions that maintain or promote the ability of the knife or the car to function well. But of course we do not mean that they are good from the point of view of the knife or the car, for knives and cars do not have points of view.

---

[3] See Plato's *Republic*, 352d–354b; Aristotle's *Nicomachean Ethics*, 1.7 1097b21–1098a20. References to Plato's works are given using the standard Stephanus numbers inserted into the margins of most editions and translations of Plato's works.

2.1.5 Now think about what an animal is. Aristotle taught us that it is possible to regard living organisms as having a function, which he identified as that of maintaining their own "forms."[4] Aristotle argued that everything, every substance whatever, can be seen as having both a "form" and a "matter." The matter is the material or parts of which it is composed, and the form is the way the parts are put together, which is what makes it the kind of thing that it is. In particular, the form is what enables the thing to serve its function. So for instance we might say that the matter of a house is a roof, walls, windows, and doors. Then we impose some form on these parts, by establishing certain relations between them: we line the walls up corner to corner, put the roof over the top, insert the door into one of the walls, so that we can go in and out—and behold!—we have an object that can function as a shelter, something in which people can keep themselves and their things safe from other people and animals and the weather.

Aristotle was also impressed by the fact that living organisms are made of fragile materials that are constantly being used up as energy or worn out or damaged in other ways. But organisms constantly take in new materials from the environment, through the nutritive process, and turn those materials into fresh parts of themselves, thus keeping themselves, for a while at least, in existence. Furthermore, living organisms also make new things like themselves—things with the same "form" as themselves—through reproduction. So Aristotle observed that we can explain a great deal about living organisms if we view them as objects that have the function of maintaining their own forms, in these two senses: first, they maintain themselves in existence, as individual members of their kind, and second, they maintain their species by producing new members of their kind.

When we view an organism as a functional object in this way, then it is like any other functional object: we can see the things and conditions that enable it to perform its function—to stay alive and reproduce—as things that are *good-for* it, in this functional sense of good-for. Just as the whetstone is good-for the knife, and being driven now and then is good-for the car, rain and sunshine are good-for the plants, and fresh air and exercise are good-for both you and your dog.

2.1.6 There are two important differences between animals and functional objects like knives and cars, however. The first difference applies to organisms generally. Although we are getting better at producing machines that are in

---

[4] These views are found in Aristotle, *Metaphysics*, Books 7–10; *On the Soul*, Books 2–3; and *Nicomachean Ethics*, 1.7.

various ways self-maintaining, generally speaking a knife does not sharpen itself, and a car does not seek out the best quality of gasoline. But a living organism does do things like that. So there is something special about the way that organisms function, which is by tending to their own well-functioning, by looking after it. In fact, unlike a car or a knife, *that is* an organism's function—to maintain its own well-functioning—or its own and that of its species. After all, that is really all that organisms do: they look after themselves and their offspring, and so keep themselves and their kind in being. There is a kind of self-referential character to an organism's functioning, for her function is more or less to continue functioning, in the way that is characteristic of her kind, and nothing more.

Or at least we can see organisms this way, a point I will come back to (2.2.5). And when we do see them this way, we see them as beings for whom things can be good or bad, in the functional senses of "good-for" and "bad-for." That is what we are doing, when we say that the rain and the sunshine are "good-for" the plants. We mean that the rain and the sunshine are helping the plants to maintain those properties that enable the plants to perform their function—which is simply to stay alive and reproduce. So the first difference is that living organisms take care of themselves.

2.1.7 The second difference brings us to what is distinctive about animals as opposed to plants (but see 2.2.3). An animal—at least as I will use the term here— is a particular kind of living organism. An animal is an organism that functions, at least in part, by representing her environment to herself, through her senses, and then by acting in light of those representations. She is guided by her representations to get the things that are good for her and avoid the things that are bad for her, in the functional senses of good-for and bad-for. In order for an animal's representational system to do its work in this way, however, it has to have what I will call a "valenced" character. That means that the things she encounters in her environment have to strike her as attractive or aversive, welcome or unwelcome, pleasant or painful, in particular ways, depending on whether and how they are good- or bad-for her. She has to be drawn by the way things appear to her to seek out the things that are good-for her and to avoid the things that are bad. So she has to perceive the world evaluatively, as a place full of things which present themselves as attractive and to-be-sought and things which present themselves as aversive and to-be-avoided.[5]

---

[5] Some readers may think I have overstated matters when I say that the animal's representations "have to" have a valenced character. Couldn't they just serve as stimuli to which the animal responds in a mechanical way, without feeling much of anything? After all, there are machines that respond to environmental stimuli, sometimes in fairly complex ways (nowadays self-driving cars inevitably

In other words, an animal experiences her own condition, and the things that affect it, as good- and bad-for her. But now they are not merely good or bad in the functional sense, but in the final sense too, since getting the things that are good-for her and avoiding the things that are bad-for her have become the ends of action. Because that is how an animal works, that is how she functions, how she goes about tending to her own well-functioning. She is "designed" to monitor her own condition (that is, her own ability to function) by representing the world in ways that will motivate her to keep her condition good. A well-functioning animal likes to eat when she is hungry, is eager to mate, feeds and cares for her offspring, works assiduously to keep herself clean and healthy, fears her enemies, and avoids the sources of injury. Don't say, "Well, of course she does!" Allow yourself to be struck by the fact that there are entities, substances, *things*, that stand in this relation to themselves and their own condition. Because what I am saying is that an animal functions, in part, by making her own well-functioning, the things that are good for her in the functional sense, an end of action, a thing to go for, a final good. The final good came into the world with animals, for an animal is, pretty much by definition, the kind of thing that has a final good—a good, in the sense that might matter morally.

2.1.8 Now I will draw one of the conclusions I promised you earlier (2.1.2). It is almost a necessary truth that for an animal who functions by taking her own well-functioning as an end, her life itself is a good for her, her very existence is a good for her, so long as she is well-functioning, and in good enough condition to keep herself that way. The reason is simple: to be well-functioning is the good, but to be well-functioning is also simply to be alive, and in reasonably good health, in the manner characteristic of your kind. So life itself is a good for almost any animal who is in reasonably good shape. That is why when you feel especially good, you sometimes say, "I really feel alive!" You feel your life, and you feel it as a good to you, as it is the nature of any animal to do.

I say "almost," because it seems possible that there are some simple animals for whom the primary conscious experiences are pains, and aversion to the sources of bad functioning, rather than enjoyment of the sources of good functioning. Such simple animals would relapse into a sort of neutral state whenever their needs were satisfied and they were safe from threats from predators or external conditions that might cause them injury—supposing that ever happens. For such

come to mind). The tropic responses of plants serve as another example. (See 2.2.3 and 11.4.4 for further discussion.) I am not sure what to say about that, so I will just say that if an organism's representations were not valenced, that organism would not have a final good. I explain the role of pleasure and pain in the final good in 9.4.

an animal, the final good would not amount to much more than avoiding the bad. But the animals that we are most concerned with in this book are not like that. For many animals, eating and drinking, sexual activity, physical activity, playing with children and with each other, warmth and comfort, and companionship are positive goods.

It is a mistake to think of life as a big empty space into which good or bad things may equally well be inserted. Life is a good, *existence* is a good, except when it is bad—and that is not a tautology.

2.1.9 So, now, let me come back to the question I raised in 2.1.3: by what standard are we evaluating a creature's life or her ends or her condition when we say that they are good, in the *final* sense of good? When we say that something is a final good, what we are saying is that it constitutes or contributes to the well-functioning of an entity who experiences her own functional condition in a valenced way, and pursues her own functional goods through action.[6] The standard is one deployed from the standpoint of *empathy* (1.4.2) because when we invoke it, we are looking at the creature's functional goods as they appear in her own view, in the way that she necessarily looks at them herself—as things worth pursuing or realizing for their own sake. Final goods exist because there are such creatures, creatures *for whom* things can be good or bad.[7]

2.2 Objections

2.2.1 Now let's consider some objections to the account I have just given, a small one, a medium-sized one, and a big one.

The small one is that the definition that I have given of what an animal is is not the same as the definition a contemporary biologist would give. An "animal," as I am using the term, is an organism that functions as an agent, where by agency

---

[6] Some readers may have doubts about whether this standard applies to the human good. The standard essentially says that the final good for an animal is to lead a healthy life of her kind in reasonably good conditions, and that may seem too "thin" to pick out the human good. I think that this standard does pick out the human good correctly, but we must remember that what counts as "well-functioning" for a creature whose self-maintenance includes the maintenance of what I call a "practical identity" is a complex matter. For the notion of practical identity, see 3.3.4. I develop the notion elsewhere, in *The Sources of Normativity*, lecture 3, and in *Self-Constitution: Agency, Identity, and Integrity*, 1.4, pp. 18–26.

[7] By empathy, I mean the ability I discussed in 1.4.2: the ability to look at things through the eyes of another and appreciate their significance from her point of view. Empathy as I understand it does not necessarily result in compassion, although it tends to. Some people associate empathy with our emotional rather than our rational nature, but I think that is a mistake, and that it involves both. In fact, although empathy comes in degrees, for reasons I will discuss in 3.5.1, it can only be achieved in the higher degrees by rational creatures, who are able to detach from their own point of view.

I mean something like representation-governed locomotion. Animals are conscious organisms who seek out the things that are (functionally) good-for them and try to avoid the things that are bad.[8] Modern science also distinguishes groups or "kingdoms" in the biological world other than animals and plants. Fungi and bacteria form separate kingdoms, and these kingdoms are distinguished not just by whether they are conscious agents, but by their modes of nutrition (animals consume other organisms, plants can make energy from sunlight or methane), features of their cell structure, and things of that kind. Some things count as animals that do not, or anyway do not obviously, fit my account of what an animal is, such as a sponge. I do not think this matters to our topic. The organisms we are concerned with when we think about whether we have duties to animals are sentient beings who perceive the world in valenced ways and act accordingly. This is the feature of organic life that I have argued places an organism in the morally interesting category of having a final good. If plants and sponges are not agents in this sense, then they do not have final goods, although in a sense they have functional goods. And if, as I will argue later, having a final good is the ground of moral standing, then it follows that we have no duties to plants and sponges.

2.2.2 The medium-sized objection concerns what I just said. Why should we think only animals (in my sense of "animals") have a final good? Why not plants and artifacts, especially things like tools and machines?[9] I have claimed that knives and cars have a functional good: when certain properties or conditions help to promote or maintain their well-functioning, then we say that those properties and conditions are good-for them. Being sharpened is good-for a knife; high-quality gasoline is good-for the car. Then why shouldn't we say that a sharp knife that is cutting or a car that is humming along smoothly down the highway has achieved its final good? Knives and cars are not guided by conscious valenced experiences, of course, but why exactly is that so important to having a final good?

I will not be able to give a complete answer to this question until later on (see 2.3 and 9.4.3). But in the meantime, I should mention that there is another reason why artifacts do not have a final good.

---

[8] Some readers will wonder what relationship I am positing between the animal's intentional states and the animal's functional good. Plainly animals do not think about what is good for them. I discuss the relation between the animal's good and the animal's purposes in 3.2.4.

[9] Purely aesthetic objects raise special issues that I will not deal with in this book. I will be speaking only about objects that are more obviously functional.

Intuitively, we do not think that a sharp blade benefits the knife. Rather, it benefits the person who is going to use the knife to do some cutting. This creates a problem for thinking about what is good-for artifacts. The problem is that when we think about what is good-for an artifact in the functional sense of good-for, it is fundamentally unclear whether we are really thinking about something that enables the artifact to perform its function, or something that would give it other properties that we would like it to have. This is because it is fundamentally unclear whether we should count, as part of its function, its having all of the properties we would like it to have. A common example of what I have in mind is when we say that something is good-for an artifact, meaning that it will enable the artifact to *keep* functioning and last for a long time (11.4.1). Is the function of a knife just to cut, or also to stay in good cutting condition for as long as possible? We prefer artifacts that last for a long time, and that makes us think of artifacts rather as if they were organisms, for it *is* part of the function of a living thing to last—that is, to keep itself alive. But self-maintenance is not, or at least not obviously, part of the function of an artifact. Or rather, it only is if we say so. Artifacts exist for our benefit and so do not have a final good of their own.

But this does not mean that there could not be an artifact with a final good. Animals are material objects, and material objects can be made. If we invented a machine that was conscious and had valenced experiences that guided her to pursue her own functional good, then she would be an animal, by my definition, and she would have a final good.

2.2.3 But don't plants have a final good? Many people, especially those who are sympathetic to the Aristotelian ideas to which I am appealing here, think that plants have a final good. And it is easy to see why, because I think we are not much inclined to accept the kind of story I just told about artifacts when we are talking about plants. Plants seem to have a good *of their own*. They do not exist for our benefit. After all, sunshine and rain are good for the weeds as well as for the flowers and the beans and the berries that we hope will grow in our gardens, and that does not seem to be because what is good for the weeds is in some way good for us. It seems like it would be true that sunshine and rain would be good for the plants even if we and the other animals did not exist. The good of plants is "final" in a slightly different sense of "final" than the one I have been discussing here. I have been talking about "final" in the sense of an end of action. A plant's good is "final" in the different sense that the explanation of what is good about the sunshine and rain seems to end with the plants themselves—it does not depend, the way the good of artifacts does, on some other good.

But there are both empirical and philosophical questions at stake in the question whether plants have a final good in my sense, which of course I cannot settle here. The tropic responses of plants—flowers turning towards the sun, roots growing towards moister soil—do involve mechanisms that are in some ways like perception and in some ways like action, and they do serve the plant's functional good. So there are questions about whether those similarities are sufficient to make plants count as agents who pursue their final good. Among other things, these include questions about whether a plant's form of responsiveness is something fundamentally different from locomotion guided by representation, or something that is on the low end of a scale or gradient whose high end is being a conscious agent. That is partly a philosophical question about the nature of consciousness itself, one I cannot attempt to answer here.[10]

2.2.4 Now for the big objection. I have followed Aristotle, and a long tradition, in talking about organisms and their parts as having functions, in particular about organisms having the function of self-maintenance. People often say that we no longer believe in "natural purposes" or natural functions. Instead we believe that organisms evolved through natural selection. In Section 1.3.3, I castigated my opponents for secretly adhering to the implications of an antiquated teleological conception of the world. But, you will object, this is exactly what I am doing myself.

I might respond that the theory of evolution does not show us that there are *no* functionally self-maintaining objects. Instead it shows us how there can be such objects even if no one designed them. We might then also be tempted to say that it also explains something else about organisms. If we regard living organisms as self-maintaining systems, we must regard them as extremely defective ones, for all individuals eventually die. If individuals are essentially self-maintaining, why should that be? What is biologically necessary for the species, or for the genes if you like, is only that there are individuals who live long enough to reproduce, and so maintain themselves long enough to reproduce. So animals are defective self-maintaining systems because natural selection only selects for self-maintenance up to the time of reproduction. But this response of course only brings out a

---

[10] Daniel Chamovich, in *What a Plant Knows: A Field Guide to the Senses*, makes the case that plants have a genuine form of sentience. It is not merely that they respond to light, smell, and touch, but that some of the genetic basis for their doing so is the same as in animals. Another recent book exploring related questions is *Brilliant Green: The Surprising History and Science of Plant Intelligence* by Stefano Mancuso and Alessandra Viola. The latter book, however, makes rather free use of mere analogies between plant and animal functioning.

deeper problem. Why call the individual organisms self-maintaining at all? Why isn't it only—or at most—the species that may be regarded self-maintaining?

In fact, for individuals there is a further problem, which is even trickier to deal with. Consider: Even if an organism were successfully self-maintaining, it could still die of an accident. It could get eaten, or burnt up in a fire, or squashed by a meteorite, or trapped in a deep pit where its needs could not be met.[11] These are just the hazards of material existence. There are a few species of organisms—the examples are controversial, but hydras, flatworms, a certain species of jellyfish (*Turritopsis dohrnii*) have been suggested—that apparently do always die of accidents and so are potentially, though never actually, immortal.[12] But most animals are doomed to die of senescence—the natural weakening of the body with age—even if they do not die of accident or disease. Perhaps this is better for the species, since an ever fresh supply of slightly different individuals enables it to adapt better to changing conditions, so that its members do not all die of accidents. But if that is true, how can the individuals of the species be character-ized as self-maintaining? For these animals, death is not just a hazard of material existence. It is, in Aristotelian terms, built into their forms.

This raises large issues about the use of the notion of function in biology, for if nothing is really biologically self-maintaining, then it is not clear what entitles us to use the concept of function when we talk about living things. But if we cannot talk about function when we talk about organisms, then we cannot talk about their functional good either. If they have no function, they have no functional good, then nothing is functionally *good-for* them. In that case, we are saying something without foundation when we say that sunshine and rain are good-for the plants, in the functional sense of good-for. (Or at most, if we grant that the species is self-maintaining, it is a shorthand way of saying that it is good-for the species.[13]) But if we cannot talk about an individual's functional good, then

---

[11] I should admit that the distinction between dying from a failure of self-maintenance and dying from an accident is a little wobbly. Aristotle thought of self-maintenance primarily as manifested in nutrition and reproduction. But we might also think of it as manifested in the body's ability to cure itself of small injuries and build up resistance to minor illnesses. Then, however, we are faced with a puzzle: why should the body's ability to heal a scrape on the knee be a manifestation of self-maintenance, but its inability to heal itself from being squashed by a meteorite *not* be a failure of self-maintenance? In a sense, these two kinds of injuries are continuous with each other. I am not sure what to say about this.

[12] We might say this about the extinction of species, too: that though it always happens, it is always because of external forces like climate change, the evolution of rival species, contagious illnesses, and so on.

[13] I discuss the question whether a species can have a good and what sort of good it can have further in 11.4. For the purposes of this chapter, I assume that it does and that the things that keep a species in existence count as good for it in the functional sense of good-for.

I cannot say that final good, and the final sense of good-for, appeared in the world when animals evolved and began to take the things that promote their functional goods as the ends of action, and to see them as things worthy of pursuit.

2.2.5 I think we can still say these things, though. I think what all of this shows is that when we talk about functional good, we are saying something contextual, and that what forms the context is a point of view. "Functional good" is what we might call a "perspective-dependent" notion.

Being perspective-dependent is not a way of being unreal, or otherwise metaphysically defective. Everyone is familiar with the question whether a tree falling in a forest makes a sound if no one is listening. One answer to that is "No": sounds exist in the perspective of creatures who can hear, although sound waves would still be bouncing around in the absence of such creatures. Similarly, we might say that colors exist only in the perspective of creatures with color vision. Without such creatures, there would still be light waves reflecting off of surfaces with certain frequencies, but there would not be colors. To take a somewhat different kind of case, chairs and tables exist in the perspective of creatures who need or use furniture. Without such creatures, there might still be, say, wooden objects shaped in such-and-such a way, but they would not be furniture. If we were oval and swam through our atmosphere like fish, there would be no tables and chairs in our world. In a similar way, values exist in the perspective of a certain kind of creature, a creature who values things, in the sense of having evaluative or valenced attitudes towards things.

When I say that the function of a knife is cutting, that a good knife has a sharp blade, and that things that keep the knife sharp are good for the knife, I am not saying anything that has to be rejected in the name of scientific naturalism. I am speaking from the point of view of a human being, who sometimes has to do some cutting. When I say that water is good-for me, since I need it to live, I say it from the point of view of a human being who wants to go on living. When I *feel* that water is good-for me, because I was dry and thirsty, and the relief from that is welcome to me, I feel it from the point of view of a creature who experiences her own condition in a valenced way, and who is genetically predisposed to seek out and to enjoy such things as water, in order to keep herself in existence for a time. I may also be genetically predisposed to senescence, but I am not predisposed to seek it out as an end of action, or to enjoy it for its own sake when it comes. Except under special circumstances, therefore, I do not regard senescence and death as part of my final good. It follows from that—or so I am about to claim—that it is not part of my functional good.

Or anyway, it need not be. A caveat here: the jury is out on whether immortality would be a good thing for people if we could have it. But that question is settled by thinking about how it relates to other things that we do experience as parts of our final good: whether it would make our lives more meaningful and interesting, our projects more worthy of pursuit, our relationships stronger and better, or whether instead it would reduce us to aimless creatures, with no ends worth struggling for, bored with existence and each other. The question here is whether we have to regard death as a final good for us, not because of the way it is related to other parts of our final good, but simply because we are "formed" by our nature to die.

But you will want to protest that I cannot be allowed, in the context of this argument, to limit the category of functional goods to the things that contribute to our final goods. This is because I have defined "final goods" in terms of "functional goods": final goods are just functional goods when taken as the ends of action. So you will accuse me of reversing the order of dependence between these two forms of goodness, functional and final. I cannot claim that final good is just functional good actively pursued, and then turn around and limit functional good to what contributes to final good, because I would have to have an independent notion of final good before I could do that.

And there is another problem. Above I suggested that senescence is not part of our final good because it doesn't appear good to us, and we do not seek it out as an end of action. But I do not want in general to identify final good with what actually appears good to us, because I want to say we, and all animals, can get it wrong. It happens all the time. Animals evolve in one set of conditions, and when those conditions change, animals may want things that are not good for them, or fail to want things that are. Notoriously, for example, human beings evolved to want to stock up on salt and fatty foods when the supplies are good, in anticipation of the lean times when they will not be. When the lean times never come, those desires do not serve our functional good, and I want to say that their satisfaction does not serve our final good either. We are wrong not to crave a leaner, blander diet, although we have a hard time seeing it as good. If we reject the idea that the leaner blander diet is genuinely good for us as individuals, then the only available explanation for the claim that it is better is that it serves the interests of the species. But if that is so, why aren't we wrong not to crave death, which probably serves the interest of the species as well?

2.2.6 The reason we are not wrong not to crave death is that when animals evolved to pursue their functional goods through action, something else evolved, namely consciousness, subjectivity, which then became essential to the individual identity of the creatures who have it. When I say that something is good-for me, even in the functional sense, the "me" that I am referring to is the embodiment of my *self*, a conscious subject and agent who is more or less (for, as we are about to see, this is a matter of degree) functionally unified over time.

Speaking a little roughly, your self is functionally unified insofar as you have an integrated point of view, at a time, and over time, that enables you to carry out your projects and stick to your commitments in a world in which you can find your way around. For a human being, this has two distinct aspects. The unity of what we may call your "acting self"—a unity that we also call "integrity"—enables you to pursue your ends effectively and maintain your projects, commitments, relationships, and values over time.[14] The unity of what we may call your "knowing self" involves the formation of an integrated conception of your environment, one that enables you to identify relations between the different parts of your environment well enough to find your way around in it. Those relations are temporal, spacial, causal, and for many animals social. By forming a unified conception of your environment, you also unify yourself as the subject of that conception. The fact that I identify with my *self*—with the agent of my projects and commitments and the subject of my conception of the world— means that there may be things about my body, such as its tendency to senescence, that are not good for *me*, even if perhaps they are good for my species or my genes. They are not good, that is, for the thing that I experience, and identify, as "me." My functional good is what maintains the aspects of me that support my having a self.

So I have not exactly reversed the order between final good and functional good. Instead what I have done is point out something that happens to the identity of an object when that object acquires consciousness and a point of view. The object acquires a new form of identity, a self. And since it is the self that experiences its condition and things in the world as good or bad, and the self that decides what to do and acts, it is the self that has a final good.

2.3 Self-Consciousness and the Self

2.3.1 Some people think that you have to be self-conscious in order to have a self. The self is not like most other things, which exist independently of your awareness of them. Your self only exists, the claim is, if you have some awareness that it

---

[14] A complication here: integrity enables you to maintain your projects, commitments, relationships, and values, but also to change them when you find you have good reason to do so. What it forbids is dropping them arbitrarily. See Korsgaard, *Self-Constitution*, especially 4.5.

is there, and that of course would have to be a kind of self-awareness. Initially, it may seem paradoxical that you could be aware of something that would not exist at all unless you were aware of it. But if you think about it, you will see why it is plausible that the self should have this "reflexive" character. After all, as I have already suggested, you acquire a self when you acquire a point of view, a form of awareness. Having a point of view introduces a distinction between yourself and the rest of the world. It identifies you, and makes you identify yourself, with a specific spot in the world, from which the rest of the world appears to you. It identifies some of the things that happen in the world as things that happen *to* you. It does this not just externally, but from your own point of view. So to have a self is to have a point of view, and to have a point of view is to be aware of the difference between you and everything else, and in that sense to be aware of yourself. What I have just been saying about the connection between having a self and having a final good seems to require that thought, since I claimed that having a self determines *what* you identify as yourself. It causes you to identify with the features of your embodiment that support the existence of a unified point of view, and to regard only those features as part of your functional good.

2.3.2 But if the self is dependent on self-consciousness in this way, can the other animals have selves? It is sometimes said that human beings are the only animals who are self-conscious. Immanuel Kant once wrote:

The fact that man can have the idea "I" raises him infinitely above all the other beings living on earth. By this he is a *person*; and by virtue of the unity of his consciousness, through all the changes he may undergo, he is one and the same person—that is, a being altogether different in rank and dignity from *things*, such as irrational animals, which we can dispose of as we please.[15]

Kant thinks that only we human beings think about ourselves. We do not know much about the thoughts of animals, or about what goes on when they are thinking. The serious study of animal minds is a young science, less than a century old. Presumably it is different for different animals, depending on what sort of cognitive powers they have. It may be true that only we human beings think about ourselves, if that means having thoughts in which we identify ourselves as "I." But even if it were, the issue is more complicated than that, for self-consciousness is something that comes in degrees and takes many different forms.

---

[15] Kant, *Anthropology from a Pragmatic Point of View*, 8:127. References to Kant will be given in the usual way by the page numbers of the relevant volume of *Kants gesammelte Schriften*, which appear in the margins of most translations. *The Critique of Pure Reason*, however, will be cited in its own standard way, by the page numbers of the first (A) and second (B) edition.

One form of self-consciousness is revealed by the famous mirror test used in animal studies. In the mirror test, a scientist paints, say, a red spot on an animal's body and then puts her in front of a mirror. If the animal eventually reaches for the spot and tries to rub it off, or looks away from the mirror towards that location on her body, we can take that as evidence that the animal recognizes herself in the mirror, and is curious about what has happened to her body. To date, apes, dolphins, elephants, and possibly some birds have passed the mirror test. An animal that passes the mirror test seems to know that a certain body is her own, or herself. She recognizes the animal in the mirror as "me" and therefore, some people think, must have a conception of "me."

But failure to pass the mirror test does not imply that an animal is not self-conscious. For one thing, many animals are not visually oriented. Imagine you are confronted with a surface which reflects back your distinctive odor. If you failed to identify that smell as "me," would that show that you are not self-conscious? More generally, I think it can be argued that even animals who do not pass the mirror test have forms of self-consciousness. In fact, I think it can be argued that pleasure and pain are *forms* of self-consciousness, since what the animal who experiences these things is experiencing is the effects of the world on himself, on his own condition. In that sense, all animals are self-conscious because they can *feel* their existence.

Again, you have self-consciousness if you have some sort of awareness that one of the things in your world is *you*. This awareness can be relational: that is, it can be knowledge in which you identify yourself as what stands in a certain relation to something else. In fact, at some level, all self-consciousness has to be relational, since what it is to be self-conscious is to be aware of standing in a certain relation to the rest of the world, to distinguish yourself from the rest of the world. Such relational knowledge is essential to action, because in order to act you have to orient yourself within the world: you have to have some sense of what your own position is in it. A tiger who stands downwind of her intended prey is not merely aware of her prey—she is also locating *herself* with respect to her prey in physical space, and that suggests a form of self-consciousness. A social animal who makes gestures of submission when a more dominant animal enters the scene is locating himself in social space, and that too suggests a kind of self-consciousness. Knowing how you are related to others in space or in a social order involves something more than simply knowing about them. It involves knowing how you stand with regard to them, and that requires some kind of conception of yourself.

2.3.3 Of course there is something right about what Kant says, when he emphasizes that having a self involves having a kind of consciousness that is unified over time. But I believe that Kant's view is too extreme, in two ways that I will try to explain: one here, and one in 2.4.

The first is that having a self is a matter of degree: a matter of how much functional unity your point of view has at a time, and over time. Here is what I have in mind. When philosophers work on questions of what we (interestingly) call "personal" identity, we identify certain factors as giving a person a certain kind of continuity over time, and so making the person one person, a person with a single self enduring. These factors are those that tend to unify the person's point of view over time. Learning, episodic memory, ongoing relationships, even long-term projects are among these factors.

But these factors may also be found, to varying degrees, in the lives of animals. Any animal who is conscious or sentient has a self, in the minimal sense of a point of view—there is something it is like to be that animal at any given time. Perhaps for some very simple animals the self, or the point of view, is something that exists at any given moment, but what-the-world-is-like-for-that-animal at one moment does not have much influence on what-the-world-is-like-for-that-animal at another. But many animals can learn, and that means that what happens to them at one moment changes the way that they respond to the world at another. Animals also do other things that systematically influence and so unify their points of view over time. They can acquire tastes, and make friends, and even take on projects and roles. If one animal bonds with another, he may feel comfortable when he encounters that other, and in some cases even feel uncomfortable when he does not. If he decides to build his nest or his dam or his burrow in some particular spot, then that becomes the spot to return to when the day's foraging is done. If he makes a mental map of a certain region to which he has been newly transported then he can find his way around there with ease. If what happens to you or what you do at one time changes your point of view on the world at another time, then your self acquires an ongoing character that makes it a more unified self over time.

Philosophers who think about what gives a human being a unified self over time like to emphasize memory, but what I am talking about does not require "episodic memory," the memory of particular events. An animal who is frequently beaten becomes fearful and cringing, or hostile and aggressive. An animal who is regularly treated well becomes relaxed and confident. These are not just changes in the animal's outward behavior: they reflect changes in the animal's way of experiencing the world, ways in which what the animal is experiencing now is informed by what he experienced in the past. An animal does not need to remember specific occasions in order for this to happen. Experience is something that accumulates, constantly modifying experience itself. The animal's point of view becomes more unified, in the sense that the animal responds to the same things in the same ways at different times.[16] But at the same time the animal's mind can also become more flexible, as the animal's repertoire of responses that are appropriate to his environment accumulate. He learns to avoid more of the things that will hurt him and seek out more of the things he enjoys.

Why does this matter to our topic? Because it changes the ways in which things can be good- or bad-for the animal. People like to say that animals live in the moment, and in one sense that is probably right: unlike human beings, they do not seem to spend a lot of time planning for the future or fretting about problems that may or may not arise. But in another sense, I do not think it is true. Or perhaps what I should say is that at least for many animals, the moment itself does not live merely in the moment, but reverberates with the character of the other moments in the animal's life. The more this is true, the more an animal's experiences build on themselves in forming his point of view, the more apt it becomes to identify what is good for him in larger temporal units. Any sentient animal has good experiences and bad ones. But the more that experience accumulates, the more it makes sense to think that the animal, like a human being, can have a good or a bad life, where a life is not just a string of good or bad experiences, but a kind of whole with an overall character of its own. This is because it becomes true that there is something it is like to live that life.

2.3.4 So far, I have proposed an account of why there is such a thing as the good. There is such a thing as the good because there are creatures in this world for whom things can be good or bad. Those creatures are animals, who pursue their functional good through action: locomotion guided by valenced representations, or in simpler terms, by sentience. We human beings have a good because we are among them—we are animals ourselves. The goodness or badness of things exists in the perspective of the animals themselves, in their valenced responses to what happens to them, and in our case, also in our evaluative judgments about our own condition and what makes it good or bad. It is tethered to that perspective. But there is nothing unreal about it, for those responses and judgments concern a matter of fact. Things are good for a creature if they contribute to the well-functioning of that creature's self, with whom the creature necessarily identifies. Having a self—that is to say, a unified self—I have suggested, is a matter of degree. Later, in Chapter 4, I will discuss what sort of practical difference those

---

[16] Someone may wish to protest that without conscious memory this could only be qualitative similarity, not an actual unified ongoing point of view. Actually, there is a puzzle about how even with conscious memory, one moment can be linked to another by anything more than a (suitably caused) qualitative similarity. This is another philosophical problem about the nature of consciousness.

differences of degree might make. But there is one more difference here that we need to discuss.

2.4 Active and Passive Self-Constitution

2.4.1 I have been arguing that Kant's view is too extreme because he does not acknowledge that the self-comes in degrees. As I said in 2.3.3, there is another way in which Kant's view is too extreme. The processes that I have just been talking about are ones that can happen more or less passively, without much active participation on the part of the animal herself. One of the distinctive features of being human, or so I am about to argue, is that we play an active and sometimes even a conscious role in determining the unity and coherence of our minds, our lives, and ultimately of ourselves.

In the *Critique of Pure Reason*, Kant tells us that the importance of the idea "I" rests in the fact that we must be able to attach an "I think" to all of our thoughts.[17] As I have argued elsewhere (although Kant himself never quite says this) a similar point holds for actions, to which we must be able to attach an "I do."[18] Part of the point here is that we claim responsibility for our own thoughts and actions, and part of what taking that responsibility involves is an active endeavor to make them coherent. Claiming my thoughts as mine, as things that "I think," is pledging myself to making them fit together. So we human beings actively try to form a coherent conception of the world as a whole, one which enables us to track the ways in which everything is related to everything else, causally, spacially, and logically. The unity here is a functional unity: it enables me to find my way around in the world and to use what is in it more effectively. If my views contradict each other, then I must change them, for then they cannot both be things that "I think."[19]

In a similar way, claiming my actions as mine, as things that "I do," is pledging myself to making them expressions of coherent principles and to fitting them together into coherent plans. The unity here is again a functional unity: it enables me to live my life without undercutting the effectiveness of my own actions in

[17] Kant, *Critique of Pure Reason*, B 131–2.
[18] Korsgaard, *Self-Constitution*, 1.4.1, pp. 18–19.
[19] Although I think rational beings play a much more active role in unifying themselves than the other animals, I do not mean to imply that they play no active role at all. An animal that is puzzled about or surprised by something in his environment and (say) moves closer to check it out is probably motivated by the desire to ensure that it is not a threat, or something like that, not by the desire to unify his conception of the world. Or perhaps I should say that even if he is simply curious, the evolutionary purpose of his behavior is to make sure that it is not a threat. Nevertheless, as a result of his curiosity, he may in fact unify his conception of the world.

achieving and respecting the values I hold most dear. The way in which human beings are self-conscious makes self-constitution, the unification of the thinking self, the knowing self, and the acting self, into a more or less self-conscious project.

In Chapter 3 I will explain why I think Kant is right about the active role human beings play in their own self-constitution. My point now is twofold: first, this does not mean that there is no functional unity to the minds and the selves of the other animals. A certain amount of functional unity is given by their instincts, and some comes naturally in other ways. So the difference between human beings and the other animals is not that the other animals do not have self-consciousness or selves. It is that we human beings play a particularly active and responsible role in constituting our selves, our own minds and identities.[20] In Chapter 3, we will take a more in-depth look at the question of what is different about being human.

---

[20] This issue is the subject of Korsgaard, *Self-Constitution*.

3

What's Different about Being Human?

I fully subscribe to the judgment of those writers who maintain that of all the differences between man and the lower animals, the moral sense or conscience is by far the most important. This sense, as Macintosh remarks, "has a rightful supremacy over every other principle of human action"; it is summed up in that short but imperious word *ought*, so full of high significance.

Charles Darwin, *The Descent of Man*, p. 70

3.1 Introduction

3.1.1 There is an old debate about what, if anything, is unique about human beings.[1] There have been many contenders: language, tool use, conceptual thought, culture, aesthetic tastes, morality, religion, self-awareness. There have been those like Descartes who have claimed that animals are not conscious at all, and those who have claimed that they have no emotions, or only fear and anger. These last two ideas seem absurd to anyone who knows a non-human animal "personally" (as we say). But all of these supposed distinguishing marks have had their scientific challengers. Scientists have found evidence that many animals use and even make tools. Birds and great apes have been taught to use language intelligently. Culture in the sense of the handing down of local traditions has been found among primates who teach their offspring how to prepare certain foods to make them edible, or which plants may be used for medicinal purposes. Defenders of human uniqueness sometimes respond by ratcheting up the criteria for what counts as having the attribute in question: it is not really language unless the animal can use syntax as well as just naming things, or unless it is used with a clear communicative intention, say.

---

[1] Some of the ideas in this chapter have previously appeared in Korsgaard, "Interacting with Animals," and "Fellow Creatures: Kantian Ethics and Our Duties to Animals."

3.1.2 It is hard not to wonder what those who respond in this way think is at stake in the question of human uniqueness. The friends of animals sometimes accuse the defenders of human uniqueness of harboring some strange form of vanity about our species, or simply trying to block the moral consequences of admitting that we are not unique. Most defenders of animals like to emphasize the continuities between human and animal life, sometimes claiming that there are no distinctively human attributes, no differences except matters of degree. We might suppose that, given the theory of evolution through natural selection, this is also what we should expect. There is scientific controversy over the question whether the process of evolution requires that all new attributes should be produced from earlier ones by gradual changes. But however those arguments turn out, it seems unlikely that when human beings evolved, nature took a single flying leap, starting from animals whose relation to their environment is wholly a matter of mechanical responses to stimuli, and moving in a single step to animals who can build rocket ships, cure diseases, cooperate on an almost global scale, write poetry, play the violin, and worry about philosophical questions. The very impressiveness of the human achievement (impressive by our own standards, that is) cries out that some rudimentary forms of these powers, or some other powers in terms of which they can be explained, must exist in the animal world. Many defenders of animals believe that the more we can show that the other animals are like us in these respects, the more we can challenge those who think we are justified in treating animals very differently than we would treat other human beings.

3.1.3 Granting all of that, it is nevertheless hard to resist the idea that there is something really different about human life. In this chapter, I will offer a sketch of what I think it is.[2] But since I am not an empirical scientist, a word of warning is in order. Strictly speaking, what I am offering here is not an account of what the difference between human beings and animals is. It is an account of two (or in a way three) different possible forms of cognition—two possible kinds of mind— and some of the effects that those forms of cognition would have on the creatures who had them. Which creatures actually *have* those forms of cognition, if any do, is an empirical question that cannot be answered by philosophy alone. I think that the distinction between these forms of cognition explains some of the other differences between people and the other animals, so I think that people have one and animals have (various versions of) the other. But this could be wrong.

---

[2] For a fuller account see *Self-Constitution*, especially chapters 5 and 6.

It might also be the case—in fact I think it probably is—that there are forms of cognition that lie between these two but that I do not know how to describe, and that some of the animals who are more like us have those.

3.2 Rational and Instinctive Minds

3.2.1 In Chapter 2, I suggested that if an animal is to be guided through the world by perception, her responses to the world must be "valenced" responses, responses of attraction and aversion. I want to be more specific now about what I have in mind.

A non-human animal, I believe, lives in a world that is in a deep way her own world, a world that is *for* that animal. I do not mean that the animal's world is necessarily favorable to her interests; often it is not. But the world as perceived by the animal is organized around her interests: it consists of the animal's food, her enemies, her potential mates, and, if she is social, of her fellows, her family, flock, tribe, or what have you. To say this is just to say that the animal's representations of things come already loaded with the practical significance of various objects for her. She confronts a world of things that are perceived directly, without calculation or conscious interpretation, as things that are *to-be-avoided, to-be-chased, to-be-investigated, to-be-eaten, to-be-fled, to-be-cared-for*, and so on. If you think of it, you will see that it has to be this way. Perception first evolved in animals who are not highly intelligent, and would have been useless if all it did was flood their minds with neutral information that needs to be processed by intelligence or reason before it can be of any use. So the world comes to an animal already practically interpreted as a world of resources and obstacles, of friends and enemies, of the to-be-avoided and the to-be-sought. The natural way of perceiving the world, as I will put it, is *teleologically*: everything has its place in a purposive order determined by the instincts of the perceiving animal herself.

3.2.2 As I have just suggested, we can use the traditional word "instinctive" for this way of perceiving and responding to the world, and it will be convenient to do so. "Instinctive" naturally contrasts with "rational." Following an ancient tradition, that is what I am about to claim is different about human beings— that we are rational. But before I can use the words "rational" and "instinctive," I need to put some warning labels on them.

Sometimes people use the term "instinctive" for reactions and movements that are wholly automatic and simply caused, not intentional, like ducking or salivating. I am not talking primarily about reactions of that kind. But it will be easier to make it clear what I am trying to get at when I add my other warning label. People sometimes contrast an instinctive response to an intelligent or learned response, and I am not doing that either. As I am using the terms, being instinctive is compatible with being intelligent, which is not the same thing as being rational.

An intelligent animal is characterized by his ability to learn from his experiences, and to solve problems by taking thought. He is able to extend his repertoire of practically significant representations beyond those with which his instincts originally supplied him. He might learn to see the porcupine as something that is *to-be-avoided* or a human companion as a member of his flock, for example. He might learn to fashion a twig into a digging stick. Intelligence so understood is not something contrary to instinct, but rather something that increases its range and ramifies the view of the world that it presents to the creature who has it.

Intelligence, on this showing, is not the same as rationality. Rationality, as I will use the term, is a normative power grounded in a certain form of self-consciousness. A rational animal is (at least sometimes) aware of the grounds of her beliefs and actions. By the "grounds" I mean the things that would directly cause her to believe what she believes or to do what she does if she were not in a position to reflect on them. This consciousness puts her in a position to evaluate those grounds and decide whether or not they count as *good reasons* to act and believe in the ways that they tempt her to act and believe.

When a non-rational animal thinks about what to do (if she thinks about what to do) she thinks about things in the world as she perceives them, not about her own attitudes towards those things. The attitudes that motivate her actions may be invisible to her, because they are part of the lens through which she sees the world, rather than being part of the world that she sees. We sometimes talk as if our own attitudes were invisible to us in exactly this way. If you say that a spider is "creepy," for instance, you speak as if your attitude towards the spider were a property of the spider itself. The particular distaste you have for the spider, the fact that it gives you "the creeps," is a lens through which you see it, causing you to think of the "creepiness" as a property of the spider. If our fear of spiders is instinctive, it is no accident that this example illustrates what I am trying to convey: this is what the kind of perception I am calling "teleological" is like. The perceived creepiness of the spider *tells you* to avoid coming into contact with it. If you think about how hard it can be to let a large spider crawl on you, even if you know she is harmless, you will see that such "instructions" can come almost in the form of commands.

In the same way, we might suppose that when an antelope flees from a lion, she is afraid. But she need not think about the fact that she is afraid, or about the fact that her fear is what is making her run. Perhaps she just sees the lion as danger, as a thing that is *to-be-fled*.[3] But we human beings are, or can be, aware of the attitudes that motivate our actions and of the facts that motivate our attitudes. We may know, in these kinds of circumstances, that we are afraid, that the possibility of being mauled by the lion is what is making us afraid, and that the fear is what is making us inclined to run. That opens up the space in which we can ask a whole new range of questions, normative questions: not only about whether a lion is a *good* thing to run away from (or a bad thing to encounter), but also about whether a lion is a *good* thing to fear, or even about whether fear, in these circumstances, is presenting us with a *good* reason to run. Perhaps, after all, we are in circumstances that make it worth taking the risk of being mauled by the lion, such as trying to save the life of a child who is in the lion's path.[4] If we are, as we take ourselves to be, rational beings, then what we actually do will be influenced by the way we answer those questions: we will, for instance, stand our ground if we decide either that we have reason not to be afraid or that we have reason not to run even if we have good reason to fear. Of course reason does not always triumph over instinct in this way, since instinct is, as I said above, commanding. But sometimes reason succeeds in facing it down.

So the difference between rationality and intelligence is this: intelligence looks outward at the world, and asks and answers questions about the connections and relations we find there—most obviously about causal relations, but also spacial and temporal and social relations. But rationality looks inward, at the workings of our own minds, and asks and answers normative or evaluative questions about the connections and relations that we find there. In particular, practical rationality raises questions about whether the attitudes and the facts that motivate our actions give us good reasons to act.

3.2.3 Rationality so understood is not the same as intelligence or the capacity to solve problems by taking thought, but rather is the capacity to ask whether something that would potentially motivate you to perform a certain action is really a *reason* for doing that action—and then to be motivated to act in accordance with the answer that you get. Rationality, in this sense, is normative

---

[3] Or the animal sees the lion as *to-be-fled* when the lion is active, or some such qualification. At least some prey animals who protect themselves by fleeing do not flee predators whenever they are aware of them, but only when it seems like they might be on the hunt. My point about these responses is not that they are inflexible or unintelligent, but simply that they tell the animal what to do.

[4] Philosophers will differ about whether the reason is provided by facts like *the fact that the lion might maul you* or by mental attitudes such as fear or the desire not to be mauled. I am not taking a stand on that here, although it is impossible to write a sentence without choosing one of these options. For my views on this matter see "Acting for a Reason."

self-government, the capacity to be governed by thoughts about what you *ought* to do or to believe. Rationality has sometimes been taken to be the attribute that makes human beings "persons" in a sense we have inherited from the legal tradition, where a "person" is something that has rights and obligations.

In fact it seems worth noting that even some philosophers who would deny that *rationality* is the distinctive characteristic of humanity would still agree that normative self-government is both definitive of personhood and distinctive of human beings. In the empiricist tradition, the tradition of John Locke, David Hume, and Francis Hutcheson, it has been common to attribute to human beings, and human beings alone, a capacity to form so-called "second-order" attitudes—for example, attitudes of approval and disapproval towards our own desires—that make them liable to normative assessment. Though I may desire to do something, I may also disapprove of that desire, and reject its influence over me, and my disapproval may motivate me not to do it after all. Or, in the more recent view of the philosopher Harry Frankfurt, the relevant second-order attitudes are themselves desires—desires concerning which of our first-order desires we should have and act on and which we should not.[5] Frankfurt identifies having such second-order desires with personhood. When I am able to refrain from acting on those desires that I do not want to act on, then I exercise the kind of self-government characteristic of a person. So, many philosophers agree that normative self-government is the distinctive characteristic of human beings, and the one that makes us "persons."[6]

3.2.4 But don't animals have reasons for what they do? In a sense, of course they do. In order to make the distinction I have in mind a little clearer, I am going to describe the two different kinds of cognition I have just been discussing in a slightly different way.

As I mentioned before, some people think of instinctive action as the mechanical and automatic response to a stimulus, like closing your eyes when something gets too near to them. In this kind of case, your behavior has a purpose, in the sense that this reaction evolved because it serves a useful purpose—it protects your eyes from harm. This is not a purpose you need to have in mind in order to engage in the behavior. It is not a purpose you need to endorse, and on a certain

---

[5] Frankfurt, "Freedom of the Will and the Concept of a Person," in *The Importance of What We Care About*.

[6] If this is indeed a difference between human beings and the other animals, it would be worth reserving the word "person" to mark it. This would be an objection to some recent proposals that we should afford animals legal rights by extending "personhood" to them. I discuss these matters in "The Claims of Animals and the Needs of Strangers: Two Cases of Imperfect Right."

kind of occasion your own purpose may be the opposite. Think, for instance, how hard it can be to keep your eye open when the eye doctor pushes his lens right up to it so that he can peer into your eye. We do not think of these kinds of reactions as "actions," exactly, but it may be that some of the "actions" of very simple animals are like that.

But although I am characterizing action based on teleological perception as instinctive, it need not be mechanical in this way. If an antelope sees a lion as something to be feared and avoided, then avoiding the lion is her own purpose as well as the evolutionary purpose of her reaction. Sometimes an animal's perception dictates a particular action: an antelope calf will, say, drop down into the tall grass when she sees a lion. Although this behavior is fairly automatic, it is possible that the animal who engages in it knows what she is doing. Such knowledge presumably makes the animal's behavior more flexible—she can decide to run away if the strategy is not working, and the lion appears to have spotted her after all. So we can distinguish:

Mechanical, Stimulus-Response Action
Instinct tells the animal:

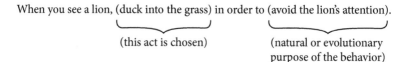

When you see a lion, (duck into the grass) in order to (avoid the lion's attention).

(this act is chosen)   (natural or evolutionary
                               purpose of the behavior)

Intelligent Action Governed by Teleological Perception
Instinct tells the animal:

When you see a lion, (duck into the grass) in order to (avoid the lion's attention).

(this act is chosen)   (animal's own purpose, as well
                               (perhaps) as natural or evolutionary
                               purpose of the behavior)

Above I claimed that a rational being is aware of the grounds of her actions, and capable of resisting her instinctive responses if she sees that there is reason to do so. One implication of this is that if she does obey her instinctive responses, it is because she has chosen to do so.[7] So rationality changes the scope of the object of choice. For an animal who acts instinctively, it is the act that is chosen, for a purpose that is given to her by nature. Even if it is her own purpose, not merely the evolutionary purpose of her behavior, it is not one she

---

[7] For further discussion, see Korsgaard, "Morality and the Distinctiveness of Human Action."

decides to adopt. But a rational being chooses the whole action, the act and the purpose together.[8] Ideally, she decides that under the circumstances, and all things considered, the purpose of the act is one that is capable of *justifying* her in performing the act. So we can add:

Rational Action

When you see a lion, (duck into the grass, in order to avoid the lion's attention)

(This whole action is chosen, as a package)
by someone who has decided that, in the circumstances,
avoiding the lion's attention is a good reason for ducking into the grass.

Another way to put this, one associated with Kant, is this: the other animals are governed by the laws given by their instincts, while we rational beings are governed by laws we give to ourselves. If an animal has instinctive cognition, that is what the law of ducking into the grass when you see a lion is—it's a law of instinct, even in the cases where the animal knows what she is doing, and the purpose is her own. But a rational being makes an assessment of the principle that she should duck into the grass when she sees a lion, asking herself whether, on this occasion, her actions ought to be governed by that principle. I will discuss how she makes this assessment later on (7.3, 7.5). In this sense, she makes the laws for her own conduct, rather than being governed by laws that are given to her by nature. This is the property that Kant called "autonomy," being governed by laws we give to ourselves. Rationality is liberation from the control, although not the influence, of instinct.

3.2.5 Rationality is the capacity to ask whether the potential reasons for our beliefs and actions are good ones, and to adjust our beliefs and actions according to the answers that we get.[9] How do we answer these questions? A theory about how we do that would be a theory about what the laws of practical reason are, and why. This is a big philosophical question, and I am not going to venture to defend a whole answer in this book, although we will be looking at some of Kant's (7.3, 8.2, 8.4) and the utilitarians' (9.2) answers later on. Some popular candidates

---

[8] I am calling things like *duck into the grass* "acts," and things like *duck into the grass in order to avoid the lion's attention* "actions." For further discussion, see *Self-Constitution*, §1.2, and "Acting for a Reason," in essay 7 in *The Constitution of Agency*, §4.

[9] Alternatively, rationality is the capacity to ask whether the potential grounds of our actions are really reasons. Which formulation is correct depends upon whether the theorist thinks reasons are constructed, or in some sense created, or not. The formulation in this note is more proper for a Kantian theory, since Kant thinks reasons are "legislated" rather than discovered.

for the laws of practical reason, just to give you a feel for what I have in mind, are that we should take the means to our ends, do what is best for ourselves on the whole, maximize the good in general, treat others as we would wish to be treated ourselves, or do what it would make sense for anyone or for everyone to do in our place. Those are all things that some philosophers have claimed that reason requires us to do. For our purposes in this chapter it is enough to suppose that there are some such laws, and that some of them—such as the law that we should maximize the good or the law that we should treat others as we would wish to be treated ourselves—are also plausible candidates for being the fundamental law of morality. Then we human beings, as rational beings, can decide what counts as a good reason to act, and be motivated accordingly, and that is what our moral nature consists in. This makes several important differences to the form of human life.

3.3 Evaluating Reasons and Evaluating the Self

3.3.1 The first difference is that when we endorse our motives and decide we have good reason to act on them, we judge their objects, the ends we have decided to pursue, to be *good*: that is, now we do not merely desire them, we value them. For that is, at least according to one theory, what valuing is—not merely wanting something, but approving and endorsing your own desire for it, and disapproving those who are indifferent to it or against it.[10] It is because we are rational that we think about what ends we should pursue and have a concept, "good," which we apply to the ends we decide to go for, the ones that in Chapter 2 I called "final goods." When we endorse our motives and decide we have good reason to act on them, we judge those actions themselves to be "right." Perhaps we judge them to be "all right" in the case where we decide that the action is permissible, or perhaps we judge them to be "right" in a stronger sense—a duty, or a requirement—in a case where we decide that it would be unreasonable *not* to do the action. So rationality, the power to evaluative our motives and the actions to which they tempt us, brings us under the government of the right and the good.

3.3.2 The second difference is that when we become aware that we can evaluate the motives of our actions, and act differently as a result of that evaluation, we become aware, in a way that the other animals are not, that our actions are *our own*—that we are their sources and authors, because what we do is up to us. Or rather, to put the point more properly, it becomes *true* in a way that it is not for

---

[10] This is a theme in the work of Simon Blackburn and Harry Frankfurt, for example.

the other animals that our actions are up to us, and that therefore they are in a special way our own. This is most obvious when you decide that the motive on which you are tempted to act is *not* a good reason for doing what you are tempted to do, and therefore refrain from doing it, or do the opposite thing. If you can override your own instinctive desires when you think that acting on them would be wrong, then you are in one sense responsible for what you do. This is when it is clearest that you are a normatively self-governing being—in Kant's term, an *autonomous* being, one who governs himself by the principles that he himself takes to be laws (7.3). If moral principles are among the laws of practical reason, as Kant himself believed, this is what makes you a moral animal.[11]

3.3.3 This in turn makes another difference. When we come to see our actions as up to us, we come to see them as expressions of ourselves—that is, of our *selves*. For because we are aware of our own attitudes and motives, or at least of some of them, our sense of our selves includes those motives and attitudes, and we are aware of this aspect of our selves as the sources of our actions. So when we turn an evaluative eye on to our own motives and actions, while at the same time coming to see those actions as up to us, we are effectively turning an evaluative eye onto ourselves. When we endorse our own motives and the resulting actions, we are pleased with ourselves, and when we act on motives that we think or later decide that we should not have allowed to govern us, we are ashamed of ourselves. Regarding ourselves as the sources and authors of our actions, and our actions themselves as good or bad, is in effect regarding ourselves as good or bad. When we take responsibility for our own actions, we see ourselves as courageous or cowardly, noble or small-minded, generous or selfish, and just plain good or bad, depending on how we act. So when we evaluate our reasons we evaluate our actions, and when we at the same time come to see our actions as having their sources in ourselves, we also come to evaluate ourselves.

When I read or hear discussions about whether there are any big differences between human beings and the other animals, I am always surprised that the one I just mentioned seldom comes up. I do not mean rationality—that has been the main contender ever since Aristotle—but the tendency to normative or evaluative

---

[11] Some people these days argue that the roots of morality, or even a primitive sort of morality itself, is observable in the social behavior of animals; most notably altruism, but also in forms of conflict resolution. See for example, Frans de Waal in *Primates and Philosophers: How Morality Evolved*, among other places, and Mark Bekoff and Jessica Pierce in *Wild Justice: The Moral Lives of Animals*. In "Reflections on the Evolution of Morality" I argue that these kinds of accounts cannot by themselves explain the origin of normative self-government. Good social behavior is part of the content of morality, but normative self-government is its distinctive form. Some non-human animals are richly social beings, but that does not make them moral.

self-conception to which it gives rise. For if this is indeed a difference between human life and the lives of the other animals—and I am tempted to think that it is—it is an *enormous* difference. Normative or evaluative self-conception does not find its expression in moral self-evaluation alone. It shows up all over the place in human life: in a teenager's desire to be cool or a ruffian's desire not to seem weak or urbanite's desire to be in fashion. We are eager that others should think well of us, and it is not (usually) because we calculate the possible benefits of that—it is because we are eager to think well of ourselves. Thinking well of yourself and thinking that others think well of you are the source of some of a human being's most exquisite pleasures. Feeling unappreciated by others is the source of enormous bitterness for many people. People can be driven to despair or suicide by the thought that they are worthless or useless or unlovely. We want to be good husbands and wives and parents and teachers and leaders and friends as well as, hopefully, good people. In a thousand ways, we are always holding ourselves to evaluative standards. None of this, I believe, is true of the lives of the other animals. I feel tempted to say that unlike us the other animals accept themselves as they are, but of course that is not the right way to put it: they do not evaluate themselves at all, so the question whether they accept themselves does not come up. A life led in the light—or the shadow—of a normative conception of the self is a very different kind of life from the one that most animals lead.[12]

3.3.4 And now we have arrived at the conclusion I promised you at the end of Chapter 2 (2.4). For if we human beings (1) regard ourselves as the source of our actions, and so (2) regard those actions as expressive of our selves, and at the same time (3) regard our actions as up to us, then we must regard it as up to us who and what we are. For whenever we choose our actions, we are deciding who—what sort of selves—we will be. That is why Kant was right in thinking that human beings play an active role in the construction of ourselves that the other animals (probably) do not play. We have what I have elsewhere called a "practical identity" that we create for ourselves.[13]

This complicates what counts as the good for human beings, for with this new form of identity comes a whole new way of functioning well or badly. We have

[12] Hobbes told a different story about how human beings acquired a normative self-conception than the one I am telling here. He thought that normative self-conception arises this way: other people place a certain amount of value on your power—your money, your influence, your strength, all of the features of your situation that make you efficacious. When you think about yourself, you associate yourself with that value, and then you come to think of it as your own value, or sense of self-worth. See *Leviathan*, part 1, chapter 10.

[13] Korsgaard, *The Sources of Normativity*, lecture 3; *Self-Constitution*, 1.4, pp. 18–26.

standards to meet and ideals to live up to, and we can function badly by having the wrong ones or failing to live up to the ones that we have.

3.3.5 But is it really true that animals lack an evaluative self-conception? Don't some animals sometimes feel pride and shame? This is a claim people sometimes make, especially about dogs. How can you feel pride or shame without thinking you've done well or badly, and that that somehow reflects on the value of your self?

I have admitted that these questions are all empirical, so there is certainly room for doubt. But let me just point out that there are some things that come pretty close, and might explain the observations on which these claims are based, without conceding that the other animals evaluate themselves.

First of all, social animals may very well want to be loved, or accepted by their group, and intelligent social animals may be aware when they have done something that would lead to anger or rejection if it were known. That could cause them to feel fearful or cast down, even if it did not lead to any thoughts about or representations of their personal worth. But I am happy to admit in any case that this is a borderline phenomenon, since in the life of a human child the beginning of normative self-conception may well involve the sense of acceptance or rejection by one's loving parents.[14] "Good boy!" we say both to our dogs and our sons. The question is whether the dog internalizes it in quite the same way a human child does, or only takes it as a signal that he's done what will serve him well in the future.

Second, animals form dominance hierarchies. Do animals higher in the "pecking order" feel that that somehow reflects well on them?[15] They are willing to fight for higher places, but of course that could just be for the privileges they bring—access to food and mating opportunities.

I am less sure about the third possibility, but it seems worth thinking about. Among human beings, there is a certain drive to maintain the appearance of self-control, even in our own eyes. This manifests itself in odd little ways. Sometimes if you make a misstep or a clumsy motion, you try to transform it into a different sort of motion, perhaps more unusual but deliberately made. You try to make it

---

[14] See the discussion of moral development in John Rawls's *A Theory of Justice*, chapter 8, sections 70–2.

[15] In "Reflections on the Evolution of Morality," I suggested that the evolution of morality may have involved the internalization of dominance instincts. The thing that animals do that looks most like they are responding to an "ought" is obeying the "authority" of dominant animals; morality involves coming to have a kind of authority over yourself.

turn out to be true that you actually meant to put your foot just there.[16] A more familiar manifestation of the tendency I have in mind is the fact that people who fall asleep in public so often hotly deny that they have done so. These reactions may be compounded by small bits of shame in the human case, but they need further explanation: after all, why should we be ashamed of stumbling or nodding off in the first place? These things bother us, I believe, simply because we are agents, faced with the job of maintaining control over our own movements. It seems possible that more sophisticated animal agents feel something like this burden as well.

3.3.6 Recall now Coetzee's imaginary philosopher (1.4), who thinks we are more important to ourselves than the other animals are to themselves. When I talked about that before, I raised the possibility that the reason we are tempted to think we are more important to ourselves is that we suppose that our lives are suffused with meaning and value, while the lives of the other animals are not. I believe that I have just described the source of that thought: it derives from the evaluative stance we take on ourselves. We do matter to ourselves in a *different* way than the other animals do, for it matters to us that we live up to our standards and meet our ideals.

3.4 Species Being

3.4.1 I have now mentioned several ways in which human beings are different from the other animals: first, we are rational, in the sense that we are aware of the grounds of our beliefs and actions, able to evaluate those grounds, and to believe and act in accordance with those evaluations. Second, this gives a different character to our actions, since we can govern ourselves by principles of our own choosing, rather than having our actions determined by instincts that tell us what to do. We are autonomous beings who may be held responsible for what we do. Third, our evaluative relation to our actions, combined with our aware-ness of ourselves as the sources of our actions, leads us to form an evaluative relation to ourselves, a normative conception of our own identity, a view of ourselves as worthy or unworthy, as good or bad things. This changes the nature of our good, for it is essential to the good of human beings, or most of us anyway,

---

[16] This might be thought to be on a continuum with something that happens in philosophical debate, which is that having said something stupid, you find yourself defending it. I realize this might be chalked up to pride in your intelligence, but I do not think that is the best explanation. Your intelligence would be better displayed, after all, in just saying, "Excuse me, I wasn't thinking, that is silly and I take it back." But this is very hard for people to do in the moment. I think the desire to maintain the appearance of control in your own eyes, and so of not having blurted something out without thinking, is at work.

to be in good standing with ourselves and at least some of our fellows. This may be part of the source of the other difference I am about to discuss.

3.4.2 The young Karl Marx, following the German philosopher Ludwig Feuerbach, argued that human beings have a property that he called "species being."[17] Human beings, he argued, are the only animals that actually think of themselves as members of a species. Any animal recognizes his own kind, of course, and sees members of his own kind as potential mates, as rivals for mates or for territory, in some cases as possible social partners of other kinds. But in the human case it is more than that. I am not sure exactly what Marx meant, but it seems clear enough that something like this is true. We identify with our species. We describe human beings as "we." We think of our lives as in a narrative way, as stories, and when we do that, the larger context in which we place that story is often the story of humanity itself—humanity has a shared history.

What exactly the story is varies from generation to generation and place to place, of course. In the Middle Ages in Christian Europe, the story was the one extending on from the Bible story—God gives the commandments to Moses, Jesus comes to save us, and eventually history comes to an end and the saved and the damned are assigned their rightful places. In the Renaissance it was a story of progress or regress depending on whether you thought ancient culture was superior to modern culture or not. In the West, since the Enlightenment, it has been a story about political and technological progress, with ever growing equality among human beings. Peter Singer was interpreting his own project in *Animal Liberation* in terms of that story when he declared that animals too are equal. We think of the members of our species as being members of a common community and, importantly, we think of our own lives as being, in various ways, contributions to the life of that larger community. We think of our lives as meaningful or not depending in part on what sort of a contribution to the life of that community they are.

All of this means that as human beings we see our lives as part of the life of the larger group, and our own good as bearing a relation to the life of that larger group. And because we are also a highly cooperative species, ready to work together to achieve our ends, we regard ourselves as, potentially at least, a kind of collective agent. When we ask whether "we" will ever achieve a permanent peace, or make it to the distant planets, or discover a cure for cancer, we are thinking of ourselves in that way. This makes the human species, potentially at

[17] See, for example, Marx's *Economic and Philosophic Manuscripts of 1844*.

least, a different kind of entity than the other animal species are: a collective agent. That fact has moral implications we will be looking at later on.

3.5 Ethics and Science

3.5.1 Finally, I would like to mention one more important human difference that comes with rationality. A non-human animal, I have suggested, perceives the world in a way that imbues it with practical significance, a practical significance determined by her own interests, as those are embodied in her instinctive responses to things. She perceives the world as populated by *her* flock or *her* pack, *her* offspring, *her* enemies, *her* food, so that she can respond to it in ways that will enable her to survive and reproduce. If you are a rational being, I have claimed, you are aware that you do this, and that makes it possible to get some critical distance on it, and so to call these instinctive responses into question. The difference made by this is even deeper than we might at first think.

Recall again the passage from *Middlemarch* that I quoted in Chapter 1. I want to remind you first of what I said then. Dorothea, an idealistic young woman who longs to do some good in the world, marries an older man, Casaubon, whom she believes is a scholar engaged in a great work. Discussing a moment when Dorothea misunderstands Casaubon's feelings, Eliot writes:

We are all of us born in moral stupidity, taking the world as an udder to feed our supreme selves: Dorothea had early begun to emerge from that stupidity, but yet it had been easier to her to imagine how she would devote herself to Mr. Casaubon, and become wise and strong in his strength and wisdom, than to conceive with that distinctness which is no longer reflection but feeling—an idea wrought back to the directness of sense, like the solidity of objects—that he had an equivalent center of self, whence the lights and shadows must always fall with a certain difference.[18]

In Chapter 1, I appealed to this passage to bring home how hard it is for us to grasp the full reality—the solidity, as Eliot puts it—of lives other than our own, especially of the lives of those whose minds, like those of the other animals, are different from our own. I wanted you to realize that it is hard for you to grasp that a non-human animal has a center of self as real as your own, where the lights and shadow might fall with a certain difference. There is a parallel point to be made here, which is that non-human animals themselves do *not*, or do not fully, grasp this sort of thing about others.

---

[18] Eliot, *Middlemarch*, p. 211.

Dorothea's revelation is not merely that Casaubon's interests, and therefore his responses to the events about which they are disagreeing, are different from her own. Her initial "moral stupidity" is grounded in something deeper than that. It is that she has failed to grasp the full significance of the fact that Casaubon does not exist in relation to her interests at all. He is not merely "the man who is going to rescue me from insignificance, and make me wise and strong." He is his own independent being, with an existence and a center of self which is completely independent of her, and which would be just as real as it is now in a world in which she did not exist at all. She is, as Thomas Nagel has put it, just one among others, who are equally real.[19] All of us *think* that we know this about others, but all of us are constantly losing track of it as well. This grasp of the full inner reality of others and its complete independence from our own concerns is absolutely essential to being a morally good person, and the fact that our grip on it is tenuous is one of the reasons why moral goodness is so hard to achieve.

But if as I have suggested, the other animals always see the world, including the other animals in the world, through the lens of their own interests, then the other animals do not have this awareness. An animal that has what psychologists call "theory of mind" may grasp that another animal sees the world differently than she does—that the other animal may not be able to see something that is visible from where she is, for instance. But if I am right, for a non-human animal, the other is always "my pack-mate," "my offspring," "my food," "my human companion," or what have you. This is one of the main reasons why the other animals cannot be moral beings.

3.5.2 A parallel point—essentially the same point—holds about a non-human animal's relation to the natural world. The capacity to get a critical distance from our own responses is what enables rational beings to grasp a terrible fact about the natural world: that *it* exists completely independently of our own interests; that it is the work of mechanical forces that operate with no regard for us or for the other animals; that it is a world in which there is no guarantee that things will turn out well for ourselves or for other human beings or for the other animals or for life itself. This grasp of the independence of the natural world from our interests, or any interests, is absolutely essential to achieving a scientific outlook on the world, and the fact that our grip on it is tenuous is one of the reasons why a genuinely scientific outlook is so hard to achieve. As for the other animals, they cannot view the world scientifically. They may understand a great deal about their environment, and even about cause and effect, but they have no conception

---

[19] Nagel, *The Possibility of Altruism*, p. 88.

4

The Case against Human Superiority

I want to describe a way of looking at the world and living in it that is suitable for complex beings without a naturally unified standpoint. It is based on a deliberate effort to juxtapose the internal and external or subjective and objective views at full strength, in order to achieve unification when it is possible and to recognize clearly when it is not ... Certain forms of perplexity ... seem to me to embody more insight than any of the supposed solutions to those problems.

Thomas Nagel, The View from Nowhere, p. 4

Your relation to your own death is unique, and here if anywhere the subjective standpoint holds a dominant position ... what I say will be based on the assumption that death is nothing, and final. I believe there is little to be said for it. It is a great curse, and if we truly face it nothing can make it palatable except the knowledge that by dying we can prevent an even greater evil.

Thomas Nagel, The View from Nowhere, p. 224

4.1 Introduction

4.1.1 In Chapter 1, I asked whether human beings are more important than the other animals, and argued that we are not. My argument was based on a point about the logic of importance and value: everything that is important must be important *to* someone; everything that is good must be good-*for* someone. Creatures, people and animals, are the beings *to whom* things are important, and *for whom* things are good or bad. Of course among the things that are important to any creature are some creatures: himself, his friends, family, the members of his pack, etc. But no creature or species of creature could be flat-out, absolutely, more important than every other unless that creature or species was more important to the members of all the other species even than they are to themselves.

Now that I have examined the question of human differences, I want to examine some other differences that some people have thought obtain between human beings and the other animals, and reopen the question whether they make what happens to us matter more than what happens to the other animals. Specifically, I am going to ask whether our moral and rational nature makes us superior to the other animals; and whether we are better off than the other animals. In the course of these discussions I am also going to raise some questions about whether, for that or for some other reason, death and suffering are worse for people than for the other animals.

4.1.2 As we saw in Chapter 2, we use the term "good," and related terms like "better" and "superior," in two different ways, which there I called "evaluative" (or "functional") and "final." It will be handy for our purposes in this chapter to express this distinction in a slightly different way. "Good" in the evaluative sense means something in the neighborhood of "excellent" or "admirable." "Good" in the final sense means something in the neighborhood of "desirable." The two questions I mentioned above are questions about the relative merits of human and animal life in each of these senses of "good."[1] The question about the evaluative sense is whether human beings are somehow superior to the other animals, more excellent as measured by some evaluative standard. The question about the final sense is whether human beings are better *off* than the other animals, whether it is better-for you to *be* a human being than it is, say, for a porcupine to be a porcupine or an eel to be an eel. I think many people get the answers to both of these questions wrong, because they make a mistake about the logic of goodness.

You might be wondering why I am bothering to raise these two questions, if I take myself to have established that even if we were superior to the other animals, or had a better life than they do, that could not make us any more important than they are. One reason is that you might not have been convinced by my argument. Another reason is that some of the defenders of animals do believe that we are superior to or better off than the other animals, and also believe that this makes a practical difference in certain kinds of cases.[2] We will

---

[1] Aristotle, in the *Nicomachean Ethics*, raises the question in which of these two senses happiness is good when he asks "whether happiness is among the things that are praised or rather among the things that are prized" (1101b 11–12). It is, of course, among the things that are prized. Maybe it is just because of the alliteration, but I like that way of making the distinction. I do not, however, want to take on board another part of Aristotle's view that seems odd to me, which is that there is some sense in which the things that are prized are better than the things that are praised (1101b 22–5).

[2] Another reason is that it is hard to dislodge the idea that superiority makes a creature more important than the ones he is superior to, even though the idea makes no particular sense.

look at some of those cases when I discuss some questions about whether it is worse to kill people than the other animals below.

4.2 Does Morality Make Humans Superior to the Other Animals?

4.2.1 Let's start with the question whether human beings are superior to the other animals, in the sense of "more excellent." There are two main grounds, I think, why people are inclined say that we are. One is because of capacities we have to a much higher degree than the other animals. The other is because of capacities we have that the other animals do not have at all. If my argument in Chapter 3 is along the right lines, and the empirical facts about what kinds of minds the other animals have are what most of us suppose them to be, then rationality and morality are in that second category. I am going to take it for granted here that the other differences are all matters of degree. Darwin, in *The Descent of Man*, argued that you can find the roots of language use, tool use, aesthetic sensibilities, and many other supposedly human capacities among the other animals and, as I mentioned in 3.1.1, many more recent scientists have followed him in this.[3] In this section, I am going to address the question whether morality makes us superior to the other animals. In section 4.3, I will come back to the question of the implications of the differences that are matters of degree.

4.2.2 So let's start with the question whether the fact that we are moral beings makes us superior beings, in a way that makes it matter more, or uniquely, what happens to us. It appears that Kant thought so, for he tells us that: "morality is the condition under which alone a rational being can be an end in itself."[4] To be an end in itself, in Kant's thought, is to have moral standing. Notice that it is a little unclear whether Kant is saying that a rational being can be an end in herself only if (or to the extent that) she actually realizes her moral capacity, or instead that only beings who have the capacity for morality can be ends in themselves. It does not matter for our purposes here, for we know from other contexts that he believed the latter claim, which is the claim we are interested in. We will look more closely at why Kant believed this in 7.4.

4.2.3 Before I go on, I want to make an important though hopefully obvious point. When I claim that human beings are moral animals, of course I do not

---

[3] Darwin, *The Descent of Man*, chapter 2.
[4] Kant, *Groundwork of the Metaphysics of Morals*, 4:443.

mean that human beings are morally good. I mean that only human beings can perform the kinds of actions that *can be* either morally good *or* bad. This is because only human beings have the kind of self-consciousness that makes it possible to evaluate the grounds of our actions and decide whether they are good reasons or not. So being a rational being means being capable of being *either* morally good or morally bad. The question is whether that capacity somehow makes us morally more important or in some way superior to the other animals.

Just to be clear, I am not claiming that our moral capacity is neutral, and that a human being is just as likely to be bad as to be good. The two properties are not on an equal footing. On my view, being moral is a form of being rational, and rationality is not a neutral property in general. When someone thinks logically or rationally, we do not need to appeal to anything except the fact that she has the capacity to think rationally in order to explain her success. But when a rational being gets tangled up in fallacies and contradictions, we do need such an explanation. I think something like this is true of morality as well. Unless people are under some special stress or threat or temptation that makes it hard to do the right thing, we do not wonder why they do it. On the other hand, when someone does something wrong we do need an explanation, although often enough one is ready to hand. But even if the capacity to act morally is not a neutral one, saying that people have that capacity is not saying that human beings are morally good.

So here is a peculiar question. Is the capacity for being morally good itself morally good? Does the fact that human beings are moral animals mean that there is something noble about our nature? There are (at least) two different reasons why you might think so.

4.2.4 Here is the first. The philosopher David Hume thought that our capacity for morality is itself morally good, for this reason. Hume believed that what makes something morally good is that we tend to approve of it, and, because we are naturally sympathetic beings, we tend to approve of things that make people happy. Hume called this tendency our "moral sense." For instance, Hume thought that we approve of beneficence and kindness, because beneficence and kindness contribute to the happiness of those to whom people are beneficent and kind. Hume also thought—I will not try to rehearse the whole argument here— that the fact that we tend to approve of beneficence and kindness makes us want to be beneficent and kind, to cultivate those properties in ourselves. When we do cultivate those properties in ourselves, of course, we are more likely to make others happy. So our tendency to approve of beneficence and kindness—our moral sense—makes people happy. Since we approve of things that make people happy, it follows that we approve of our own moral sense. So by our own standards, our own moral nature is morally good.[5,6]

That argument works if you think that what makes something morally good is that we tend to approve of it. But many philosophers disagree. Many philosophers think that what makes our actions, and the motives or personal characteristics behind them, morally good is that they tend to maximize happiness, or accord with principles on which everyone can agree, or treat all people (or all people and animals) as having equally important interests, or something of that kind. On these views, motives and actions are not morally good because we approve of them—rather, we approve of them because they are morally good, having one of these properties. Morality itself cannot be morally good in the same way.

Still, one might say, the argument can be generalized. We *do* approve of the motives and characteristics that motivate people to do the right thing. And our moral nature does motivate people to do the right thing. So it is natural to think of our moral nature as being a morally good thing.

4.2.5 That brings us to the second reason. You might think something like this: there are certain standards governing the ways we ought and ought not to act, and non-human animals do not conform to those standards. Cats, for example, toy with their prey before killing them. Baby birds shove their siblings out of the nest to their deaths, so that they do not have to share food and their parents' attention with them. Male lions kill lion cubs that are not their own, so that their mothers will come into heat and bear their own cubs instead. Hyenas, lions, and chimpanzees eat their prey while the prey is still alive. We find such actions horrifying. It is not their fault, of course, because they do not know any better. But surely it is better to be a creature who does know better, if it means you are more likely to act the way you ought. So that means there is something good about having a moral capacity—namely, it motivates and enables you to act as you morally ought.

But this argument assumes something that is not true. It assumes that moral standards apply to the actions of animals, even though the animals themselves cannot see that. But they do not. It makes no more sense to say that animals act wrongly when they do these things than it does to say that tornadoes and volcanoes act wrongly when they kill people at random.

---

[5] These views can be found in *A Treatise of Human Nature*, especially Book 3, part 3, section 6, and *Enquiry Concerning the Principles of Morals*, especially part 2, section 9.

[6] The moral sense should make us approve of anything that tends to make animals happy, too, since according to Hume we can sympathize with animals. I say more about Hume's views on ethics and animals in 7.2.2 and 11.1.2.

4.2.6 There are two kinds of evaluative standards: internal and external.[7] An internal standard applies to something because of the thing's own nature. The standards of functional goodness we looked at in Chapter 2 are internal. Knives should be sharp because they are for cutting—that is their nature. Cars should be fast and easy to handle because they are for getting people swiftly and safely to places they cannot easily reach on foot. Cakes and cookies should taste good, because their role in our lives is to serve as treats. Teachers should be clear and interesting because that is how you make people learn, and so on. All of those standards are internal. If you do not understand why knives should be sharp, cars should be fast, cakes should be tasty, and teachers should be clear, then you do not understand what knives, cars, cakes, and teachers are, or the role they play in our lives. Internal standards also have this implication: something that meets an internal standard is good *as* that kind of thing. Knives that are sharp are good knives. They are good *as* knives. Cars that are fast are, to that extent anyway, good cars. They are good *as* cars.

External standards apply to things when we have some special purpose for them, or they play some special role in our lives, something that their nature does not make them especially suited for. If you want to use your stapler for a doorstop, it is good for it to be heavy and stable. If you want to use a kitten for a paperweight, the kitten should be more inclined than kittens usually are to stay put.[8] If you want to hide from the police in your laundry hamper, it is good if it is unusually tall. External standards do not have the "good-as" implication. Kittens who are inclined to stay put are not especially good as kittens, and 6 feet-high laundry hampers are not good as laundry hampers, since it is difficult to reach inside them.

I believe that moral standards are internal standards of human action.[9] To put the point at the most general level, it is the nature of human actions to be done for reasons, so the standards defining what counts as a good reason apply to them in virtue of their nature. So if moral laws are laws of reason, moral standards apply to actions internally. A moral action is good as a rational action.[10] But as we saw

---

[7] The internal ones are also sometimes called "constitutive." I discuss this distinction in the Introduction to *The Constitution of Agency*, section 1.3, "The Normativity of Instrumental Reason" (essay 1 in *The Constitution of Agency*), pp. 57–62; "Self-Constitution in the Ethics of Plato and Kant" (essay 3 in *The Constitution of Agency*), pp. 112–13; and in *Self-Constitution*, 2.1.

[8] I did not make this example up. The character Penny Sycamore uses a kitten as a paperweight in the movie *You Can't Take It with You*.

[9] Korsgaard, *Self-Constitution*, chapter 5.

[10] I believe a moral action is also good as an action (without the qualifier "rational"), but I do not need the stronger conclusion for my purposes here.

in Chapter 3 (3.2), animal actions are not, in the same way, based on reasons. So moral standards do not apply to them internally.

This is not to say that animals cannot do the wrong thing, or what they ought not to do. In Chapter 2 I argued, with Aristotle, that we can regard animals as functional objects. When we do, we see their actions as having a function: to promote the animal's good, in the way characteristic of that animal. If animal action has a function, it is subject to an internal standard. So when an animal does something that is contrary to her own good, perhaps because her instincts evolved to make her fit for a different environment than the one she lives in now, she does the wrong thing, although of course it is not her fault (2.2.5).[11] But, distasteful as it seems to us, cats who toy with mice, birds who push their siblings out of the nest, and lions who kill other lions' cubs are doing just what they ought to do.

Of course, in a sense, nothing stops us from applying moral standards to animal actions, externally. But what would be our purpose in doing so? Apart, that is, from making us feel as if we were superior to the other animals.

4.2.7 One creature is superior to another when there is some standard they are both supposed to meet, and the first creature meets it and the second one does not, or the first one meets it to a greater extent than the second one does. John, who spends lots of time playing with his children, reading to them, and helping them with their homework, is a better father than George, who pays little attention to his children. But John is not a better father than Michael, who has no children. Notice also that it makes sense for John to set a high value on being a father, as a role that enriches his life and gives it value, and that he can do this without thinking that he is superior to Michael. In the same way, we can set a high value on our moral nature, as something that enriches our lives and gives them value, without thinking that we are superior to the other animals. Our moral nature does not make us superior to the other animals, because the standard it sets for us does not apply to them. It is just a way in which we and the other animals are different.

4.3 The Implications of Cognitive Sophistication

4.3.1 I now turn to the capacities we have to a higher degree than the other animals. The one I am going to focus on, for reasons that will become clear below, is intelligence. First we should ask, are human beings more intelligent than the

---

[11] See Korsgaard, *Self-Constitution*, 5.5.3.

other animals? It seems pretty obvious, but I suppose one might quibble about the claim. One issue here is that intelligence is not really a single attribute, but a cluster of cognitive abilities—insight, memory, calculative ability, logic, diagnostic judgment, other kinds of good judgment, creativity, and so on. What a person has is some collection of these, and what an intelligent person has is a large collection, or one that works together well. But some of the other animals have at least some of these—notably, memory—to a greater extent than people do. Pigeons have prodigious memories, for instance, and scientists have discovered that squirrels really do remember where they bury a lot of those nuts. Still, it seems clear that as a species, human beings have a set of cognitive skills that places us far above any other animal in terms of intellectual ability. Does that make us superior beings? And could that make us matter more morally?

Why should it? Intelligence seems to *us* to be a really important property—but then, it is the nature of human beings to live by our wits, or by that and our capacity for cooperation. We do not regard the other species as superior to us in some general way because they tend to have this or that property—strength, speed, memory, agility—to a higher degree than humans. More importantly, though, as far as the concerns of this book go, it just does not matter. We certainly do not think that individual human beings who are more intelligent than others therefore have a higher moral standing or anything like that.

4.3.2 In spite of that, many people plainly have the intuition that it is worse to torment or kill a more "cognitively sophisticated" animal than one who is less so. Even most defenders of animals tend to agree that it is worse to kill a human being than another sort of animal, and our superior cognitive capacities are sometimes proposed as the reason why. But the point is not just about human beings. Many people believe there is a general hierarchy of importance, with the more "cognitively sophisticated" non-human animals being more important than the less sophisticated ones. People who wish to argue that we should not eat, kill, or torment a certain kind of animal often point to the animal's cognitive abilities and achievements as providing a reason. I have been putting "cognitively sophisticated" in scare quotes because it is an evasive phrase one encounters in the literature. No one seems to be sure exactly which cognitive powers matter and why they should matter in this way. But many of us share the intuition that there is something worse, for example, about harming or killing a gorilla than a hamster, and then again something worse about harming or killing the hamster than an insect.

Of course, this last point might just be an expression of prejudice, born of a suspect relation between size and the arousal of squeamishness. Insects are so small, and so different from us, that it might just be harder for us to perceive their miseries. They do not weep or whimper or scream when we stick pins through their bodies or tear off their wings. Similarly, defenders of fish point out that their expressionless faces make it difficult to empathize with them. It even makes it possible for some people to doubt that they experience the pain that their thrashing bodies seem to express so clearly.[12] Perhaps the sense that there is some sort of hierarchy here is just based on the fact that some animals are more like us, and we find it easier to empathize with them.

4.3.3 But suppose that is not the answer, or anyway, not the whole answer, and that there is something right about these intuitions. What would explain it? I am going to tell you about an answer I am tempted by, and then tell you why I also think there is a problem with it.

In Chapter 2, I argued that the extent to which a creature has a self is a matter of degree. To have a self is to have a unified point of view on the world, so you have a self to the extent that your point of view is unified, both at a time and over time (2.3.3). Many philosophers share the intuition that which things can be good or bad for a creature and how good or bad they can be depends on how much psychological unity the creature has.[13] The fact that human beings are linked to their past and future selves by memory and anticipation is one of the standard reasons why death is supposed to be worse for people than for the other animals. Having a more unified self, and so a more substantial self, the human being, we might think, has more to lose. In fact we might even go further. In 2.4 and 3.3.4, I argued that human beings play a more active role in the constitution of our own identities or selves than the other animals do. You might think that this piece of "cognitive sophistication" gives us a special sort of stake in ourselves. We are, as it were, our own creators, so we matter to ourselves in a special way. Or to take another example, if an animal really did have disconnected experiences, so that the badness or goodness of one of his experiences had no ramifications for the badness or goodness of his other experiences, then perhaps the experiences themselves would be less good or bad *for that animal*. For a more psychologically disconnected creature the badness of being tormented once a week would be the intermittent badness of the experiences. For a more psychologically connected creature, however, it would be the badness of being a creature who is constantly being tormented. Even if, by some standard, the amount of pain being meted out on each occasion is the same, it would be worse for the creature who is more

---

[12] See Victoria Braithwaite, *Do Fish Feel Pain?*, p. 8; and Jonathan Balcombe, *What a Fish Knows*, part 1.

[13] I will discuss the ideas of Peter Singer and Jeff McMahan on these questions in 12.3.

connected. An isolated pain, neither resented nor remembered, ceases to trouble you the moment it is over. But for the more connected creature, the torments determine what his *life* is like, in the sense that the fact that he experiences them colors his outlook on the world.

Of course there are other ways in which the nature of your mind and the resulting character of your experiences can make pain either worse or less bad. Many people suppose that the fact that human beings have reflective capacities makes a difference of that kind. The fact that besides being aware of our suffering, we are aware *that* we are suffering, can make it worse. But the lack of reflection does not always make suffering less bad. In some cases, animals may suffer less because they do not reflect on the fact that they are suffering, and suffer in turn from that reflection. But in other cases, they may suffer more because they do not know that it will be over in a moment. And as many have pointed out, they cannot understand why they are suffering, and that it might be good for them, say if they are undergoing a medical treatment. Animals cannot laugh at their pains; we do it all the time.

Still, there are some reasons for thinking that suffering and death can be worse for more psychologically connected creatures. Some philosophers also think such comparative judgments can play a legitimate role in our practical thinking. Suppose, for instance, that for some reason you had to choose between killing a human being and killing a rabbit. One thing that might be relevant to your decision is that death is likely to be a worse thing for the human being than it is for the rabbit.[14]

4.3.4 I am pointing all this out here because I think that it helps to explain the intuition that cognitive sophistication is relevant to our assessment of how we should treat various animals. The point is that the kinds of properties that give some creatures more psychologically connected selves over time also tend to make those creatures more intelligent. Memory and the ability to modify your conception of the world through learning tend to unify your conception of the world over time, and so to unify you as the holder of that conception. But they also, by the same processes, make you smarter. So the suggestion I am tempted by is that the cognitive differences that are relevant to the intuition that it is worse to harm more "cognitively sophisticated" animals are the ones that tend to give an animal a more unified ongoing self.

If we did think this, here is how the confusion would arise. Because there would then be good reason to save the human being in preference to the rabbit,

---

[14] Other things might be relevant—the fact that the person is an autonomous rational being with the right to choose what things he is willing to die for, say, or species solidarity.

we would tend to think of the human being as being more important than the rabbit. That would not really be the reason—the reason would really be that death is worse for the human than it is for the rabbit. But it would seem as if we were treating the human as more important. Then because the properties that give us good reason to save the human being in preference to the rabbit are also properties that make the human being more intelligent, we would be tempted to conclude that the reason why human beings are more important is that we are more intelligent. The trouble with that conclusion is that it is ridiculous. But it is not ridiculous to think that the psychological properties that make us and the "higher" animals more intelligent also make it possible for us and the "higher" animals to be more profoundly affected by certain goods and evils.

4.3.5 In Chapter 1, I argued that people are not more important than animals, that more generally, it makes little sense to say that some creatures are more important than others. Can we accept the argument I have just proposed without conceding that some creatures are more important than others after all? I believe that we can. As I noted in 1.2.4, one way to put the response would be to say that you are treating two creatures as "equally important" so long as you think it is equally important that each of them gets the things that are important to her. What the argument we have just looked at suggests is not that the rabbit's death matters less than the human's because the rabbit is absolutely less important than the human, but that the rabbit's death matters less because it matters less *to the rabbit herself* than the human's does to him. The argument is supposed to show that what can be important *to* an animal herself varies with the extent to which she has a self, which in turn depends on her level of cognitive sophistication.

4.3.6 I said before that I was going to present an argument I am tempted by, and then explain why I think there is a problem with it. I have just described the argument I am tempted by, so now for the problem. My view is not exactly that people and animals are equally important, as, say, Peter Singer might put it.[15] My view is that it makes (almost) no sense to rank creatures in a hierarchy of importance, because creatures are the entities *to whom* things are important. Singer himself, offering one explanation of why we think it is normally worse to kill a person than an animal, says:

a rejection of speciesism does not imply that all lives are of equal worth. While self-awareness, the capacity to think ahead and have hopes and aspirations for the future, the

---

[15] I am referring to the slogan that serves as the title of the first chapter of *Animal Liberation*, "All Animals are Equal." Later (9.2) I will argue, as others have done, that this is not really Singer's view: his view is that all interests are equal.

capacity for meaningful relations with others and so on are not relevant to the question of inflicting pain...these capacities are relevant to the question of taking life. It is not arbitrary to hold that the life of a self-aware being, capable of abstract thought, of planning for the future, of complex acts of communication, and so on, is more valuable than the life of a being without these capacities.[16]

But if, as I argue, everything that is good must be good for someone, we have to ask, *for whom* is the life with these capacities more valuable? I have been arguing that the human life is more valuable to the human being than the rabbit's life is to the rabbit. But when you think about it, you will realize that the fact that untimely death will be a greater loss to the human than the rabbit, even if it is a fact, need be of no importance whatever to the rabbit. The problem I pointed out in Chapter 1 still stands: the human being's life is not more important from the rabbit's point of view. Nothing can make the human being's life *absolutely* more important than the rabbit's unless the human being's life is also more important than the rabbit's life from the rabbit's point of view.

4.3.7 Let me try to clarify the point I am trying to get at by putting it in a different way. In moral philosophy, especially since Kant, we often say that human beings (or rational beings or sentient beings) have an inherent or an intrinsic value. Here it is important to make a distinction. In Chapter 3, I discussed the fact that human beings, or rational beings, have an evaluative self-conception: we think of ourselves as worthy or unworthy, morally good or bad, attractive or unattractive, interesting or boring, and so on (3.3.3). The kind of value I am talking about now is different from that. This is the kind of value each of us is supposed to have as what Kant called an "end in itself."[17] When we accord a creature this kind of value, we commit ourselves to respecting her rights, taking her interests into account in our deliberations, promoting her good when we have the chance, and things like that. We also commit ourselves to the idea that this creature should not be used as a mere means to the ends of others. This is what it is to have moral standing.[18]

We often say that people have *equal* value as ends in themselves. Kant, however, firmly distinguished this kind of value, which he called "dignity," from "price." He said that dignity "is raised above all price and therefore admits of no equivalent."[19] On that showing, the value we have as ends in ourselves is not so much "equal" as "incomparable." Now I will explain why that matters.

---

[16] Singer, *Animal Liberation*, p. 20.

[17] Stephen Darwall distinguishes these two attitudes as "Appraisal Respect" and "Recognition Respect" in "Two Kinds of Respect."

[18] See also 9.2.   [19] Kant, *Groundwork of the Metaphysics of Morals*, 4:434.

4.3.8 When we think of a creature as an end itself, as having moral standing, we think of the creature herself as having a kind of value. We also sometimes speak of *lives* as having value. We do not always distinguish these two things carefully. After a catastrophe, we might say: "So many lives were lost!" rather than "So many people lost their lives!" The second formulation makes a distinction that the first formulation blurs over: the distinction between the life and the creature who lives it. To see the importance of this distinction, consider the fact that most of us think that killing a person wrongs that person. It is not just a morally bad thing to do, but an offense against the person whose life it was, a violation of that person's right. If all that killing does is prematurely end a valuable life, we might wonder why the killing especially wrongs the person who got killed, rather than just wronging all of us collectively, by removing something of value from the world.[20] So the value of the creature and the value of the life are different. The creature is, as Tom Regan puts it in *The Case for Animal Rights*, the "subject of the life," the one who lives and experiences it.[21] So we might ask, what is the relation between the value of the creature, and the value of the life, assuming there is one?

Once we think of things this way, we see that the value of the subject of the life does not depend on the value of what is in the life. Neither fortunate nor accomplished people are any more "ends in themselves" than unfortunate or ordinary ones. Human lives do not matter more because they have more valuable stuff *in* them. Rather, what is in a life matters because it matters to the subject of the life, and he matters. When we combine this thought with the requirement that a creature who is an end in itself should never be treated as a mere means to the ends of others, this has an important implication: that the value of a life is, first and foremost, its value *for* the creature *himself or herself*. But therein lies the problem. For even if the rabbit's life is not as important to her as yours is to you, nevertheless, for her it contains absolutely *everything of value*, all that can ever be good or bad for her, except possibly the lives of her offspring. The end of her life is the end of all value and goodness for her. So there is something imponderable about these comparisons.

Kant's claim that the value involved in being an end in yourself is not a mere price with a certain equivalent is not merely a rhetorical flourish. We cannot pay for a rabbit's death with a human being's life. Not straightforwardly, anyway. Although for most purposes the idea that creatures have an "equal" value does

---

[20] I do not believe that utilitarians have an answer to this question.
[21] Regan, *The Case for Animal Rights*, 7.5.

successfully capture the idea that one creature is not more important than another, if we take it to suggest that we can trade one creature for another, it leaves something very important out (9.2).

4.3.9 In fact, the situation may be even more paradoxical than these considerations make it sound. In 2.2.5–2.2.6, I argued that we need not take death to be part of our good, even though it is in a sense written into our "forms." As I mentioned there, this does not settle the question whether or not death might be good for us. The question whether death is good for us also depends on a different issue, namely whether there is something essentially finite or limited about the human good. It could be that human good has to take a certain definite sort of shape that is incompatible with immortality. Jeff McMahan has argued that death is worse for a human being than for another sort of animal because human life has a sort of narrative structure. He says:

the lives of persons typically have a narrative structure that may demand completion in a certain way. People autonomously establish purposes for their lives, form patterns of structured relations with others, and thereby create expectations and dependencies that require fulfillment. The importance of later events in a typical human life may thus be greatly magnified by their relation to ambitions formed and activities engaged in earlier. The goods of a person's expected future life may assume a special significance within the life as a whole if they would bring longstanding projects to fruition, extend previous achievements, resolve conflicts, harmonize hitherto dissonant ambitions, redeem past mistakes, or in general round out or complete the narrative structures established earlier... In the lives of animals, however, this potential for complex narrative unity is entirely absent. There are no projects that require completion, mistakes that demand rectification, or personal relations that promise to ripen or mature. Rather, as Aldous Huxley once put it, "the dumb creation lives a life made up of discreet and mutually irrelevant episodes." Each day is merely more of the same.[22]

But of course the reflection that human life has a narrative structure could lead us to the opposite conclusion, for a narrative structure requires a beginning, a middle, *and an end*. McMahan says it himself: things that are narratively structured "demand completion."[23] We would need to know much more to make this argument: why human good depends on life having a narrative structure, and why a narrative structure requires a completion. But if something like this is only true of human life, as McMahan supposes, then it is possible that death is good for us,

---

[22] McMahan, *The Ethics of Killing: Problems at the Margins of Life*, p. 197. For further discussion of this passage, see my "Keeping Animals in View."

[23] For another, related account of why human life might require death to make it meaningful, see Bernard Williams, "The Makropulos Case: Reflections on the Tedium of Immortality," in Williams, *Problems of the Self.*

or anyway necessary to our good, in a way that it is not for the other animals. For we can also turn the other part of McMahan's observation upside down. It might seem, for instance, as if a non-human female mammal could find such joy as she is capable of in raising a litter of cubs or pups every year for all eternity, though most of them are doomed to die and probably to be forgotten, even by their mothers.

4.3.10 Here is another consideration along the same lines. In 3.4, I endorsed Marx's contention that human beings are characterized by "species being." We think of ourselves as members of a species, and think of our own lives as parts of the history of that species. We see humanity as engaged in a sort of collective project, and may see our own lives as contributions to that project. Especially when this feature of our nature is combined with our moral nature, one of the implications of this is that for human beings, there are things worth dying for. We are prepared to die for the sake of justice, or freedom, or to risk death in the exploration of unknown territory. Because we see ourselves as participating in the larger, common life of our species, there can also be some compensation for death in the thought that you have left a legacy—made an important discovery, produced a work of art or literature, set a wrong right, passed on your skill or knowledge to the next generation, or just contributed in a positive way to the ongoing life of humanity. None of these compensations, except possibly contributing to the welfare of offspring, is available to the other animals. For them, death is more absolutely the end than it is for us.

So because of the narrative structure of human life, death may be good for us in a way that it could not be for the other animals, and because our lives are contributions to the ongoing life of the human species, death may be less bad for us than it is for them.

4.4 Are Humans Better Off than the Other Animals?

4.4.1 I have been considering the idea that death and pain might be worse for creatures with more psychologically connected and substantial selves. But the passage I quoted from Singer gives a different reason why the death of a human might be worse than the death of another sort of animal. He says: "It is not arbitrary to hold that the life of a self-aware being, capable of abstract thought, of planning for the future, of complex acts of communication, and so on, is more valuable than the life of a being without these capacities." If we suppose that this means (or anyway should mean) "more valuable to the creature who has these capacities," it brings us to the second question. Are human beings better off than the other animals? Is a human being a better thing to be, in the sense of better for the human being himself, than it is to be another kind of animal?

John Stuart Mill famously claimed that it is better to be a human being dissatisfied than a pig satisfied.[24] Mill believed this because he believed that human beings have access to what he called the "higher pleasures," and that this is a good thing for us. The pleasure of reading poetry, for example, is "higher" than the pleasure of eating a bowl of chips. The higher pleasures, Mill thought, are always preferred by those who have experience of them. It is only those who lack the experience, the training, the cultivation, to appreciate the objects of the higher pleasures who prefer the lower ones. In fact Mill believed that the higher pleasures are so much better than the lower ones that it is worth having the capacities that give us access to them even if having those capacities also makes us subject to greater dissatisfaction. Mill says:

Few human creatures would consent to be changed into any of the lower animals for a promise of the fullest allowance of a beast's pleasures; no intelligent person would consent to be a fool, no instructed person would consent to be an ignoramus, no person of feeling and conscience would be selfish and base, even though they should be persuaded that the fool, the dunce, or the rascal is better satisfied with his lot than they are with theirs.[25]

Mill argues that because human beings are also animals, we have experienced the kinds of pleasures that the other animals are capable of: we are familiar with the pleasures of eating, drinking, sex, physical activity, and affection. But only human beings are familiar with the pleasures of music and poetry and art and literature, scientific discovery, intellectual understanding, and moral goodness. The fact that we would never choose to be another sort of animal shows that these things must be better in some way, especially because the capacity for them also brings with it the capacity for certain specifically human dissatisfactions, and yet we prefer them even though they bring those dissatisfactions in their wake.

But, we may ask, for whom are the higher pleasures better? Would it be better *for the pig* if she were human, because she would then have access to poetry? Poetry is not good for a pig, so it is not something valuable that is missing from the pig's life, that she would get access to if only she could be changed into a human being. Temple Grandin, in her book *Animals Make Us Human*, reports that there is nothing pigs love more than rooting around in straw. She says: "Pigs are obsessed with straw. When I threw a few flakes of wheat straw into my pen of piglets, they rooted in it at a furious pace...So far, no one has found anything that can compete with straw for a pig's interest and attention." We could just as well say that rooting around in straw is something valuable that is missing from

---

[24] Mill, *Utilitarianism*, chapter 2, p. 10.   [25] Mill, *Utilitarianism*, p. 11.

your life, and that you would get access to if only you could be changed into a pig. So it would be better for you to be a pig.[26]

But isn't reading poetry a higher pleasure than rooting around in straw? If what makes a pleasure "higher" is, as Kant and others have suggested, that it cultivates our capacity for even deeper pleasures of the very same kind,[27] then we must have that capacity before the pleasure can be judged a higher one for us. Since the pig lacks that capacity, poetry is not a higher pleasure for a pig. Of course, we might try the argument that, so far as we can tell, none of the pig's pleasures are "higher" in Mill's sense. But then perhaps it is only for us jaded human beings that the lower pleasures seem to grow stale. So long as the straw itself is fresh, pigs apparently *never* lose their enthusiasm for rooting around in straw.

4.4.2 I suggested in section 4.1.2 that people go wrong both about the question whether human beings are superior to the other animals and about the question whether human beings are better off than the other animals because they make a mistake about the logic of goodness. I am now ready to explain that remark. In 4.2.7, I argued that one creature is only superior to another when there is a standard that applies to both of them, and one of them meets that standard and the other does not, or one of them meets it to a higher degree than the other one does. Our moral nature does not make us superior to the other animals because moral standards do not apply to them at all. In the same way, for one creature to be better off than another, there has to be something that is good for them both, and one of them has it and the other does not, or the first has more of it than the second. In some cases the second creature does not have the good thing because he does not realize that it would be good for him, like a person who does not know how deeply he could enjoy poetry if only he were taught how to. But one creature cannot be better off than another simply because different things are actually good for him. Mill's error was to confuse those two cases.

Of course human beings can be better off than the other animals in terms of having better access to goods that we and the other animals share. Human beings, at least in the developed world, eat more regularly, have more reliable shelter from the elements, do not have to worry much about getting eaten, have access to medical care, and nowadays have much lower rates of infant mortality than the other animals do. These are things that are good for all animals, and we have more of them. But this is just the opposite of what Mill thought—he thought we

---

[26] Grandin, *Animals Make Us Human: Creating the Best Life for Animals*, pp. 185–6.
[27] Kant says: "we correctly call these joys and delights more refined because they are more under our control than others, do not wear out but rather strengthen feeling for further enjoyment of them," in *The Critique of Practical Reason*, 5:24.

are better off because of the things that are good only for us, not because we have better access to the things that are good for both people and animals. Where there are no shared capacities or standards, these ideas make no sense.[28]

4.4.3 There is another way to put the point I have just been making. There are two possible views about the good, in the final sense of good, the sense that means something roughly like "desirable." One is that what is good-for you is relative to your nature—your capacities—and the other is that it is not. In the case of things that are good-for you in a more humble sense of "good-for"—namely, healthy— the first view seems obvious.[29] Vegetables are good for you but not for your cat, who is an obligate carnivore. But many philosophers do not extend this kind of relativity to "good-for" in the final sense. According to views like Mill's, some things (objects, activities, experiences) are good in themselves, and your capacities determine whether you have *access* to those goods. This seems to suggest that the final good is not relative to your nature; rather, your nature determines which goods you are able to experience and enjoy. According to views like the one I argued for in Chapter 2, by contrast, your capacities determine what is good for you. What is good for you is relative to your nature.

People who hold the view that your capacities determine your access to things which are good independently of anyone's nature characteristically think that human beings are just flat-out better off than the other animals. They think we are better off not because we have greater access to the kinds of things that are good for both people and animals, but because we are able to engage in intrinsically valuable activities, like reading and writing poetry or doing science and philosophy, to which the other animals lack access because of their limited capacities. Of course, these philosophers would probably not say that, say, reading poetry would be good for porcupines, if only they could do it. To describe their view more correctly but also more paradoxically, they think that we humans are better off because certain things which are intrinsically good are also good for us.[30]

---

[28] Someone might reply to my argument this way: one creature can be better off than another not only by having more of something that is good for them both, but by having a better quality of something that is good for them both. That's what Mill is arguing: pleasure is good for both people and animals, but people have access to a higher quality of it than animals. So it is like having access to a higher quality of food or water. To address this objection, I need to explain what is wrong with the idea that pleasure is the good. As I have already suggested in Chapter 2, I think what is good for a creature is his functional good and the things that promote it. Pleasure is an incompletely reliable perception of that (2.2.5). But there is a more complicated story to tell about this, which I tell in 9.4.

[29] For a discussion of the relation between good in the sense of healthy and good in the sense of final good see Korsgaard, "On Having a Good."

[30] I have to admit that I am swimming against the tide here. Mill borrows his argument from Plato, who, in chapter 9 of the *Republic*, uses it to establish that the pleasures of philosophy are

This view is fairly common in the literature on animal ethics. I think it is at work in the passage I quoted from Singer in 4.4.1. Here is another example. Describing the view that what is wrong with death, and therefore with killing, is that the victim is harmed by the loss, Jeff McMahan says approvingly:

> The Harm-Based Account has certain virtues. For example, it offers a credible explanation not only of why the killing of persons is in general more seriously wrong than the killing of animals but also of why the killing of animals of certain types is generally more objectionable than the killing of animals of other types. Because animals vary considerably in their capacities for well-being, some may be harmed to a greater extent by death than others. For example, because a dog's life is normally richer (in pleasure, social relations, and so on) than a frog's, dogs generally suffer a greater harm in dying.[31]

McMahan thinks it's better to be a dog than a frog. But better for whom? Would it be better for the frog if he could enjoy richer social relations?

4.4.4 You might wonder whether I am really saying that there is just no fact of the matter about whether, say, the best possible human life is a more desirable thing than the best possible life of a pig or a dog. Basically, yes, I am. If everything that is good must be good for someone, until we ask, "Better for whom?" the question which life is better is not a well-framed question. Does it follow that there is no way, or anyhow no self-interested way, to decide the question whether you would prefer to be a human being or a dog?

Perhaps not quite, because one sort of animal might in general be more likely to get the things that are good for her. Although by that measure, it is not clear that we human beings have the advantage over the dog. Dogs appear to enjoy their lives immensely. Well, you might ask, but wasn't that exactly Mill's point—that we would prefer to be human even though the dog is less subject to dissatisfaction than we are? But we judge the situation from the point of view of human beings, who have the human sort of good, and judge in terms of it. Part of the reason that we have a hard time getting a grip on this question is that we tend to think about mammals, and there is a lot of overlap between things that are good for different kinds of mammals, so it makes it seem like we can compare the two sets of goods. The fact that one sort of animal is more likely to get the things that are good for her than another might be relevant if we were thinking about which of the two creatures we would prefer to be, in a case where both of them had a good which

---

greater than the pleasures of profit or honor (*Republic* 9, 581c–583a). Aristotle assures us that although there are people for whom the political life is best, the contemplative life is the best life, so it is better to be someone for whom the contemplative life is best (*Nicomachean Ethics*, Books 1 and 10). These are people I usually try to avoid disagreeing with, but here I find myself with no choice.

[31] McMahan, *The Ethics of Killing*, p. 192.

was more deeply unlike our own. Try asking yourself whether it is better to be a butterfly or an octopus, say, assuming that those are creatures who have final goods.

But, in general: there is no way to answer the question which kind of life is better until we ask "Better for whom?" If that seems wild to you, consider this. Suppose you are trying to think about whether you would like to have been Napoleon. What is it you are trying to decide? If it is whether you would have liked to have been someone a lot like Napoleon, but with your own memories and tastes and preferences and feelings, you are not asking whether you would have liked to have been Napoleon, since Napoleon did not have your memories and tastes and preferences and feelings, so it was different for him. On the other hand, if you are asking whether it was good to have been Napoleon with Napoleon's memories, tastes, preferences, and feelings, all you are asking is whether Napoleon found his life to be good.[32] So if you are asking whether you would like to be a dog, but with your memories, tastes, preferences, and feelings, the answer is almost certainly no. You would miss your human pleasures, and probably dislike eating kibble all the time. But if you are asking whether the dog finds his life good, the answer is very likely yes. As I have already noted, dogs appear to be quite enthusiastic about their lives.

4.4.5 There is one kind of case in which I think it does make some sense to say it would be better to be someone for whom something different is good. Earlier I considered the case of someone who does not enjoy poetry, because he has not been taught how to appreciate it. In a way, poetry is not good for him, and he would be better off if it were. But that is still because of something about him, something that is relative to his nature: he's a human being, and has the capacity to derive satisfaction and inspiration from a good poem. Most cases in which we urge someone that he would be better off if he changed his (individual) nature are like this: when we tell someone he would be happier and better off if he developed more interests, or thought more about the good of other people, we are urging him not so much to change his nature as to perfect it, or to overcome some defect in it. He has the capacities that make this sort of thing good. But now consider a person who cannot appreciate poetry, or enjoy some other specifically human pleasure of the sort Mill thought higher, not merely because he has not learned how to, but because he is damaged or disabled in some way that makes that

---

[32] In fact, if all you are asking when you ask whether you would like to have been Napoleon is what it was like to have been Napoleon, with Napoleon's memories, tastes, and feelings, we could just as well say that you were Napoleon. That state of affairs in the world—that someone with Napoleon's memories, tastes, or feelings was Napoleon—was realized. The example is suggested by Derek Parfit's discussion of being Napoleon in *Reasons and Persons*, chapter 11.

impossible. He cannot enjoy music because he is deaf, or painting because he is blind, or higher learning because he mentally deficient.[33] Music, or painting, or higher learning is not good for him, given his nature, nor could it be. There is a sense in which he would be better off if these things were good for him. But that too is because of something in his nature: he is the kind of being for whom these things are ordinarily good, although he's not a fully functioning being of that kind, and that is a fact about him. To put it another way, there is such a thing as having a defective nature, and not just a different nature. We will come back to that thought later on (5.2.3) when it is time to discuss a somewhat different issue in animal ethics, the so-called argument from marginal cases.

So there are cases in which you can benefit a creature by changing his or her nature. But there are also limits on that. A squirrel in my garden would not be better off if we turned him into Aristotle. He would simply have been replaced by Aristotle. Where exactly do we draw the line between the changes that can improve things for you and the changes that would merely make different things good for you because they made you different? It is important to recognize that this is a version of one of the very oldest philosophical questions in the world, one with which Parmenides, Plato, and Aristotle struggled. What is the difference between merely changing something and destroying it and putting something else in its place? In the case of creatures, where do we draw the line between changing them and simply substituting something else for them? This is a hard question, but I believe that the boundary line is somewhere in the region of species membership, even though that is itself a somewhat fuzzy boundary line. If this is right, you are replacing a creature rather than changing him if you make him into a different species.

4.5 Conclusion

4.5.1 In this chapter, I have advanced some arguments that I know many readers will find paradoxical. I have rejected the idea that our moral nature makes human beings superior to the other animals. I have offered an argument intended to make sense of the idea that it is worse to kill a human being than another sort of animal, or

---

[33] I am aware, of course, that there are those who claim that these are not disabilities, or that they are only disabilities relative to social conditions that we could fix. Certainly the concept of a disability has fuzzy edges. People who wear glasses nowadays do not consider themselves disabled, because glasses are widely available, although they are sometimes covered by health insurance, which suggests we regard them as a response to a disability. Health insurance, however, does not cover the step stools and long-handled reaching devices, that being short, I have to buy to move comfortably through a world designed for a person taller than me. I do not want to argue about particular cases, but I think we need the concept of a disability, and generally, as I will argue later, the concept of a defective nature. See also *Self-Constitution*, 2.1.8, pp. 33–4.

more generally that things can be better or worse in a deeper way for creatures with more sophisticated cognitive faculties than for creatures with less sophisticated ones. But then I criticized the use of that argument to decide practical dilemmas, or at least ones about killing, in favor of the more sophisticated creatures, because it ignores the fact that, for a sophisticated and an unsophisticated being alike, death is the loss of pretty much everything to her, while the fact that death is worse for someone else may not matter to her at all. Finally I argued against the idea that it is better to be a human being than another sort of animal, because it ignores the way in which what is good for any creature is relative to that creature's nature and capacities.

I have already pointed out that the case against human evaluative superiority and the case against the idea that human beings are better off than the other animals are based on a common point about the logic of goodness. We cannot judge animals to be inferior to us because they do not meet an evaluative standard that applies only to us, and we cannot judge the other animals to be less well off than we are because they lack access to things that are good only for us. In both cases the problem is that we cannot make comparative judgments unless the two things are subject to a common standard.

Behind this thought, in turn, is a deeper idea that also informs my attack on the argument that the lives of more cognitively sophisticated animals matter more than the lives of less cognitively sophisticated ones. Value is a perspectival notion: values arise from the point of view of valuing creatures. And the values that arise from one point of view can be discordant with values that arise from another. There may be a way in which it is true that a more cognitively sophisticated creature loses more by death, but there is also a way in which both the sophisticated creature and the unsophisticated one lose everything that matters. In fact, we can see ethical life as an attempt to bring some unity or harmony into our various evaluative perspectives, by choosing those ends that are good for all of us. If we view ethical life in this way, it is not surprising that things become more difficult when we try to take the other animals into account (8.8.3; 12.1).

In Part II, I am going to argue that the idea of constructing a good that we can share is at the center of Kantian ethics. That is one way to think about the Kantian project of creating the Kingdom of Ends. I believe this can help us to understand both why Kant thought that only rational beings can have moral standing and, also, why he was wrong.

PART II

Immanuel Kant and the Animals

5

Kant, Marginal Cases, and Moral Standing

> The fact that man can have the idea "I" raises him infinitely above all the other beings living on earth. By this he is a *person*; and by virtue of the unity of his consciousness, through all the changes he may undergo, he is one and the same person—that is, a being altogether different in rank and dignity from *things*, such as irrational animals, which we can dispose of as we please.
>
> Immanuel Kant, *Anthropology from a Pragmatic Point of View*, 8:27

5.1 Human Beings as Ends in Themselves

5.1.1 Perhaps no theme of Immanuel Kant's ethical theory resonates more clearly with our ordinary moral ideas than his dictum that a human being should never be used as a mere means to an end.[1] "You are just using me!" is one of the most familiar forms of moral protest. Nearly any modern person, if asked to make a list of practices that are obviously wrong, would put slavery on the list, and Aristotle never seems so alien to us as when he complacently tells us that "the slave is a living tool."[2] A person, we now feel strongly, is not just a tool to be used for the achievement of other people's ends. Of course we do use each other as means to our ends all the time: the cab driver who drives you to the airport, the doctor who treats your illnesses, the banker who lends you money, all do things that help you to promote your own ends. But to treat someone as a *mere* means, as Kant understands it, is to use her to promote your own ends in a way to which she herself could not possibly consent, or for ends that she could not possibly share.

Kant argued that treating a person as a mere means violates the dignity that every human being possesses as an "end in itself" (4.3.7–4.3.8; 8.3). And he enshrined this idea in one of his formulations of the Categorical Imperative,

---

[1] The material in this section previously appeared in "Fellow Creatures: Kantian Ethics and Our Duties to Animals."

[2] Aristotle, *Nicomachean Ethics*, 8.11 1161b 4.

the Formula of Humanity, which runs: "So act that you always treat humanity, whether in your own person or in the person of any other, always at the same time as an end, never merely as a means."[3] Respect for a human being as an end in himself or herself, Kant argues, demands that we avoid all use of force, coercion, and deception, that is, all devices that are intended to override or redirect the free and autonomous choices of other people. People should decide for themselves what ends and projects they are going to promote or pursue, governed only by their own reason, and we should not try to force or trick them into doing what we want them to do or what we think is best. Respect for humanity therefore demands respect for the legal rights that protect people's freedom of choice and action. Finally, Kant believed that respect for humanity also demands that we help to promote the ends of other people when they need our help, at least where that is consistent with the other ends we have reason to promote. This is because an essential aspect of respecting your own humanity is regarding your own ends as good and worthy of pursuit (8.4). When that same respect is accorded to others, it demands that we regard their ends as good and worthy of pursuit as well.[4]

Kant describes rational beings who respect one another's humanity as forming what he calls the "Kingdom of Ends." Like the Kingdom of God on earth, the Kingdom of Ends is a spiritual or notional community, constituted by the relations among human beings who share a commitment to a conception of ourselves and each other as ends in ourselves. But with a characteristic Enlightenment twist, Kant reconceives this spiritual kingdom as a kind of constitutional democracy, in which each citizen has a legislative voice. When we act on moral principles, Kant believes, we act in a way that is acceptable from any rational being's point of view, and therefore we interact with them on terms that they can accept. So moral laws may be viewed as the laws, legislated together by all rational beings in congress, of the Kingdom of Ends.

5.1.2 When people are confronted with this account of morality, the question always immediately arises: But what about non-rational beings? If the value of human beings as ends in ourselves is associated with our capacity to be governed

---

[3] Kant, following a tradition that goes back to Aristotle, tends to identify human beings and rational beings. But it is clear that it follows from Kant's view that if there were creatures, say on other planets, who were "rational" in the normative sense described in Chapter 4, they would also count as persons and as ends in themselves. We will be looking at the argument for the Formula of Humanity in Chapter 8.

[4] I discuss in more detail how Kant reaches these practical conclusions from the Formula of Humanity in "Kant's Formula of Humanity," essay 4 in *Creating the Kingdom of Ends*, and in "Valuing Our Humanity," forthcoming in *Respect for Persons*, ed. Oliver Sensen and Richard Dean.

by autonomous rational choice, what are we to say about those who, we suppose, have no such capacity? What about infants who are not yet rational or the very old and demented who are rational no longer? What about the cognitively disabled and the incurably insane? And what about the non-human animals? Are none of these to be regarded as ends in themselves? If not, does that mean that we are permitted to use them as mere means to our ends? If what it means to have moral standing is to be an end in oneself, do none of these creatures have moral standing?

In fact, it has become a commonplace in the animal ethics literature to challenge Kant's conception and others like it by arguing that it is inconsistent to refuse moral standing to animals while granting it to human beings whose rational capacities are undeveloped or defective or damaged in these various ways. The strategy goes all the way back to the early utilitarian Jeremy Bentham, who asserted that "a full grown horse or dog is beyond comparison a more rational, as a well as a more conversable animal, than an infant of a day or a week or even a month, old."[5] According to what has come to be called the "Argument from Marginal Cases," whatever property we choose as the ground of moral standing, there will be some human being who lacks it, or some other kind of animal who has it. There is no property, Peter Singer has urged, that is possessed by all and only human beings, and so no possible grounds for assigning moral standing to human beings alone.[6]

In my view, this kind of argument is metaphysically flawed, for several reasons, which I will spell out in Section 5.2.

5.2 Against the Argument from Marginal Cases

5.2.1 In the first place, it is important to realize that words like "rational" and "reason" have both a normative and a descriptive use.[7] When we say that someone "is rational" in the descriptive sense, we mean that there is some consideration which she believes to be relevant to what she should do or believe, and on the basis of which she decides to act or forms a belief. We ordinarily also believe that she knows what that consideration is, and that she would offer it in answer if you asked her why she believes or does what she does. That consideration is her "reason" for what she does. In this sense, when we say of someone that she made a decision "rationally," we mean that she thought it through and chose on the

---

[5] Bentham, *Introduction to the Principles of Morals and Legislation*, chapter 17, note 122.
[6] Singer, *Animal Liberation*, p. 237.
[7] A version of this discussion is forthcoming in Korsgaard, "Rationality," in Lori Gruen (ed.), *Critical Terms for Animal Studies*.

basis of her principles or at least on the basis of considerations she is able to articulate. When we mention someone's reason in this sense, we are explaining how the situation looked through her eyes, and how what she did or believed was a response to that.

When we say that a human being acts "rationally" in this sense, the contrast is with being out of control, or engaging in some form of expressive action—slapping someone in rage, screaming in terror—or acting in an automatic, unreflective way—ducking, wincing, or doing something entirely out of habit. In these kinds of cases we can explain what the person does, but the explanation does not take the form of citing a consideration on the basis of which she made a decision. More generally, acting rationally in this sense contrasts with performing actions that are not based on considerations that the agent consciously takes into account. Actions of this kind are not descriptively rational, though their perpetrators may be. If I am right in thinking that the actions of non-rational animals, like some of the human actions I just mentioned, are grounded in the ways they instinctively perceive the world (3.2.1), animal actions are not descriptively rational.

But sometimes, when we say that someone made a decision "rationally," we mean that he made the decision *well*, that the principles on which he acted were the correct ones, and that his reason for what he did or believed was a good one. That is the normative sense of "rational." Acting "rationally" in this sense contrasts with doing or believing things for bad or silly reasons.

We use the terms both ways. Suppose, for instance, that you and your friend Henry are having a political argument. Henry plans to vote for a candidate whom both you and Henry think is racially prejudiced, ignorant of foreign affairs, overly influenced by certain lobbies, and so on. You ask him why he would vote for such a person. He replies that the candidate is the nominee of the Populist Party, and that he always votes for the nominee of the Populist Party. Henry is rational in the descriptive sense: his action is based on a consideration that he takes to be relevant, namely that the candidate has been nominated by his favored party. He articulates this consideration in response to your question "Why?" You may pose an objection to his plan either by saying "That is a bad reason to vote for him" or "That is no reason to vote for him." If you say, "That is a bad reason to vote for him," you are using the term "reason" in the descriptive sense, to refer to a consideration on the basis of which someone decides to act. If you say, "That is no reason to vote for him," you are using the term "reason" in the normative sense, essentially to mean a good reason.[8] Someone can reason badly and still be

---

[8] There is one kind of case that cuts across the distinction in an interesting way: cases in which someone believes or acts on the basis of a consideration, but one whose efficacy for him he is not

"a rational being" in the descriptive sense. And someone who is not in a condition to make his decisions well may still be a rational being in the descriptive sense, in the sense that he is capable of acting on considerations he can articulate. You do not cease to be a rational being if you fall asleep or become unconscious, though your rational capacities are unavailable to you then. You do not cease to be a rational being if you get drunk or high, though you may not be able to reason very well in these conditions. Being in a condition that makes you bad at reasoning—say, one of mental deficiency—even if the condition is permanent, does not necessarily make you a non-rational being in the descriptive sense. Kant's claim about the value of rational beings is about rational beings in the descriptive sense.

5.2.2 Of course the argument I just gave does not apply to all of the categories of human beings who have been deemed "marginal." Very young infants, for instance, do not just reason badly: they cannot reason at all. But infants, I believe, are not even candidates for being the type of entity that should have moral standing. A human infant is not a particular kind of creature, but a human creature at a particular life stage. I believe that it is not proper to assign moral standing, and the properties on which it is grounded, to life stages or to the subjects of those stages. Moral standing should be accorded to persons and animals considered as the subjects of their whole lives, at least in the case of animals with enough psychic unity over time to be regarded as the subjects of their whole lives.[9] Nor, except perhaps in the case of extremely simple life forms, should we think of the subject of a life merely as a collection of the subjects of the different temporal stages of the life. As we have already seen, for most animals having a self is not just a matter of being conscious at any given moment, but rather a matter of having a consciousness or a point of view that is functionally unified both at a particular time and from one moment to the next (2.3.3). That

---

aware of and whose relevance he might consciously deny. We think of Freudian slips, prejudices, implicit biases, and various forms of self-deception as working in this way. Perhaps Henry is in fact drawn to vote for the Populist candidate because the opposing party's candidate is a woman and Henry unconsciously views women as incompetent to hold office. A critic of Henry might say that that is "the real reason" he is voting for the Populist candidate. The consideration is in a sense operating as a cause, rather than as a reason, because Henry is not aware of its influence, but it makes his conduct intelligible in something like the way a reason does: it shows us how the situation looks through his eyes, and how his action is a response to that.

[9] Tom Regan's term "subject of a life" for the sort of thing that has moral standing is felicitous in this respect. The fact that Regan himself excludes young infants and the permanently comatose from the category on the grounds of their present lack of certain characteristics suggests that he himself does not use it in the sense that I have in mind, however.

ongoing self is the thing that should have or lack moral standing, or be the proper unit of moral concern.

Why should we take the person or animal, considered as the subject of the whole life extended over time, as the proper unit of moral concern? Earlier I argued that the extent to which an animal's point of view is connected over time is related to the temporal unit we appeal to when we think of the animal's good: the more functionally unified the animal's self is over time, the more sense it makes to think of the animal's whole life as a thing that can be good or bad (2.3.3). I also think that once we think of the whole life as good or bad, we are more likely to consider the value of particular experiences and conditions in terms of their impact on the life as a whole. Many hedonistic utilitarians think of this overall impact as a matter of the effect of the experience on an aggregate total: Did the experience add to the overall total of pleasure you experienced in your life, and if so, how much? That is why they (and many others) think it makes sense for you to forego certain pleasures at one moment in order to get even more pleasures later on. It is because the good you are concerned with is the good of your life as a whole.

Although the argument I am making here does not depend on this point, those who doubt that the quality of life can be understood in terms of an aggregate will be even more inclined to think of the value of experiences and conditions in terms of their impact on the life as a whole. Consider, for instance, the kind of experience we would characterize as "formative." Going to college, say, is something that is good for you not merely in the sense that you enjoyed it while you were there, but in the sense that it makes a difference to the whole character of your life. That difference will certainly *include* things like whether you enjoyed your life during the stretch of time you were in college, but it may also include things like the fact that you developed a wider and better informed outlook on the world that changes the way you see the world for the rest of your life. When you think about whether college was good for you, you are taking those larger effects on the character of your whole life into account. Or think about someone who says, "It is better to have loved and lost than never to have loved at all." Such a person is talking about the impact of experiencing love not just on himself as he was at the time, but also its impact on his *life*. He is not just saying that the pleasure of having loved outweighs the pain of losing it; he is saying that his life as a whole is a better thing for him *because* he had this kind of experience. It is not clear that the good of such things can be understood in terms of their impact on an aggregate total. Instead of thinking of the value of our lives as a kind of sum of the value of the particular good things in it, it may make better sense, at least in some cases, to think of the particular things themselves as being good or bad depending on what kind of contribution they make to the value of the whole. But as I said before, the argument does not depend on this point. Whether or not we think of the impact of particular good things on our lives in aggregative terms, we do think of the good and bad things in our lives in terms of their effects on our lives as a whole. If to have moral standing is to be someone whose good matters for its own sake, then the unit of moral standing, the object of moral concern, should be the subject of a whole life.

It is only when the connectedness of the self over time is minimal or absent that we might reasonably be tempted to treat the subject of a life stage rather than the subject of the whole life as the proper unit of moral concern. We might, to take a rather vivid case, puzzle ourselves over the question whether the goodness of a caterpillar's life makes any contribution to the goodness of the butterfly's life (assuming such creatures are sentient), or whether those are just separate matters. But, as a matter of fact, the animals we are most often concerned with in the domain of animal ethics do not undergo these kinds of radical transformations. They are connected over time and are the unified subjects of their entire lives.

For all of these reasons, we should not ordinarily ask whether a person or animal at this or that life stage, say, infancy or senility, has moral standing. Someone who treated a human infant the same way he would treat a dog on the grounds that the infant "lacks rationality" would be doing something wrong. An infant's developing brain is the developing brain of a rational being, and if the way you treat the infant is not responsive to that fact, you are doing something wrong. The point here is not, as people sometimes say, that infants are "potentially" rational beings. They are, of course, but that is in virtue of properties they have now. Being human, they are already rational beings: they are the kind of creature who is "designed" by the evolutionary process to function in a certain way. The argument applies as much to people with extreme senile dementia at the other end of life, who will never choose rationally again. Except in cases like the caterpillar and the butterfly, or perhaps to extremely simple creatures devoid even of the ability to learn, moral standing does not belong to particular life stages or to particular conditions, but to the subjects of whole lives.

5.2.3 There is a third reason for rejecting the argument from marginal cases, and it is the most important. A creature is not just a collection of properties, but a functional unity, whose parts and systems work together in keeping him alive and healthy in the particular way that is characteristic of his kind. Even if it were correct to characterize a human being with cognitive defects as "lacking reason," which usually it is not, this would not mean that it was appropriate to treat the human being as a non-rational animal. Rationality is not just a property that you might have or lack without any other difference, like blue eyes. To say that a creature is rational is not just to say that he has "reason" as one of his many properties, but to say something about the way he functions. He thinks about the things he is inclined to believe or to do, assesses them by rational standards, and believes or acts accordingly. A rational being who lacks some of the properties that together make rational functioning possible is not non-rational, but rather defectively rational, and therefore unable to function well. He is unable to make good decisions about what to believe or to do. Children, for example, gradually acquire the kind of self-consciousness that makes us rational—they are, increasingly as they grow up, aware of the grounds of their beliefs and actions. As we saw before (3.2), it is because of this form of self-consciousness that human beings need reasons in order to believe and act, and principles from which to derive those reasons. A child who has the relevant form of self-consciousness but is not yet able to understand the principles that should guide his choices is unable to make good decisions, and therefore needs the help of adults to decide what to do.[10] Having developed one aspect of rationality before the other, he is not yet functionally unified. An addict, on the other hand, may be able to evaluate her desires correctly, but may be unable to refrain from acting on them. A comatose person does not have a different way of functioning, but rather is unable to function at all. It is not as if you could simply subtract "rationality" from a human being, and you would be left with something that functions like a non-human animal. A non-rational animal, after all, functions perfectly well without understanding the principles of reason, since he makes his choices in a different way. He is "designed" by the evolutionary process to be guided by the ways he instinctively perceives the world, rather than by reason (3.2).

In fact, this reflection gives me a way to bring out the point I am trying to make. I have been suggesting that the argument from marginal cases wrongly treats a way of functioning as if it were just a property you could have or lack without other changes. In general, it treats a living thing as a heap of properties rather than a functional unity. The picture it suggests is this:

Properties of a dog: alive, sentient, emotional, intelligent.
Properties of a human being: alive, sentient, emotional, intelligent, rational.
Subtract rationality from the human being: you are back to something essentially like the dog.

To see what is wrong with that, you need only consider the following analogy:

Plant: alive, capable of nutrition and reproduction.
Dog: alive, capable of nutrition, reproduction, and action.

[10] Tamar Schapiro, "What Is a Child?".

Subtract the capacity for action from the dog: you are back to something essentially like the plant.[11]

No, you are not back to something essentially like the plant. Subtract the capacity for action from the dog, and the dog will die. The most obvious reason for this is that the way the dog carries out the function of nutrition is through action. A dog has to be able to go and get his food, and before he can digest it he must eat it, and those are actions. A dog who was, say, paralyzed, and therefore unable to act, would, without assistance, starve to death. In the same way, a severely mentally defective human being could not simply revert to functioning completely instinctively. It is not like we could decide: well, he is not quite fit for human society, but if you just let him loose in the forest he will be fine. Many things about the human being, including the way that we act, are changed by the fact that we are rational. In a much more extensive way than the other animals, we have to figure out what to do, and a severely mentally defective person cannot do that. That is why we have to take care of such people. They are rational beings with defects that make them unable to function rationally. If they were not rational beings, they would not have a problem.

The Argument from Marginal Cases ignores the functional unity of creatures. A creature who is constructed to function in part by reasoning but who is still developing or has been damaged is still a rational creature. So the Kantian need not grant and should not grant that infants, the insane, the demented, and so on, are non-rational beings. The point is not, of course, that we should treat infants and people with cognitive disabilities exactly the way we treat adult rational beings, because they too are rational beings. The way we treat any creature has to be responsive to the creature's actual condition. But the creature's condition itself is not given by a list of properties, but also by the way those properties work together. The moral issues raised by the fact that creatures grow up through developmental stages, the moral issues raised by the fact that all creatures are subject to illness and handicap and damage, and the moral issues raised by the fact that creatures come in different species are very different kinds of moral issues, and should not all be treated alike.[12]

---

[11] We sometimes describe people who have lost certain brain functions as being in a vegetative state, but that does not literally mean they are like plants. Plants can normally function without help. People in a vegetative state will die without help.

[12] Of course, there may be human children born so defective that they cannot be said to have any aspect of rationality. But it is even more obvious that they cannot be compared to non-rational animals, since they are completely non-functional. The way to explain their condition is still as defectively rational beings, or perhaps as defective animal beings, not as non-rational beings.

5.3 Atemporal Creatures

5.3.1 According to the arguments I have just given, moral standing properly belongs not to the subjects of certain phases of a life (say, for example, those during which a creature is rationally competent), but to the subject of the life as a whole, the ongoing self who has a good. Moral standing is not something that is acquired and lost as you go through life: it belongs to you as the creature whose life it is. If I am right, that may seem to have implications that many people would find objectionable about another ethical issue. Many people think that the question whether and when it is permissible for a person to have an abortion turns on the question when her developing fetus becomes a person, and thereby (according to one theory) acquires moral standing. If we say that moral standing is something you have in virtue of the kind of being you are, and cannot be acquired or lost, must we say that a creature has it right from the moment of conception?

To explain why not, I need to clarify something important about the position I am advocating here. I am not claiming that moral standing is something that endures as long as the creature's life. I am claiming that moral standing is something atemporal. Our lives are furled out in time, but considered as the subjects of those lives, we are not. So the position I advocate does not settle any questions about when a creature's life begins, or when we take the creature herself to begin to exist.

5.3.2 I am aware that what I am saying is going to sound paradoxical to many readers at first. Human beings inevitably think of the world temporally, and this makes it easy for us to confuse something's being atemporal with something's being immortal or eternal, something's having always been there. But how can a creature's moral standing have always been there, when the creature herself has not always been there, and (unless you believe in some extravagant form of determinism) might never even have been born? The problem is that this way of thinking about atemporality is a mistake. "Has always been there" is a temporal notion. It is not what being atemporal means.

Suppose I say, "Alexander the Great is alive." At the moment, that is false. But for a time, it was true. In particular, it was true from 356 to 323 BC. But now suppose I say, "Alexander the Great lived from 356 to 323 BC." When was that true? That is an ill-formed question. It is an atemporal truth. In particular, it is one that treats Alexander the Great as an atemporal object, and tells us how that object is related to a certain thing that did take place in time, namely his life.

We can think and talk about ourselves in both ways, but when we think and talk of ourselves as subjects, first personally, we think of ourselves atemporally.

I mean this to apply both to ourselves as the subjects of our experience, and to ourselves as the subjects of sentences and propositions. It can be hard to see, because we can think both temporal and atemporal thoughts *about* ourselves. If I say, for instance, "I am a little uncomfortable," I mean something like "I am a little uncomfortable right now." I am saying that is true now. I am not saying that it is an atemporal truth that I am uncomfortable. But if I say, "I was born in 1952," I am not saying something that I take to be true of me right now. I am saying something I take to be atemporally true. So why do I say that even in the first case, when I am thinking a temporal truth about myself, I am thinking and speaking of myself atemporally? It is simple: because if you ask me when I am uncomfortable, I can answer. I can say "right now" or I can say, "On March 26, 2017." When I give those answers, I stand outside of time, see it unfurled before me, and locate the events of my life in it. You and I look down at time together, at the unfurling of my life through time, and I point to a spot in that unfurling and I say "There. March 26, 2017. That is when I am uncomfortable." I think of myself not as a sequence of moments or events, but as the individual who is marching through them.

If we think of ourselves as atemporal insofar as we are subjects, the subjects of experience and the subjects of thoughts, sentences, and propositions, then we should think of the subjects of lives as atemporal also.

5.3.3 Here is one reason why that matters. There is an old debate, going at least back all the way to Aristotle, about whether a person can be affected for good or evil after his death. Aristotle apparently favors the view that "evil and good are thought to exist for a dead man, as much as for one who is alive but not aware of them."[13] Aristotle says the cases he has in mind are "honours and dishonours or the good or bad fortunes of children and in general descendants."[14] For example, we might plausibly think it is a bad thing for you if someone spreads evil rumors about you after your death, especially if it happens in a community of people whose opinions you cared about, or if you had some hopes of setting a good example to others. This case fits the argument lurking in the remark from Aristotle I just quoted: it would be bad for you if someone spread evil rumors about you while you were alive, even if you were unaware of it, so why wouldn't it be bad in the same way if it happened after you were dead? Aristotle also thought it plausible to say it is a bad thing for you if your children suffer unhappy fates after you have died, presumably because the good of your children was important to you. What was important to you was not just "the good of my children during

---

[13] *Nicomachean Ethics* 1.10 1100a 10–32.   [14] *Nicomachean Ethics* 1.10 1100a 20–1.

my lifetime."[15] That, after all, is why you made provision for them in your will—which brings us to another obvious example. It seems plausible to say that you are wronged if your last will and testament is not carried out after your death, say because someone forges an alternative will in order to get your money for himself. These kinds of examples suggest that you can be both harmed and wronged after your death.

Some people think that you cannot be harmed or wronged after your death because there is not anybody there to be harmed or wronged. In other words, they think that people along with their moral standing are temporal objects, and therefore that the existence of a person coincides with his life. (Keep in mind here that the alternative claim is not the religious claim that people *continue* to "exist" or live in time after they die, but rather the logical claim that people should be thought of as atemporal objects.) Those who believe that the existence of a person coincides with his life must deny that the people I described in the paragraph above are harmed or wronged after their deaths.[16] In fact, they must deny the intuitively plausible view that what is bad about death or at least untimely death is the loss to the person who suffers it. After all, they think there is no one (still) around to whom that loss can accrue. On the other hand, if we think of ourselves as atemporal objects, the claim that we can be harmed or wronged by untimely death or after our deaths becomes unproblematic.

Once we can make claims about the harms or wrongs you can suffer after your death, we can also ask whether you can be benefited or harmed, or treated rightly or wrongly, before your birth—or rather, I should say, so as not to foreclose any questions in advance, before the beginning of your life, whether that coincides with what we ordinarily call your "birth" or not. These are the kinds of questions to which certain issues about abortion and future generations give rise.

5.3.4 Before I go on, let me mention one issue just to lay it aside. I have been talking about both harms and wrongs, but there are actually two separate questions here: whether a person (or an animal) can be benefited or harmed before his life begins or after his death, and whether a person (or an animal) can be wronged or treated rightly before his life begins or after his death. There are

---

[15] It seems plausible to say that it is bad for you if, say, after your death, your child is arrested and executed for a crime she did not commit. But Aristotle worries that this sort of judgment gets increasingly less plausible as your descendants get increasingly distant from you, both because of the distance itself and because of possible shifts in their fortunes. Do you become better off when your grandchildren 19th do really well and then worse off when your grandchildren 20th fall into hard times?

[16] This view was famously held by the ancient philosopher Epicurus in his *Letter to Menoeceus*.

disputed questions about the relation between being harmed and being wronged. One is whether you can be wronged without being harmed. Or to put it more properly, about whether when you are wronged there must always be some harm to you independently of the fact that you are wronged. That is the proper way to put it, since we might think that being wronged is itself a kind of harm. I will not try to argue for it here, but I do not believe you are wronged only when you are, independently of that fact, harmed. Suppose someone asks you if he can "borrow" (as people say) a paperclip from the box on your desk, and being a curmudgeon, you say "No." If he takes one from your desk anyway as soon as your back is turned, he has wronged you, by violating your property rights, although the loss of the paperclip is very unlikely to do you any harm. Of course we might also wonder whether you can be harmed by someone's actions without being wronged, but that seems pretty clear. Suppose someone succeeds in attracting the romantic attention of the person you were courting, or gets a job you were seeking. If you would have succeeded were it not for the competition, then arguably the loss is a harm to you, but you are not wronged. I do not want to argue about these issues now, because settling them is not necessary to my view, but I want to point out another way in which harm and wrong can, as it were, occur independently of each other. Even if you think that a person or an animal can only be harmed by events that occur during her lifetime, it might still be that she could be wronged by actions that occurred before her lifetime, actions that foreseeably brought about the harms that she suffers during her life.

5.3.5 Now I am ready to state my view. Since I believe that the subjects of lives and their moral standing are atemporal, I believe this: once you exist, once your life begins, you have a moral standing that is itself atemporal. That means in effect that you can be wronged by actions that take place either before or after your life. I think this is true even if you can only be harmed by events that occur during your lifetime, although like Aristotle, I do not think that is plausible. You can be wronged by actions prior to your life because actions that occur prior to your life can harm you in a way that wrongs you during your lifetime. I will come to some examples of that shortly. And actions that occur subsequent to your life might wrong you even if they do not harm you. Some may think that the action of a lawyer who ignores your last will and testament to give your money to somebody else is like that, although arguably you are both wronged and harmed in this case.

There are a variety of familiar problems that an atemporal conception of moral standing solves or helps to solve. For instance, some philosophers are puzzled by what is sometimes called the "procreation asymmetry." Suppose you learn that any child you conceive will have a birth defect that will make his life not worth living: say, he will end up being in constant pain, will require endless medical treatments to keep the pain from being even worse, will be so cognitively disabled that he cannot do much without acute frustration and the need for help, and so on. It seems plausible to say that you have a reason, and even a duty, not to conceive a child.[17] On the other hand, suppose you are so situated that you have every reason to believe that any child you conceive will have an extremely happy, satisfying, and useful life. Even so, if you do not wish to have a child, you certainly do not have a duty to have one just because she will be happy; in fact it looks as if you do not even have a reason. Why exactly is it that the foreseeable harm to a future, not-yet-existent child provides a reason and even a duty not to bring him into existence, while the foreseeable benefit to a future, not-yet-existent child provides no duty or even a reason to bring her into existence? Suppose we say that the reason you do not have a duty to bring the happy child into existence is that prior to conception there is no child there for you to owe the duty to, or no child who is harmed by the fact that you failed to bring her into existence. Then to some people, it looks as if we are stuck with the view that you have no duty not to bring the miserable child into existence, since prior to conception there is no child there to be wronged or harmed by conception.

We could try to address this problem with moral theory. We could argue, for example, that our duties not to inflict harms on people are much more stringent than our duties to confer benefits, or some such thing. While that might seem plausible, I do not think it is necessary to make that argument here, because the answer is much simpler, and does not depend on which moral theory you hold. If you bring a child into existence, foreseeing this will be harmful to him, there will be someone in existence who will then have an atemporal moral standing and who therefore will have been wronged by your action. If you fail to bring a child into existence, although you foresee that existence would be a benefit to the child if you did, there will not be a child in existence who has failed to receive this benefit. Even if we had a duty to confer benefits, it would not matter: there is no one in existence on whom you fail to confer this benefit.

A related problem philosophers worry about these days is the "non-identity" problem. It is a familiar thought that, given the dependence of your existence on events affecting the moment of your conception, you might easily not have been born. If your father had not been delayed by the rain one particular day, he would never even have met your mother—that sort of thing. Now suppose we take extensive measures to curtail climate change. Arguably, if we did this, all kinds of

---

[17] To many of us, it also seems plausible to say that if you are in this condition, you have a duty to abort any child you conceive by accident, but that requires a further stretch of argument.

things would be done differently, and as a result, different people would be born. (If you want to make the case really vivid, suppose one of the measures we take to curtail climate change is to control the growth of the human population.) Now suppose instead that, after all, we *do not* take these extensive measures to control climate change, and the people (and animals) of the future find themselves on an overheated planet, with all of the devastation that will bring. The "non-identity problem" in this case stems from this thought: those people will not have been wronged by the fact that we failed to curtail climate change, since if we had taken measures to curtail it, they most likely would never have been born.

In this case, the problem about being affected by events and actions outside the boundaries of your life intersects with another set of problems. One is that the judgment that someone has been harmed requires a decision about the benchmark: when we say that someone is harmed we are saying that their situation is worse than it would have been if ___. But how do we fill in that blank—if *what* exactly? In the case of the procreation asymmetry, I avoided this problem by simply stipulating that life itself is a harm to the person we bring into existence. But in the climate change case, presumably life is still worth living for at least some of the members of future generations. Climate change makes conditions worse for whoever is around, but it may not make life cease to be worth living. So the worry is that people in future generations cannot say "I am worse off than I would have been if the people in the previous generation had taken measures to curtail climate change," since if that had happened, they would likely never have been born at all. They would not *personally* have benefitted from the better state of affairs we would have produced had we taken measures to curtail climate change, since they would not have existed. So to get the right conclusion in this case, we do need a contribution from moral theory. We need to argue that sometimes we owe duties to people in their capacity as occupants of a role, and therefore that sometimes people can be harmed and wronged in their capacity as occupants of a role. We owed the duty to curtail climate change to "the members of future generations, whoever they might be" and it is in his capacity as "a member of future generations" that the future person has a complaint. Once that is in place, however, this is another example of cases in which someone is harmed or at least wronged by actions that take place before he begins to exist. Whoever comes to exist in the future will have an atemporal moral standing which we will have violated when we foreseeably made the world so much worse.

5.3.6 Now let's think about abortion. Here is a familiar problem. Suppose that we want to preserve two ideas. First, a person has a right to have an abortion, at least during a certain portion of the earlier stretches of pregnancy, and for certain reasons, which I will leave unspecified here. Second, a person who knowingly does something that damages her fetus in some horrible way and then brings the fetus to term anyway has done something wrong, and in fact has wronged the person that that fetus becomes. The view that moral standing is temporal makes it very hard to preserve both of these ideas. If we give the fetus temporal moral standing too early, it is hard to preserve the thought that the person has a right to abortion. I am not saying it is impossible, for there are some arguments that purport to show that a person has the right to an abortion even if her fetus does have moral standing, and we would have to give those a hearing before we decided.[18] I am just saying it is hard to do. On the other hand, if we give the fetus temporal moral standing too late, it is hard to preserve the thought that by harming the fetus you have wronged the person that fetus becomes.

On the other hand, suppose that moral standing is atemporal, and you may be wronged, and possibly harmed, before you begin to exist or after you die. Then we have this possibility: that things that happen to the fetus are things that can harm and wrong the resulting person, even if the fetus is not yet the person and does not yet have moral standing. The mother who knowingly damages her fetus in some horrible way, while still intending to bring the fetus to term, has done something wrong, and has wronged the resulting person. But the mother who decides not to bring the fetus to term has not wronged anyone,[19] since no person with moral standing emerges from her pregnancy. Or we could even say, if you prefer, that the fetus that is eventually brought to term does have atemporal moral standing, the standing of the person, but only because it was eventually brought to term.

As I said at the beginning of this discussion, settling the question whether moral standing is atemporal or not is not the same as settling the question when something with moral standing begins to exist. In some cases, of course, it is obvious when something begins to exist. The fact that World War I lasted from July 28, 1914 until November 11, 1918 is an atemporal truth, but unless some form of very hard determinism is true, there is a time when that truth came into existence. It started to come into existence in 1914, or perhaps earlier if something earlier made it inevitable, and got finally settled in 1918. But in that case there are pretty hard lines to draw, if we take wars to begin when they are declared and to end when the treaties say so. A human being develops from conception gradually. Some may think that the fetus begins to be a person or

---

[18] The classical example is Judith Jarvis Thomson, "A Defense of Abortion."

[19] Unless of course there are others besides the mother and the fetus involved—say a father to whom the mother had promised not to end the pregnancy.

anyway something with moral standing when it begins to be sentient or independently viable. But it is possible that nothing about the biology or the metaphysics of that development is going to enable us to draw a plausible line telling us when a person begins to exist.

In the law, we sometimes have to draw hard lines where only soft borders are to be found: say, at what point you reach majority and become a legal adult. In those cases, we sometimes make our decision not only by appeal to facts about the people whose status is being settled, but to facts about their social circumstances and the bearing of the decision on others. The voting age in the United States was lowered from 21 to 18 in 1971, because young men were being drafted to serve in the war in Vietnam, and people felt they could not be asked to serve if they had no voice in the political process. The difficulty could have been solved the other way, by raising the draft age, but people thought the younger soldiers were needed. That is not a very edifying example, perhaps, but it makes the point. In my own view, there would be nothing amiss in making the decision when a person with moral standing begins to exist not just on the basis of the stage of development the embryo or fetus has reached, but also on the basis of how the decision will affect lives of women, given the current circumstances of the culture.

But I am not trying to convince you of that. You can think that there must be hard lines, and you can think that every human entity is a person from the moment of conception. My point is just that deciding that persons and their moral standing should be understood atemporally does not settle the question when these atemporal entities come into existence. That is a different matter altogether.

5.4 What Is Moral Standing Anyway?

5.4.1 Though I have been talking at length about the notion, I sometimes doubt whether there is such a thing as moral standing. The trouble with the idea is that it suggests an on/off property, something that a creature (or whatever) either has or lacks. There are problems with both the idea that it is a property and that it is on/off, and I will discuss both, but I am going to start with worries about its being on/off. The problem here is that you might think instead that there are appropriate ways to treat nearly anything, given its nature. Although I have not yet made my argument, you have probably already figured out that I am going to argue that the fact that animals have moral standing has something to do with the fact that they, just like us, have a final good. But plants, as we have seen, at least have a functional good. Indeed on Aristotle's conception, as we saw in Chapter 2 (2.1.5), pretty much any substance or thing has a functional good, since what makes a thing a *thing* is that its parts are functionally unified. So why shouldn't there be right and wrong ways to treat any sort of thing, depending on what sort of good it has, rather than thinking that "moral standing" is something that some things have and some do not?

At the risk of being thought a complete lunatic, let me admit that I am tempted by this thought. We do have normative responses to plants, for instance; a drooping plant in need of a drink seems to present us with a reason to water it; a sapling growing from what seems to be almost sheer rock makes us want to cheer it on. Is this because we cannot help animistically imagining that the plant experiences its good? Or is it perhaps because the shared condition of *life itself* elicits these responses? Could it even be that we have duties, not only to our fellow creatures, but to our fellow organisms, and to even our fellow entities? Granted, it sounds absurd to suggest that we might have duties to machines, yet still there is something in the far outer reaches of our normative thought and feeling that suggests this. We have a general discomfort in the face of wanton destructiveness, a tendency to wince when objects are broken, a sadness at the sight of uninhabited homes, an objection to the neglect or abuse of precision tools. These responses are not rooted completely in the idea of economic waste, perhaps not even in any sort of human-centered or animal-centered waste. Again it might be suggested that such feelings result from a kind of animistic imagin-ation, that we imagine that the tool feels the badness of being broken, say. But what is it that calls forth that animistic imagination, unless it is a distant form of respect for functional unity itself, a condition we share with all entities? Perhaps we *should* treat every kind of thing in accordance with its nature, in accordance with the kinds of good and evils to which it is subject.

As I said, I am somewhat tempted by such thoughts. But I am also convinced that there is something special about the kind of good to which something is subject when it is a conscious being with a self, and that it is conscious beings who have selves, or rather are selves, that make moral claims on us.

5.4.2 Now for the problem about moral standing being a property. First of all, consider the fact that some philosophers have suggested that moral standing comes in degrees. Characteristically, those who believe this think that animals have a lower moral standing than humans, or that there is some general hierarchy of moral standing among animals, with humans at the top.[20] This view is just a philosophical rephrasing of the view, which I rejected in Chapter 1, that people are more important than the other animals. I call it a "philosophical rephrasing" rather than a theory because all by itself it does not do anything to *explain* the

---

[20] This is the view I discussed in 4.3 but with a different explanation than the one I proposed there.

intuition that people are more important than animals. It just restates it using the technical term "moral standing." Consider:

Question: "What explains the intuition that a human death matters more than an animal's?"
Answer: "A human being has a higher moral standing."
Question: "What does it mean to have a higher moral standing?"
Answer: "It means that what happens to you matters more."

Obviously, this is getting us nowhere fast. But when we notice this, it brings out a more general problem about the idea of moral standing. The whole idea can look as if it is either unhelpful or completely otiose, or both.

Here is one way to put the problem. According to a well-known philosophical thesis, endorsed by Hume and Kant and many others, natural facts by themselves do not have normative implications.[21] In other words, you cannot derive an "ought" directly from an "is." There is a gap between the natural and the normative, or between fact and value, to put it another way. The problem is that people sometimes use the term "moral standing" as if it were the name of a metaphysical property that is supposed to provide a sort of bridge that gets us over that gap. Suppose, for instance, you think that the ground of moral standing is sentience, or the ability to feel pleasure and pain. Then you might think: a mouse is sentient, and *therefore* the mouse has moral standing, and *therefore* you should not hurt the mouse. Moral standing, in that formulation, appears to form a bridge between the natural property of sentience and the normative fact that you should not hurt the mouse. Unsurprisingly, the term "person" also sometimes gets used in this way in the literature on practical ethics: as if it served as a bridge between some natural property, say rationality or self-consciousness, and normative conclusions about the way we should treat the one who has that property: say that we should not kill him, or we should accord him certain rights.

The trouble with this way of thinking emerges when we ask whether the claim "a mouse has moral standing" is *itself* a natural claim or a normative one. If it is a natural claim, then you might think there is still a gap between the claim of moral standing and its normative implications. How do we get from "a mouse has moral standing" to "you should not hurt the mouse" without violating the principle that you cannot reason directly from an "ought" to an "is"? On the other hand, if it is a normative claim, it seems to be otiose: it does not *explain* why you should not hurt the mouse. It more or less just *says* that you should not hurt the mouse.

---

[21] For Kant see *Groundwork of the Metaphysics of Morals*, 4:387–88 and 4:406–11; and *The Metaphysics of Morals*, 6:378. The locus classicus of the claim that you cannot derive an "ought" from an "is" is in Hume, *A Treatise of Human Nature*, Book 3, part 1, section 1, pp. 469–70.

Furthermore, we are left with no explanation of how we arrived at this normative conclusion. How did we get from the natural claim that "the mouse is sentient" to the normative claim that "the mouse has moral standing"? I am not saying that these arguments are decisive, or that no one could come up with replies to them. But there is a worry here about whether the idea of moral standing can do any work.

5.4.3 I am not suggesting that we should abandon the concept of moral standing, or at least, not for this reason. Rather, we should recognize that "moral standing" is a stand-in, a kind of variable, for whatever it is that explains why we have obligations to the members of some group of entities, or more generally for whatever it is that determines how we should treat the members of some group of entities. To fill in that variable, we have to say not only which property confers moral standing, but why it does so.

From this point of view, there is one thing helpfully suggestive about the term "moral standing." It suggests an analogy with the notion of "standing" in the law. In the law, someone has standing when he is in a position to bring a lawsuit for the enforcement of some law. Ordinarily, in the United States at least, a person has standing only if he himself is in some way personally affected by the violation of the law. Thus the legal notion brings together two ideas: that the person is in some way being harmed or affected by the principles people act on, and that because that is so, he is in a position to make a claim on the community. The second of those two ideas is a relational one. Indeed, in general, "standing" is something we have in relation to particular others; in ordinary talk, your standing with respect to someone is something you can lose by mistreating him in certain ways. For example, you can lose your standing to demand an apology for bad behavior from someone if you have mistreated him in exactly the same way yourself. So the idea of moral standing suggests something important about the kind of explanation we are looking for when we fill in the notion of moral standing. Someone who claims that, say, sentience, or rationality, or autonomy, is the ground of moral standing must be prepared to explain why a creature's being sentient or rational puts that creature in a certain kind of relation to others. That is what the "fellow" in "fellow creatures" does—it gestures at a relation in which we stand to each other (8.7.2).

Kant believed that the properties of rationality and autonomy place people in relations of reciprocity with each other, whereas the properties we share with the other animals place us only in relations of "analogy" with them. He thought that in the absence of relations of reciprocity, the analogies between people and animals do not ground duties to the other animals, although they do call out something that we owe to ourselves. In the next two chapters of the book we will look at his arguments for these ideas, and then in Chapter 8 we will see why he was wrong.

6

Kant against the Animals, Part 1
The Indirect Duty View

> When [the human being] first said to the sheep, "*the pelt which you wear was given to you by nature not for your own use, but for mine*" and took it from the sheep to wear it himself, he become aware of a prerogative which...he enjoyed over all the animals; and he now no longer regarded them as fellow creatures, but as means and instruments to be used at will for the attainment of whatever ends he pleased.
>
> Immanuel Kant, "Conjectures on the Beginning of Human History," 8:114

> Any action whereby we may torment animals, or let them suffer distress, or otherwise treat them without love, is demeaning to ourselves.
>
> Immanuel Kant, *Lectures on Ethics*, 27:710

6.1 Animals as Mere Means

6.1.1 In 5.1.1, I gave a sketch of Kant's moral view. We saw that Kant assigns moral standing to rational beings as ends in themselves, who reciprocally legislate moral laws for themselves and one another in a Kingdom of Ends. We then considered an objection to which this account gives rise: that it implies that infants, the demented elderly, the insane, those with severe cognitive defects, and the other animals have no moral standing. I argued that when the ideas of rationality and moral standing are properly understood, Kant's account does not leave not out any human beings. All human beings are constructed to function rationally, although some may have defects that make that difficult or impossible for them. There is a difference between being a defectively rational creature, and being a different kind of creature altogether. But although we should keep in mind that it is an empirical question, it seems likely that only human beings are rational. So that part of the question still stands: If we human beings are ends in ourselves because we are rational, then do the other animals lack moral standing?

Kant himself thought so, for in the argument leading up to the Formula of Humanity, he says:

Beings the existence of which rests not on our will but on nature, if they are beings without reason, have only a relative worth, as means, and are therefore called *things*, whereas rational beings are called *persons* because their nature already marks them out as an end in itself, that is, as something that may not be used merely as a means.[1]

Animals are among the beings whose existences "rest on nature," and so here are declared to be "things" which may be used as mere means.

Kant makes his position even clearer in his essay, "Conjectures on the Beginnings of Human History." Here Kant speculates about the emergence of humanity from our animal past.[2] Using the story of the Garden of Eden as his model, Kant describes a process leading from the origins of self-consciousness to the development of morality, which comes in four stages.

At the first stage, human beings become self-conscious in the sense we looked at in Chapter 3 (3.2), that is, we become aware of our own attitudes and their grounds. This gives us the ability to compare the objects to which we are instinctively drawn with other objects that resemble them, and that draws us to those other objects, motivating us to try them. Self-consciousness enables Eve to reflect on the fact that she is instinctively drawn to, let's say, eating pears, and then, having noticed that apples are similar to pears, she gets the idea that she might like eating one of those, too. The fateful result is the first free choice—that is, the first choice not governed by instinct—ever made in history.

---

[1] Kant, *Groundwork*, 4:428. The contrast in the first line of this quotation is between our own desired ends, whose existence does depend on our will, and the things we find around us, whose existence rests on nature. Kant has already, at this point, claimed that the value of our own desired ends is not absolute, but depends on our desires themselves. We will look more closely at this argument in Chapter 7.

[2] Perhaps you are wondering how Kant can be "speculating about the emergence of humanity from our animal past" seventy-three years before the publication of Darwin's *Origin of Species*. I put it that way because Kant says this: "Initially, the newcomer [in the Garden of Eden] must have been guided solely by instinct, that *voice of God* which all animals obey" (8:111). Kant insists he is just speculating for the sake of the light it throws on philosophical issues, not offering a real history. But in fact, both Hume and Kant conceived the general idea of natural selection. Hume describes the idea in part 8 of the *Dialogues Concerning Natural Religion*. After remarking that the common structure among animals "reinforces our suspicion that they are actually akin," Kant proposed that a natural scientist "can make mother earth...emerge from her state of chaos, and make her lap promptly give birth initially to creatures of a less purposive form, with these then giving birth to others that became better adapted to their place of origin and to their relations with one another, until in the end this womb itself...confined itself to bearing definite species that would no longer degenerate" (5:419). Obviously, Kant thought that the environment was unchanging and that therefore the process would stop when forms perfectly adapted to that environment, and to each other in that environment, were achieved. But otherwise, he had the basic idea: new species that appear as organisms become better adapted to their environment and each other.

Kant speculates that this kind of self-consciousness also brings with it the ability to inhibit the expression of our impulses, which in turn brings sexual sublimation and with it romantic love and the sense of beauty. That is the second step. Next we begin to anticipate the future, acquiring both the capacity to be motivated by concern for the future and the terrifying knowledge of our own mortality.[3] And then, Kant says:

The fourth and last step which reason took, thereby raising man completely above animal society, was his realisation that he is the true *end of nature*... When he first said to the sheep "*the pelt which you wear was given to you by nature not for your own use, but for mine*" and took it from the sheep to wear it himself... he became aware of a prerogative which, by his nature, he enjoyed over all the animals; and he now no longer regarded them as fellow creatures, but as means and instruments to be used at will for the attainment of whatever ends he pleased. This notion implies... an awareness of the following distinction: man should not address other *human beings* in the same way as animals, but should regard them as having an equal share in the gifts of nature...

Thus man had attained a position of *equality with all rational beings*... because he could claim to be *an end in himself.*[4]

Kant here firmly links our realization that we are to be treated as ends in ourselves with the moment when we ceased to regard the other animals as fellow creatures, and began to consider them as mere means instead. It is particularly haunting that Kant imagines Adam *addressing* his remarks about the pelt *to* the sheep, as if that one last vestige of the peaceable kingdom, the ability to communicate with the other animals, was still in place at the moment when we turned our backs on them.

6.2 How Kant Thinks We Ought to Treat Animals

6.2.1 But when Kant spells out his views about how we should actually treat the other animals, we get a surprise.[5] Kant claims that we have the right to kill the other animals, but that it must be quickly and without pain, and must not be for the sake of mere sport. Recreational hunting would therefore be wrong in Kant's view, as well as sports like dog-fighting and cock-fighting that may lead to the animal's painful injury or death. Kant does not say why we should kill animals,

---

[3] These remarks summarize Kant, "Conjectures on the Beginning of Human History," 8:111–14.

[4] Kant, "Conjectures on the Beginning of Human History," 8:114. I have changed Nisbet's rendering of the German *Pelz* from "fleece" to "pelt," although the German can go either way, because I think that the rendering "fleece" softens Kant's harsh point; a sheep may more easily share her fleece.

[5] The main discussions are at *The Metaphysics of Morals*, 6:442–4 and *Lectures on Ethics*, 27:458–60 and 27:710.

and he does not discuss the question whether we may eat them, but presumably that is one of the reasons he has in mind.[6] He does not think we should perform painful experiments on non-human animals "for the sake of mere speculation, when the end could also be achieved without these."[7] He thinks we may make the other animals work, but not in a way that strains their capacities. The limitation he mentions sounds vaguely as if it were drawn from the Golden Rule: we should force them to do only such work as we would force ourselves to do.[8] And if they do work for us, he thinks that we should be grateful. In his course lectures, Kant sometimes told a story about the philosopher Leibniz carefully returning a grub he had been studying to the tree from which he had taken it when he was done, "lest he should be guilty of doing any harm to it."[9] Both in his lectures and in *The Metaphysics of Morals*, Kant has hard words for people who shoot their horses or dogs when they are no longer useful.[10] Such animals should be treated, Kant insists, with "gratitude for . . . long service (just as if they were members of the household)."[11] He remarks with apparent approval that "In Athens it was punishable to let an aged work-horse starve."[12] He tells us that: "Any action whereby we may torment animals, or let them suffer distress, or otherwise treat them without love, is demeaning to ourselves."[13]

6.2.2 But as that last phrase suggests, Kant thinks that these moral duties are not owed directly *to* the other animals, but rather to ourselves. They are duties *with respect* to the treatment of animals, but not duties owed *to* them. In a similar way, you might imagine we have duties with respect to beautiful paintings—not to deface them, to keep them clean and well-preserved—but of course we would not owe these actions *to* the paintings. Kant thinks our moral relationship to animals is like that. Animals belong to a category of objects that inspire feelings

---

[6] The question of eating animals comes up indirectly when Kant mentions the fact that in England butchers are not allowed to serve on juries because their profession is thought to habituate them to death (*Lectures on Ethics*, 27:459–60).

[7] Kant, *Metaphysics of Morals*, 6:443. It is not clear whether these two requirements are meant to function together or separately, so it is a little hard to know how much of a limitation Kant intends this to be.

[8] Kant, *Metaphysics of Morals*, 6:443.   [9] Kant, *Lectures on Ethics*, 27:459.

[10] Kant, *Metaphysics of Morals*, 6:433; *Lectures on Ethics*, 27:459.

[11] Kant, *Metaphysics of Morals*, 6:443.

[12] Kant, *Lectures on Ethics*, 27:710. It is particularly surprising that Kant approves of this, since his official view is that coercively enforced laws are justified only to preserve equal human freedom. It is also unclear what he could possibly be referring to. The accounts I have seen suggest that there were no animal welfare laws anywhere in the world until 1635, when the Irish made a law against tying horses to the plow directly with their tails and pulling the wool off of sheep instead of clipping it, partly because of the cruelty of these practices.

[13] Kant, *Lectures on Ethics*, 27:710.

in us which Kant thinks we should cultivate because they are conducive to good moral conduct. This category of objects includes plants and beautiful natural objects as well as animals. In the case of plants and beautiful natural objects, the feeling in question is the love of the beautiful. The love of the beautiful, according to Kant, is a disposition to love something even apart from any intention to use it.[14] Perhaps his idea is that this disposes us to love people for their own sakes, and not just for what they can do for us. In the case of what he calls "the animate but non-rational part of creation," Kant says: "violent and cruel treatment of animals is...intimately opposed to a human being's duty to himself...for it dulls his shared feeling of their suffering and so weakens and gradually uproots a natural disposition that is very serviceable to morality in one's relations with other people."[15] In his course lectures, Kant made the same point by saying that non-human animals are "analogs" of humanity, and that we therefore "cultivate our duties to humanity" when we practice duties to animals as analogs to human beings.[16] So animals who work for us are analogs of human servants ("members of the household"), to whom we owe gratitude. Animals who might suffer needlessly at our hands are analogs of possible human victims, to whose welfare we must attend. And beautiful natural objects, which seem to exist for their own sake alone, might be thought of as analogs of rational beings in our capacity as ends in ourselves.

6.2.3 The view I've just described combines two theses—first, that we owe the duty of treating animals well in various ways to ourselves rather than directly to the animals; and second, that the ground of the duty rests in the effects of the way we treat animals on our own characters, or on those of our emotions that are "serviceable to morality." Taken together, these two theses are sometimes called "the indirect duty" view. But notice that the two theses are separate, logically speaking. We could owe it only to ourselves, not directly to the animals, to treat the animals well, and yet the duty could be to treat them kindly for their own sakes, not for the sake of the effects on our own characters or emotions.

Why did Kant believe that we cannot owe duties directly to the animals? Kant thought that the other animals, not being rational, cannot participate in the reciprocal "legislation" from which moral laws emerge. I will discuss this argument in Chapter 7. But it is not clear why Kant also held that the ground of our duties with respect to the other animals is the effects of our treatment of animals on our own characters. As I mentioned in Chapter 5, there are some philosophers

---

[14] Kant, *Metaphysics of Morals*, 6:443.   [15] Kant, *Metaphysics of Morals*, 6:443.
[16] Kant, *Lectures on Ethics*, 27:459.

who believe that you cannot be wronged unless you are harmed (5.3.4), and for them it may be natural to suppose that all duties to the self must be grounded in possible harms or benefits to the self. So they might think that if we owe it to ourselves to be kind to animals, it must be because we are somehow harmed by being cruel to them, and the injury to our own moral characters or emotions would be such a harm. Kant, however, does not tie being wronged to being harmed in this way. He believes we can be wronged in a number of ways that do not necessarily involve any independent harm—we can be treated disrespectfully, lied to, paternalized, and so on. So it is unclear why he holds the second part of the "indirect duty" view. Of course, if our duties with respect to animals were *not* grounded in harms to the self, we would have to find some other reason why the abuse of animals is, in Kant's own surprising words, "demeaning to ourselves."[17] In Chapter 8, we will see that there is such a reason, although Kant himself did not see this.

6.3 An Incoherent Attitude

6.3.1 Many people have criticized the indirect duty view for having the wrong conclusion. Even people who believe our duties to animals are rather weak—that all that we owe to the animals is to avoid "unnecessary" cruelty—think we owe that duty, such as it is, directly to the animals. But I believe that the indirect duty view has another problem, which is that it is almost incoherent. Or at least, the attitudes it invites us to have are almost incoherent.

Take the claim that we should love beautiful things, because it fosters the general disposition to love things independently of any intention to use them. Can we at once love the beautiful things without intending to use them, and yet at the same time intend to use loving them as an occasion for improving our own characters? The problem is even worse in the case of animals, at least if we take Kant to be urging us to love them, and not merely to treat them as if we did.[18] The way you love an animal for his own sake involves not merely appreciating him like an aesthetic object, but caring about his welfare and his interests for his sake—that is, for the sake of the animal himself. So if we do love animals, we will

---

[17] Kant, *Lectures on Ethics*, 27:710.
[18] Notoriously, Kant thinks that love as a feeling cannot be commanded. But he says love can be cultivated by moral practice: "The saying 'you ought to love your neighbor as yourself' does not mean that you ought immediately (first) to love him and (afterwards) by means of this love do good to him. It means, rather, do good to your fellow human beings, and your beneficence will produce love of them in you (as an aptitude of the inclination to beneficence in general)." *Metaphysics of Morals*, 6:402.

want to treat them well for their own sakes, independently of the effects of doing so on our characters. There is surely some tension between loving a creature for his or her own sake, and seeing that love as a way to "preserve a natural disposition that is very serviceable to morality in one's relations with other people." Perhaps Kant does not mean that we should deliberately *cultivate* love and sympathy for animals for the sake of improving our characters, but rather that we should indulge them when we do experience them, knowing that these attitudes will improve our characters? I'm not sure that helps.

There are related but much deeper questions here about whether love is fully detachable from moral concern at all. Can you love someone without thinking that his or her welfare is something that matters for its own sake, and can you think that his or her welfare matters for its own sake without thinking that it has a moral claim on you, irrespective of your love?[19] From there, some would argue, all you have to do is generalize: if you think your own dog's welfare matters irrespective of your love for him, why wouldn't every other dog's welfare matter in the same way? Granted, many people appear to love their own dogs who are perfectly prepared to be brutal to the other animals—people who eat meat from factory farms, for instance. Do they really love their dogs, for the dogs' own sakes? Or do they just regard them as a kind of especially cute living toy? Of course we can raise the same kinds of questions about the personal and family loves of evil people. We are in dark territory here, about which no one is very clear what to say.

6.3.2 But that is not the end of the problem. Consider Kant's claim that we should be grateful to animals who work for us, and be motivated by that gratitude to give them a comfortable retirement. I think we have to assume that Kant thinks that their services make gratitude an *appropriate* response to animals. For we do think that our emotions and attitudes are subject to standards of appropriateness. We say things like "That's nothing to be afraid of!" "You shouldn't be angry at him," to indicate that someone has attitudes and feelings that he should not have. To see what I have in mind, imagine someone who refuses to send his old car off to be mined for spare parts and scrap metal, citing his gratitude for the long service it has given him. Instead he insists on keeping it in a well-heated garage, and washing it every Sunday, even though he can no longer use it. We would think this person was dotty. "Put it under the wrecking ball, it's just a car," we might say. Now I have to admit that in the days when people made extensive use of work horses, there probably were plenty of people who would have said "send it to the glue factory, it's just a horse" to the man who insists on giving his

---

[19] See the discussion in T. M. Scanlon, *What We Owe to Each Other*, pp. 164–5.

worn-out work horse a comfortable retirement. But would it really be quite the same? The man who says "Send it to the glue factory, it's just a horse" at least can be heard as urging the farmer to face up to a regrettable economic necessity, but that is not what we mean when we say "It's just a car." My point is just that the person who wants to give his horse a comfortable retirement seems *intelligible*, even to people who like to think of themselves as unsentimental about animals, in a way that the man who wants to provide a retirement for his car does not. In any case, I think Kant must have thought so, for he does not urge us to cultivate dispositions that will be serviceable in our relations with people by attending to the welfare of our machines and tools, or by being grateful to them. The idea that it is appropriate to feel grateful to animals who serve us seems be part of what Kant has in mind when he says that animals (but not machines and tools) are "analogs" of human beings.

6.3.3 But if the services of animals make gratitude an *appropriate* emotion, why don't we owe that gratitude—and the comfortable retirement that it calls for—directly to the animals themselves? To see the problem, consider the following piece of reasoning:

1. It is appropriate for us to be grateful to the animals who serve us.
2. Being grateful to someone involves wanting to do something for him in return for his services.
3. It is appropriate for us to want to do something for animals who serve us.
4. If it is appropriate for us to be grateful to the animals who serve us, it is inappropriate for us to fail to be grateful to the animals who serve us.
5. If it is inappropriate for us to fail to be grateful to the animals who serve us, it is inappropriate for us to fail to want to do something for the animals who serve us.
6. If it is inappropriate for us to fail to *want* to do something for the animals who serve us, it is inappropriate for us to fail to *do* something for the animals who serve us, unless we have some very good reason why not.
7. If it is inappropriate for us to fail to do something for the animals who serve us, then we ought to do something for the animals who serve us, unless we have some very good reason why not.

This is not a Kantian style of reasoning; in fact it is loosely derived from Adam Smith.[20] It is also not absolutely airtight—there are steps about which you could

---

[20] See Smith, *The Theory of Moral Sentiments*, part 2, section 1.

quibble—but it seems like a pretty natural line of thought.[21] But notice that I reached the conclusion that we ought to do something for the animals who serve us from the premise that it is appropriate to be grateful to the animals who serve us, without going through some detour about the effects on our own characters.

Of course, the claim that a certain attitude is "appropriate" or "inappropriate" has at least a quasi-normative, or even a vaguely moral character: that is what enabled me to reason from it to an "ought" in the last step. Exactly how to understand the normative dimension of emotions and attitudes is a whole philosophical subject in its own right, and one that I am not going into in any detail here.[22] But however we understand that, I think Kant has to be making the assumption that gratitude towards animals is appropriate in a way that gratitude towards machines and tools is not. But if animals are the proper objects of gratitude, then it seems as if the gratitude and the resulting actions are owed directly to them. So the attitude Kant is inviting us to have to animals seems inherently unstable, if not absolutely incoherent. It is as if Kant were inviting us to love animals quite wholeheartedly and genuinely, just as if they were people, while at the same time telling us that we are just pretending they are people. It is as if he were telling us to love animals the way a child might love a doll.

6.4 The Problem of the Moral Filter

6.4.1 Of course, it has to be admitted that there just *is* some instability in our attitudes towards animals. To see this, imagine someone replying to the argument

---

[21] For instance, one place we might quibble is this: there might be a case in which you want to do something for someone to whom you are grateful, but it would be inappropriate to actually do it, because it would make it seem as if you were paying him for the service, and that would seem to undermine the generosity of what he did. It's a delicate business, gratitude, when it is directed to people.

[22] There is a closely related question at issue here about how attitudes like gratitude, which are at least partly emotional, are related to morality. Kant, in a passage I quoted earlier, mentions dispositions to feeling that are "very serviceable to morality in one's dealings with people." There, and in other places, he seems to conceive of emotions as at best instrumentally useful to moral practice: pity, say, makes you more alert to the occasions when kindness is required, or makes you a more sensitive judge of what counts as kindness, or makes it easier to bring yourself to be kind when the acts required are distasteful. Others, notably Aristotle, have argued that virtue directly requires certain feelings; one who does not feel them is morally lacking. He would say that inappropriate fear signals the vice of cowardice, for example. I do not discuss this disagreement here because the problem I am discussing in the text arises either way. Whether attitudes like gratitude are only aids to good moral character or part of its essence, the attitudes have to be appropriate to both people and animals if the indirect duty argument is to work. For discussion of the disagreement between Aristotle and Kant about how emotions are related to morality, see my "From Duty and for the Sake of the Noble: Aristotle and Kant on Morally Good Action," essay 6 in *The Constitution of Agency*.

I just made by pointing out that animals do not serve us voluntarily—that is why they are *only* a kind of analog of human beings who do us services, and the gratitude is not really owed directly to them. When we feel grateful to them, we are, as it were, pretending they intended to be serviceable to us.

This possible reply raises an interesting question. It may seem as if the proper object of your gratitude is *voluntary* or *intentional* services that are offered for the sake of your own good. Suppose someone pulls you out of the river *only* because you were sitting in his expensive car when you went in and it is just as easy for him to hoist it out without removing you first. Gratitude may seem superfluous at best. Animals do not (usually) serve us by their own choice, although they may do so willingly enough (dogs perhaps especially) if the work is to their taste. Since they serve us because they have to, they do not serve us for the sake of our good. But for that matter, we might suppose that the household servants Kant had in mind serve the family only as a way of making their own living. And household slaves, like household animals, do not serve the family from choice at all. If we are members of the family in question, should we be grateful to our servants or our slaves for their services? Perhaps we should be grateful only if, or only because, they at least serve us cheerfully and ungrudgingly, without always trying to do the minimum they can get away with? Or perhaps gratitude to our servants and slaves is appropriate anyway, as long as serving us is really what they are intentionally doing, regardless of their motives for doing it. Would such gratitude extend to the services of animals? To all of them, or only the willing ones? To the seeing eye dog, but not the leeches, perhaps? Not to Leibniz's little grub after all?

6.4.2 Some of these points, admittedly, are problems about gratitude, not problems about our attitudes towards animals. Gratitude is a complicated subject in its own right. Still, the whole issue is even more complicated when we raise questions about gratitude to animals, in a way that Kant does not seem to take into account. It is part of a family of issues about our "personal" (as we interestingly call them) feelings for non-human animals that arise from the following fact. Certain of our feelings for people are either aroused originally in response to people's moral qualities, or are put through what I will call a kind of "moral filter." Say, for instance, you are angry at someone who has acted against your interests, until someone points out to you that he had a perfect right to do what he did, and so is not a proper target of your rage. You withdraw your anger after putting it through a moral filter. Or suppose you are deeply attracted to someone who is physically beautiful or socially charming, but eventually the knowledge that he is a bad or shallow person either destroys the attraction or makes you dismiss it as a weakness in yourself.[23] You have put your attraction through a moral filter, and dismissed it or distanced yourself from it as a result. You bask in the admiration of people whose good opinion you know deep down is not worth having, until a friend points this out. You are grateful for a service that was not voluntarily given, or not really done for your sake, until you reflect on the motives for which it actually was done. In all of these cases, your response to another person is either directed to the moral character of his motives and actions, or at least constrained and limited by them. That is what I mean when I say we put our responses to people through a moral filter.

We also respond naturally to the other animals with feelings that, were we to have them towards other people, we would feel pressured to put through that moral filter. We love animals, enjoy their love, are flattered by their love and attention, get mad at them, and feel grateful to them. If the objects of these feelings, when we feel them towards people, are people's moral qualities, or if the feelings when we have them towards people are constrained and shaped by our responses to people's moral qualities, then we might worry that the feelings are inappropriate ones to have towards animals, or anyway we might feel that there is something puzzling about them. You should not get mad at your dog, since nothing is his fault; but by the same token, you should not really love him for who he is, since nothing is to his credit. It is silly to feel flattered by his love for you, since it is not based on an appreciation of your virtues or anything else about you, and in fact he would love anyone who fed him. You should not dislike your neighbor's dog for being aggressive or barking, because it is just his nature, or the result of bad training which was no fault of his own. I am overstating things here, but I suspect many people will recognize such thoughts. We are not sure what it makes sense to feel in the absence of the moral filter.

6.4.3 Of course, sometimes people do respond to what they see as the "goodness" of animals, and are inspired with love and admiration by animals who do altruistic or heroic things. Kant himself remarks that "the more we devote ourselves to observing animals and their behavior, the more we love them, on seeing how greatly they care for their young."[24] In 1996, a stray cat named Scarlett became world famous when she repeatedly returned to a burning building to

---

[23] For one account, based on Hume's view of the emotions, of how a moral "filter" would work in the case of love, see Korsgaard, "The General Point of View: Love and Moral Approval in Hume's Ethics," essay 9 in *The Constitution of Agency*.

[24] Kant, *Lectures on Ethics*, 27:459.

carry each of her five kittens to safety, getting severely burned herself in the process. Some 7,000 people expressed interest in adopting her, and an award for Animal Heroism was created in her honor.[25] Was she "heroic"? Compared to what? Other felines in whom the mother instinct is not as strong—or in whom the self-preservation instinct is stronger? Guilty human mothers who wonder what they would have done in her place?

Suppose you think that our feelings towards animals do not make sense, because we cannot put them through the moral filter, or because when we do put them through the moral filter, nothing that we can strongly identify with comes out. Then you might also be tempted to think that people who claim that our feelings for animals are "sentimental"—based on crass anthropomorphism, or even largely imaginary—might be right. Or, to take a more moderate view: If, in the case of people, we put these feelings through a moral filter, then when we feel these same things towards animals, there is something slightly disconcerting about the fact that the moral filter is not there. We filter out the anger, reminding ourselves that it is stupid to blame a dog for anything, since nothing is his fault, but we do not filter out the love and gratitude, even though his virtues are not to his credit and his services were not offered with a view to our good. Isn't that cheating, to filter out the negative attitudes, and leave the positive attitudes in place?

Some of this discomfort is dispelled when we recollect that the kind of love we feel at least for the animals we live with, see regularly, or work with, is family love. We do not need anything like a reason to love our family members and those we have grown up in intimacy with, although we need a reason not to.[26] The moral filter plays less of a role here, too: family love often survives the realization that its object is a jerk. And after all, animals themselves experience love, anger, sometimes apparently even gratitude, towards us and towards each other, although they are not capable of wondering whether the objects of their love and gratitude are really worthy of those attitudes or not. So perhaps what we feel for them is just the kind of thing that they feel for us and each other. In fact, one of the reasons that we enjoy the company of our pets is precisely the fact that their feelings *for us* are *not* put through a moral filter—unlike our feelings for each other. They are not, as we say, judgmental.

---

[25] Wikipedia: Scarlett (cat) Last edited July 19, 2017. <https://en.wikipedia.org/wiki/Scarlett_(cat)>.

[26] Not all of the worries I have mentioned are dispelled by the thought that the love of animals is a kind of family love. You might still wonder whether it makes any sense for you to hate your neighbor's aggressive dog. I think that it does not, for a reason I have gestured at in the text. Love and hate are often regarded as opposites, but there is this difference between them: hate needs a justification, while love does not. Since the dog's bad behavior is not the dog's fault, you have no justification for hating your neighbor's dog.

6.4.4 Fortunately, we can raise the same question about another of Kant's examples—I mean the question about whether our feelings for animals are appropriate—without getting mired in these complexities. As we saw, Kant says that a person should avoid cruelty to the other animals because "it dulls his shared feeling of their suffering and so weakens and gradually uproots a natural predisposition that is very serviceable to morality in one's relations with other people." There is surely no reason to doubt that empathy for the suffering of animals is an appropriate response.[27] So when we think about the suffering of animals, the instability of the indirect duty position becomes overwhelming. For if (1) the natural predisposition in question is a tendency to empathize with suffering and therefore to want to prevent it, and (2) if human suffering is something to which there is a rational and moral objection, and (3) if animal suffering is "analogous" to human suffering, then why isn't there a rational and moral objection to animal suffering as well? If we ever subject our empathy with suffering to the moral filter—and it is not clear that we should, even in the case of people—but if we ever do, it is to withdraw our empathy because the suffering one has done something to deserve his suffering. But animals cannot deserve to suffer, for they can do nothing morally wrong.

6.5 Desert and the Worthiness to Be Happy

6.5.1 Actually, in the strictest sense, if animals are not moral beings, they cannot deserve anything, good or bad. I know that sounds peculiar, but here is what I have in mind.

Saying that animals do not "deserve" anything sounds peculiar because there are different uses of the term "deserve." I believe it is worth paying attention to these differences, because we will find ourselves thinking things we shouldn't if we conflate them. In what I will call the "strong" sense, to say that someone deserves to be treated a certain way means that he ought to be given (or subjected to) that treatment because he has behaved well or badly in some way that is relevant. Using "deserve" in this strong sense, we may say that criminals deserve punishment and benefactors deserve gratitude and services, meaning that their conduct (somehow—I am not theorizing here about how) makes those outcomes and responses appropriate.

---

[27] Unless you doubt that they feel pain. But such doubts, especially in the case of mammals, birds, and fish, are largely just bad faith. For an account of our reasons for believing that mammals, birds, and fish feel pain, see Victoria Braithwaite, *Do Fish Feel Pain?*

One step away from this, we use the phrase "deserve," or more commonly "doesn't deserve," when someone has forfeited an ordinary right or entitlement. Everyone has the right to be protected from violence, for example, but if a person has used violence against us himself, or if he has used it against the innocent, we might in certain contexts say that he does not "deserve" any protection, or at least any protection from us. The difference here is that although we say *now* that he "does not deserve" protection, we do not mean to imply that he "deserved" it before in the strong sense, the way the benefactor deserves gratitude. You do not have to *earn* the right to protection; it is not a reward for your goodness. You just have to be vulnerable in some way. So I will call that the "middle sense" of "deserve"—someone deserves something in the middle sense if it is an ordinary right and he has not forfeited it.

One step further out, and you find people saying things like "every dog deserves a good home." I think this means that every dog has a right to a good home, but even if you do not think that animals have rights, you might think it is right and proper that every dog should live in a good home. But either way, it certainly does *not* mean that every dog has done something good, because of which he should be rewarded a place in a good home. Nor does it even mean that no dog has forfeited his right to a good home, since, arguably, no dog can do that, because no dog can do anything morally bad. So call that the "weak" sense of deserve—someone is said to "deserve" something simply if it is right and proper that he should have it.[28]

I think it would be better if we did not use "deserve" in all of these ways, because when we confuse them with each other, they promote a certain moralized picture of the world, in which what gives you moral standing or entitles you to happiness more generally is moral goodness.[29] It is a familiar picture, according to which the world has a moral structure, given by the idea that goodness will be deservedly rewarded and evil deservedly punished. This moralized picture of the world is harsh and cruel quite apart from the issue of our relationship to the other animals. It vaguely suggests that every bad thing that happens to everyone is somehow "deserved" in the strong or at least the middle sense. It makes people ask "What did I do wrong?" or "Am I a bad person?" when bad things happen to them, and makes

---

[28] I do not know the source of the popular saying "Every dog deserves a home, but not every home deserves a dog" (internet sources say it is anonymous). Notice that if what I say in the text is correct, the saying uses "deserves" in the weak sense in the first clause, but in the middle sense in the second—some people behave in a way that makes them forfeit their ordinary right to have a dog.

[29] Readers who were offended when I made fun of the reaction to Scarlett the heroic mother cat should keep in mind that the picture of the world I am describing here was the target of my remarks there. Scarlett "deserved" a good home, but so does every other cat.

children wonder if it is "their fault" when their parents' marriages fall apart. It tempts people to turn a blind eye to poverty and suffering, thinking it is probably somehow "deserved." You do not have to "deserve" a good life in the strong sense of desert in order for it to be right and proper that you should have one. If you are a human being, you can *fail* to "deserve" a good life in the middle sense of "deserve": you can forfeit your right to it, by doing evil things. But if you are an animal only the weak sense applies. If the argument I am going to present in Chapter 8 works, and you are a non-human animal, all you have to do in order to "deserve" a good life is to exist.

6.5.2 Kant himself identified moral virtue, without any real explanation, with "the worthiness to be happy."[30] If "worthiness" is thought of as a synonym of my "middle" sense of "deserve," this would be, in my opinion, perfectly acceptable. It would indicate only that human beings can lose their claim on happiness by being morally evil. But it would not indicate that a creature has to earn his claim on happiness by being morally good, and therefore that the other animals can have no such claim.

Kant apparently does not understand the claim in this relatively benign way, however. Kant argued that morality sets an ultimate end for us, an end that he called "the Highest Good." The Highest Good is a world in which all human beings are morally good, or are progressing towards virtue, and are happy in proportion to their virtue.[31] I will not try to rehearse the whole argument here, but Kant's religious theory is based on the idea that we can have no hope of achieving such an end unless we have faith in a God, who would make the laws of nature cooperate with our morally good intentions, and an immortal life, in which we ourselves could progress endlessly towards greater moral perfection.[32] In this way Kant's theory overturns the familiar idea that morality is

---

[30] Kant identifies virtue with the worthiness to be happy at *Critique of Practical Reason*, 5:110 and the good will with the "worthiness to be happy" at *Groundwork*, 4:393. In some of my early essays (for example, "Aristotle and Kant on the Source of Value" and "Two Distinctions in Goodness," essays 8 and 9 in *Creating the Kingdom of Ends*), I read Kant's claim that morality is the "condition" of all value as implying that morality is in a sense the source of all value. If that is taken to mean that the goodness of your happiness depends on your moral character, I now think that is wrong. If it means that human beings confer absolute value on relative values by making moral laws, I think it is true.

[31] Kant, *Critique of Practical Reason*, 5:108–10.

[32] I believe that Kant's religious theory conflates or anyway equates two ideas: the idea that in the morally best world people would be happy in proportion to their virtue, and the idea that in the morally best world, our efforts to achieve good ends by morally justifiable means would always succeed. You can see this equation at work in the long passage I am about to quote in the text. In effect this means that the Kingdom of Ends—the world in which everyone acts rightly—would coincide with the Highest Good. Although I will not pursue the issue here, the identification of those

based on religion, arguing instead that it is the other way around: our faith in God is grounded in our sense of moral obligation. It is necessary to have faith in God because we must see ourselves as promoting the Highest Good through moral action, but we cannot see how we could do that without God's help. Here is one of the passages, from the *Critique of Judgment*, in which Kant explains his thought:

Consider the case of a righteous man...who actively reveres the moral law [but] who remains firmly convinced there is no God and...no future life...He does not require that complying with the law should bring him an advantage, either in this world or in another; rather, he is unselfish and wants only to bring about the good to which that sacred law directs all his forces. Yet his efforts encounter limits: for while he can expect that nature will now and then cooperate contingently with the purpose that he feels...obligated...to achieve, he can never expect nature to harmonize with it in a way governed by laws and permanent rules...Moreover as concerns the other righteous people he meets: no matter how worthy of happiness they may be, nature, which pays no attention to that, will still subject them to all the evils of deprivation, disease, and untimely death, just like all the other animals of the earth.[33]

With a breathtaking lack of empathy, Kant consigns "all the other animals of the earth" to the unrelieved cruelty of nature, while holding out the hope that human beings will be exempted from it. So he seems to think that a creature's happiness is not part of the final good unless the creature deserves it in the strong sense of "deserves."[34]

6.6 Treated Like Animals

6.6.1 Here is another place where the "analogy" view is at work. Consider the common use of the phrase "treated like an animal." People whose rights are violated, people whose interests are ignored or overridden, people who are used, harmed, neglected, starved, or unjustly imprisoned standardly complain that they are being treated like animals, or protest that after all they are not mere animals. If they mean to complain that they are not being treated as ends in themselves, why don't they say that they are being treated like objects or instruments or tools? It is because they *need* the analogy between people and animals in order to make their complaint. Complaining that you are being treated "like an

---

two ideas needs to be justified. In general, I do not think Kant's argument succeeds. For further discussion see Korsgaard, *Self-Constitution*, 5.2.

[33] Kant, *Critique of Judgment*, 5:452.

[34] For further discussion of this passage and a comparison to the attitude of Hume mentioned in 11.1.2, see Korsgaard, "Just Like All the Other Animals of the Earth."

animal" conveys a meaning that is not conveyed by complaining that you are being treated "like a tool," because a tool has no interests of its own that can be ignored or overridden. In the sense intended, an object *cannot* be treated badly, while an animal can. But then the curious implication of the phrase seems to be that animals are the beings that it is *all right* to treat badly, and the complainant is saying that he is not one of *those*.[35]

6.6.2 In 4.3.7, I argued that the value Kant assigns to people as ends in themselves is not so much "equal" as "incomparable." "Dignity," as Kant calls it, is not a kind of price, not even an equal price. One implication of that is that we do not compete for this kind of value—it is not something of which you have less because someone else has more. It is not like social status, say. But if I am right about the phrase "treated like animals," we are contrasting ourselves with beings whom we take to have a lower value when we use it. Kant himself identifies the moment in which human beings first realized we are ends in ourselves with the moment when we first made a contrast between ourselves and the other animals, and "no longer regarded them as fellow creatures, but as means and instruments to be used at will for the attainment of whatever ends he pleased"[36] (6.1.1). Kant also makes a comparison when he says that if we have no faith in God, then we must believe that people will ultimately suffer "all the evils of deprivation, disease, and untimely death, *just like* all the other animals of the earth"[37] (6.5.2). In this case, Kant is using the analogy with animals to deplore the lack of a contrast, just like people who complain that they are being treated like animals. In fact, in a way, he is making the complaint himself. He is complaining that the godless cosmos is treating us like animals.

It is as if we were unable to assert our own claims to dignity and respect without invoking a contrast with other creatures who *could* conceivably be treated with respect, or kindness, or consideration, but, morally speaking—or so we suppose—need not be. It is as if Kant himself failed to understand the full implications of his own concept, the concept of an end in itself. We do not need to contrast ourselves with animals in order to appreciate our own value, which is, in any case, incomparable. In fact I am going to argue that it is the reverse: we cannot appreciate our own value without also appreciating the value of animals as ends in themselves (8.5.3, 8.6.1). There is more than an analogy at work here. Animals, like us, have a final good.

---

[35] The idea of this section first appeared in Korsgaard, "Getting Animals in View."
[36] Kant, "Conjectures on the Beginning of Human History," 8:114.
[37] Kant, *Critique of Judgment*, 5:452; my emphasis.

6.6.3 Earlier I said that the indirect duty argument has two parts: the claim that we cannot owe duties directly to the other animals, and the claim that the grounds of our duties to treat the other animals well in various ways is the effect of doing so on our own characters. I have been arguing against that second claim, on the grounds that the attitude it invites us to take to animals is unstable at best. I have granted that there are some natural instabilities in our personal feelings about animals. When we interact with animals personally, we respond to them with love, hate, gratitude, resentment, or anger—the kinds of feelings and attitudes that, when we have them towards people, we at least sometimes feel should be shaped and controlled by our assessment of their moral characters, put through what I have called a "moral filter." That kind of moral filter is out of place when we are dealing with animals, and it can leave us puzzled about whether our reactions to them are appropriate or not. But there is no such worry about our empathy with their suffering and their joy. It makes little sense to suggest that we should care about their joy and suffering for their own sakes, and yet do that caring for the sake of something else, our own characters.

In Chapter 7, I am going to take up the other side of the indirect duty argument: the claim that we cannot have duties directly to the other animals, because they cannot participate in the reciprocal legislation that creates the Kingdom of Ends.

7

Kant against the Animals, Part 2

Reciprocity and the Grounds of Obligation

> a human being has duties only to human beings (himself and others), since
> his duty to any subject is moral constraint by that subject's will.
>
> Immanuel Kant, *The Metaphysics of Morals*, 6:442[1]

7.1 Introduction

7.1.1 In Chapter 6, we saw that the "indirect duty view" consists of two theses:
First, we owe the duty of treating animals well in various respects to ourselves
rather than directly to the animals, because we cannot have obligations to
animals. Second, the ground of the duty to treat animals well rests in the effects
of the way we treat animals on our own characters, or on those of our emotions
that are, in Kant's words "serviceable to morality in one's relations with other
people."[2] In Chapter 6, I criticized the second of those two theses on the
grounds that the attitude it invites us to take to the other animals is at least
unstable, if not incoherent. The argument depends on the idea that animals, as
"analogs of human beings,"[3] are the *proper* objects of kindness, empathy,
gratitude, and love. But if that is the case, we should care about the animals
for their own sakes, not just for the sake of the effects of that caring on our own
characters.

It is hard to resist the thought that the second thesis of the indirect duty view is
a product of desperation—an attempt to explain the everyday intuition that we
really *do* have at least some obligation to be kind to animals, within a moral
framework that allows obligations to exist only between people, or between
rational beings. If that is right, the pressure to adopt the second thesis comes

---

[1] See also *Metaphysics of Morals*, 6:241.   [2] Kant, *Metaphysics of Morals*, 6:443.
[3] Kant, *Lectures on Ethics*, 27:459.

from the first thesis—the idea that we can have obligations only to people, or only to rational beings. In this chapter, I am going to look at the argument for that idea.

7.2 Reciprocity Arguments

7.2.1 Arguments to the effect that we can have no duties that we owe directly to the other animals, or that our duties to them are limited in certain ways, frequently appeal to the idea that morality or justice, at least in the case of duties to others, essentially involves relations of reciprocity in which animals cannot participate.[4]

Reciprocity arguments may be used in various ways: to show that we have no duties at all to the other animals; to show that we have duties of kindness but no duties of justice to the other animals; or to show that animals should not or could not have legal rights. To some extent, these differences in the exact conclusion of the argument are based on the fact that the philosophers who appeal to the argument categorize our rights and duties in different ways. For now, I will discuss the form of the argument in general, without worrying too much about the exact formulation of what it is supposed to prove.

Perhaps the simplest example of a reciprocity argument is one that portrays morality or justice as arising from or involving a kind of bargain or agreement, or a social contract. Why am I obligated to respect, say, your liberty and your property, or more generally your rights? Because we have made an agreement: I agree to respect your liberty and your property and your rights, but only on condition that you agree to respect mine; you agree to respect my liberty and my property and my rights, but only on condition that I agree to respect yours. So we are bound to each other by something like a reciprocal exchange of promises, and that obligates us to respect one another's rights. Animals, the argument goes, cannot be a party to an agreement with that kind of content, because they cannot enter into agreements, and because they could not understand the content of this particular agreement even if they could. Since they are not part of the social contract, they are not part of the moral community, so we can have no duties, or perhaps no duties of justice, to them.

That version of the argument is subject to a fairly standard objection. The argument undertakes to derive moral obligation from the fact that we have made

---

[4] Kant also thinks we have duties to ourselves. In 8.5.2, I will explain how those are in some ways like our duties to others, and others' duties to us.

an agreement, but for that very reason it cannot explain why we are obligated to keep that first agreement. We cannot without obvious circularity say that we are obligated to keep our agreements by the fact that we made an agreement to keep our agreements. It may of course be in my interest to keep such an agreement, so long as you keep the agreement too; and in your interest to keep it so long as I do. But as soon as it is not in my interest to keep the agreement, the obligation vanishes as well.

7.2.2 This is one problem with a version of the reciprocity argument that David Hume claimed shows why we do not have duties of justice to animals. Hume argued that the duties of justice only hold in certain conditions, conditions which John Rawls later called "the circumstances of justice."[5] Hume makes the argument in order to prove that the duties of justice are grounded in considerations of interest and utility. We expect people to conform to the duties of justice only under certain conditions, Hume argues, and those conditions are exactly the ones in which conforming to the duties of justice is useful to all concerned. One of these conditions is an approximate equality of power between the parties to the agreement, which renders it in the interest of all parties to make and maintain the agreement. If you had enough power to completely control someone else, it would not be in your interest to make any concessions to him, and Hume thinks you therefore would not owe him anything. On these grounds, Hume argues that we do not have duties of justice to the other animals:

Were there a species of creatures intermingled with men, which, though rational, were possessed of such inferior strength, both of body and mind, that they were incapable of all resistance, and could never, upon the highest provocation, make us feel the effects of their resentment; the necessary consequence, I think, is that we should be bound by the laws of humanity to give gentle usage to these creatures, but should not, properly speaking, lie under any restraint of justice with regard to them ... Our intercourse with them could not be called society, which supposes a degree of equality; but absolute command on the one side, and servile obedience on the other. Whatever we covet, they must instantly resign: Our permission is the only tenure, by which they hold their possessions: Our compassion and kindness the only check, by which they curb our lawless will: And as no inconvenience ever results from the exercise of a power, so firmly established in nature, the restraints of justice and property, being totally useless, would never have place in so unequal a confederacy.

This is plainly the situation of men, with regard to animals; and how far these may be said to possess reason, I leave it to others to determine.[6]

---

[5] Rawls, *A Theory of Justice*, chapter 3, section 22.
[6] Hume, *Enquiry Concerning the Principles of Morals*, pp. 190–1.

Hume's version of the argument seems subject to the objection that if some group of people acquired sufficient power over the rest of us, they would cease to have duties of justice to us, because they would cease to have an interest in entering into cooperative relations with the rest of us. Suppose, for example, that a small coterie of people obtains joint control over the only remaining nuclear weapon, and uses the threat of deploying it to blackmail the rest of us into submission to their wills. Since it is not in their interest to cooperate with us, by Hume's argument, they are not obligated to act justly towards the rest of us. Hume seems even to invite that objection, for he emphasizes that in order to have the kind of superior power that frees people from the obligations of justice, it is not enough that the members of one group are stronger *individually* than the members of the other: they must also be sufficiently *organized* and unified among themselves, and arguably, must be just among themselves, to maintain their force against the members of the weaker group. He says:

In many nations, the female sex are reduced to ... slavery, and are rendered incapable of all property, in opposition to their lordly masters. But though the males, when united, have in all countries bodily force sufficient to maintain this severe tyranny, yet such are the insinuation, address, and charms of their fair companions, that women are commonly able to break the confederacy, and share with the other sex in all the rights and privileges of society.[7]

Hume is obviously having a little fun here, but the point is a serious one when we come to think about the claims of animals. It is obviously an important feature of the human relationship to animals that the almost complete control that we are able to exercise over them springs from our superior capacity for cooperation— and so from our ability to remain united.

These versions of the reciprocity argument fail, or at least have implications that most of us find unacceptable. But the Kantian version, as we will see, is not so easy to dispose of.

7.3 Kant's Account of Moral Choice

7.3.1 Before I can explain the role that reciprocity plays in Kant's argument, I need to say a little more about how Kant's moral theory works. In 3.2.4, I distinguished rational action from two kinds of instinctive action. Here is a formalization of what I said there:

---

[7] Hume, *Enquiry Concerning the Principles of Morals*, p. 191.

Mechanical, Stimulus-Response Action

Under circumstances C, (do act A) for the sake of   (end E)

(this act is chosen)   (natural or evolutionary
                                  purpose of the behavior)

Intelligent Action Governed by Teleological Perception

Under circumstances C, (do act A) for the sake of   (end E)

(this act is chosen)   (animal's own purpose,
                              as well (perhaps) as natural or
                              evolutionary purpose of the behavior)

Rational Action

Under circumstances C, (do act A for the sake of end E)

(this whole action is chosen, as a package),
in light of the circumstances

If this is right, the difference between rational action and instinctive action is this: the other animals are governed by the laws given by their instincts, while we rational beings are governed by laws we give to ourselves. Even in cases where the animal knows what she is doing, the purpose is her own, and she is intelligent enough to respond flexibly to conditions in deciding how to pursue it, the purpose is still given to her by her instincts. But a rational being makes an assessment of the whole principle, of the "maxim," as Kant calls it, of doing this act for the sake of this end on this kind of occasion, and decides whether to act on it or not. The fact that rational beings choose in this way has two important consequences. First, there is a sense in which rational beings choose which ends to pursue. Our ends may be suggested by instinct or desire, but we can reject those ends if we decide we must not act on the maxims in which they appear. That means that when we *do* decide to pursue an end, there is a sense in which we have chosen to do so. Second, more generally, a rational being selects the laws that govern her own conduct, rather than being governed by laws that are given to her by her instincts. This is the property that Kant called "autonomy," being governed by laws we give to ourselves.

The nature of autonomy becomes even clearer when we consider how Kant thinks we decide which maxims to accept and which to reject. As I said in Chapter 3, rational beings are aware of the grounds of our beliefs and actions, the possible reasons for doing and believing things. This is what a maxim expresses—a possible reason for an action. The role of the principles of practical reason, as I said before, is to provide standards of evaluation for possible reasons, and different theories of practical reason propose different standards. The standard Kant proposes is a formal one, as I will explain below. Since a proposed maxim is a possible law governing your conduct, Kant believes we should evaluate maxims by asking whether we could will that they should serve as universal laws, laws that everyone could or should act on in relevantly similar circumstances. This standard is embodied in the first formulation of the categorical imperative, the Formula of Universal Law, which runs roughly like this:

> Act only on a maxim which you are able to will as a universal law.

In other words, the reason embodied in your maxim is a good one if, and only if, you are able to will that everyone who is in the same circumstances as you are should act on it too.[8] If you are able to will your maxim as a universal law, the action it describes is permissible—it is "all right" for you to act on it. If you are not able to will it as a universal law, it would be wrong for you to act on it. In that case, you would have a duty to refrain from the action, and in some cases to do the opposite action—to keep your promise when you find it would be wrong to break it, for example.

The test is supposed to be a "formal" one for two reasons. First, the categorical imperative does not directly tell us to do, or not to do, this or that particular action. Instead, it tells us how to *identify* principles that correctly tell us to do, or not to do, this or that particular action. Such principles are ones that can take the "form" of a law, which is universalizability. The agent is "autonomous" because his choice of principles, and ultimately his conduct, is based on his own assessment of whether his proposed principles qualify to be laws.

To see what this means, imagine that you and a friend find a wallet on the street, empty of money but full of photographs and credit cards and a passport, and you say "We really ought to return this to the owner." And imagine that your friend asks, "Why should we do that?" There are two different kinds of answers you can give him. On the one hand, you could say, "Well, the owner will probably want his cards and his passport back, and maybe he cares about the wallet itself,

---

[8] Some commentators argue that Kant is not entitled to assume that maxims must be universalizable in this sense: they think that all that his argument to this point shows is that if I take a consideration to be a reason for me, I must grant that it would also be a reason for you in similar circumstances, but not that I must be able to will that you should act on it. I do not take up that question here. I have addressed it elsewhere under the heading of the question whether reasons are "private" (the normative force of my reasons is only for me) or "public" (the normative force of my reasons extends to everyone). See Korsgaard, *The Sources of Normativity*, 4.2; and Korsgaard, *Self-Constitution*, chapter 9.

it's a pretty nice one, so he'll probably give us a reward." Notice that in this case what you are doing is inviting your friend to join with you in adopting a certain maxim. You are inviting your friend to adopt the maxim: "When you find a wallet whose owner you can identify, return it, in order to get a reward." But suppose instead that you answer this way. You say, "Well, you know, if you lost your wallet, you would want someone who found it to return it to you." There are three important features of this reply. First, unlike the appeal to the prospect of a reward, this is a recognizably *moral* appeal. Second, you are implicitly appealing to what you suppose to be your friend's conception of a law. When you say, "You would want someone who found your lost wallet to return it to you" you are suggesting to your friend that *he himself* would will it as a law that anyone who finds lost property should help the owner to recover it. His own will commits him to this law, since it commits him to the principle that *he* should be helped in this way if he lost his wallet. Third, and importantly, you are also suggesting that that is why he should return the wallet, that should be his motive: *just* because he himself thinks it is a law that people should return lost property, and for *no* other reason. This is what Kant thinks moral motivation is like. When we appeal to a person's moral motives, we appeal to his autonomy, in the sense that we invite him to govern himself in accordance with his own conception of law.

The second reason why the principle is "formal" is that the reason why you could not will certain maxims as universal laws is supposed to be that doing so would introduce a contradiction into your own will.[9] Suppose, to take one of Kant's own examples, I need some money, and I know you will lend it to me if I promise to pay you back next week. Suppose also that I know I will not be able to pay you back next week, so if I say that I will, I will be making a false promise. According to Kant, I should evaluate this maxim by asking whether I could will it as a universal law that everyone who needs some money should make a false promise as a way to get it. Kant thinks that if I willed this as a universal law, I would contradict my own will. He argues that if everyone who needed money made a false promise in order to get hold of it, no one would make loans on the basis of such promises—I'll call them "repayment promises." People would just laugh at such promises as "vain pretenses," because so many people would have lost their money in such transactions in the past.[10]

---

[9] Kant thinks that the universalizations of some maxims are directly self-contradictory while others contradict the agent's will. This is not the place to go into details about this distinction or the many other questions that arise about this method of "testing" maxims. See Korsgaard, "Kant's Formula of Universal Law," essay 3 in *Creating the Kingdom of Ends*.

[10] Kant, *Groundwork of the Metaphysics of Morals*, 4:422.

The reason why willing the universalization of your maxim would introduce a contradiction into your own will is that you *also* propose to will to act on the maxim yourself. Kant thinks that in willing the universalization of your maxim, you are willing a state of affairs in which no one accepts repayment promises. If you will to get money by making a false repayment promise, and at the same time will a state of affairs in which no one accepts repayment promises, you would in effect be willing to undercut the effectiveness of your own method of achieving your end. The contradiction is a practical one. The test shows that you are not proposing to act in a way that you could will for everyone to act, and therefore not acting on what you take to be a universal law, but instead making an exception of yourself.

It's important to keep in mind that Kant is not suggesting that this practical contradiction is your actual, practical reason for not making a false promise. In the real world, the fact that you act on a certain maxim does not actually lead to the universalization of that maxim or its untoward implications. The test is a thought experiment. What the discovery that your maxim would lead to a contradiction if it were universalized does is force you to look at your action from the point of view of others. If it would be unacceptable to you if others did this, then it would be unacceptable to others if you did this. Moral laws are laws that are acceptable from everyone's point of view.

7.3.2 The idea that reasons must be universal, in the sense that what counts as a reason for you must count as a reason for anyone similarly situated, is a familiar one. We appeal to it in the realm of theoretical reason as well. If the fact that your DNA was found at the scene of the crime is a good reason for me to conclude that you were present at the crime scene, then it is also a good reason for the jury to conclude that you were present at the crime scene. On the other hand, if the fact that I dislike you intensely is not a good reason for the jury to believe that you committed the crime, then it is not a good reason for me to believe it either. Reasons for belief must be the same for everyone.

Here is one (very informal) way to see why you might think that a universalizability test is the correct standard for evaluating a person's reasons for action. If you do something wrong, you have wronged someone; and that means someone has a legitimate complaint against you.[11] You need to know what the right thing

---

[11] This sentence assumes, as Kant himself does, that all duties are duties owed to someone—either oneself or others. They are "directed." Some philosophers believe that there are duties that are not owed to anyone in particular. Since Kant thinks of duties as grounded in laws we make for ourselves and each other, on his view the idea of an undirected duty does not make sense.

to do is, in order to avoid being in this position. But how are you to know what the right thing to do is? That looks like a problem.

But in fact, the solution is given by the very formulation of the problem. In order to do the right thing, all you have to do is act in such a way that no one has a legitimate complaint against you. If you act on a maxim that you could will that anyone could act on, then you are acting on a maxim that anyone could will that you should act on. Trying to see whether you can will your maxim as a universal law is just a way of seeing whether your proposed conduct is acceptable to everyone involved in the transaction. When you discover that your method of achieving your end would not even work if everyone tried to use it, you discover that the use of this method could not be acceptable to all concerned. But if your maxim does pass the test, then you are acting in a way that is acceptable to everyone, and if you are acting in a way that is acceptable to everyone, then no one has a legitimate complaint against you. If no one has a legitimate complaint, then you have done nothing wrong. Moral standards are just the standards of conduct that we can all agree that people should adhere to. But it is not, as you might have thought, that we can all agree to this conduct, because it is morally right. Rather, it is morally right *because* we can all agree to it.[12]

7.4 Kant on Reciprocal Legislation

7.4.1 What does all this have to do with reciprocity? The connection emerges when we reflect on the fact that moral laws are supposed to be laws on the basis of which we can make *claims* on one another, claims that are supposed to give rise to *reasons*. When I make a moral claim on you, I appeal to a purported moral law which says that you have an obligation to treat me in the way that I demand.

Now, generally, my appeal to a law only gives you a reason to do what I demand in the name of that law under certain conditions. First, and most obviously, objectively speaking, that law really has to have authority over your conduct. Furthermore, this has to be true in virtue of something about *you*. I can make a demand on you in the name of the laws of France, but unless you are French or at present on French territory, that demand will just bounce off

---

[12] A parallel move is made in T. M. Scanlon's theory, where an action is right because it is justifiable to everyone, rather than justifiable to everyone because it is right. See Scanlon, *What We Owe to Each Other*. Note that I am offering this as a way of making it seem intuitive that the categorical imperative is the standard of right and wrong action. But I am not offering it as an argument for the categorical imperative. A foundational argument has to show why there is such a thing as right and wrong, whereas the argument in the text assumes there is.

of you without any effect. The law applies to you, if it does, *because* you are French or in France. Second, I must be able to show you that, or I will not succeed in motivating you to meet my claim. Third, and maybe a little less obviously, I have to acknowledge the authority of that law, over the conduct of anyone in your circumstances, including myself if I should find myself situated that way.

Actually, that is a needlessly cumbersome way to put it, but I put it that way to make room for a certain kind of case in which we are most immediately under different laws. Suppose I claim something from you on the grounds that you are French and laws of France demand that you do this, but I am not French myself. Have I succeeded in giving you a reason? Only if there is some further law whose authority we do both grant, such as "everyone should obey the laws of his or her country." Otherwise I am just manipulating you. Or suppose we are soldiers, and I am a general and you are a private. I can claim your obedience on that basis in a way that gives rise to a reason for you to obey me, only if I concede that if you were the general and I was the private, you would have the right to command me. If I do not concede this, I am not granting that our relationship as general-to-private is a reason-giving relationship, and so I have not succeeded in offering you a reason after all.[13] In this way we arrive at the idea that for one individual to owe something to another, in the sense that makes it possible to make a reason-giving claim, they must conceive themselves as being under shared laws, grounded in some authority that is acknowledged by them both.

None of this seems like a problem for the possibility of making claims on each other under the moral law. Kant thinks that rational beings are all under the authority of the moral law, simply by virtue of the fact that we are rational beings. It is the nature of rational beings to choose autonomously, to make laws for ourselves, and the categorical imperative simply tells us how to do that: how to decide which of our maxims qualify to be laws. Since we are all under the authority of the moral law, of course we can make moral claims on each other.

But the matter is not quite as simple as that. As I said above, the categorical imperative is not a substantive principle that tells us to do or avoid this or that particular action. It is a principle that tells us *how* to identify the substantive principles that do tell us to do or avoid this or that particular action. The reason we act on these substantive principles is because we ourselves, as individuals, recognize them to be laws: the kinds of principles that we would will for everyone to act on. An autonomous agent is, first and foremost, under her own

---

[13] Here I am drawing on ideas from Stephen Darwall, in *The Second-Person Standpoint: Morality, Respect, and Accountability* and Michael Thompson in "What Is It to Wrong Someone? A Puzzle about Justice."

authority—the authority of her own mind—to act on the laws she makes for herself. The fact that we are under the authority of the moral law is just the same fact as the fact that we are under our own individual authority.

How is it, then, that we can make claims on each other? First of all, since the test for qualifying to be a law is one of consistency, every rational being should arrive at the same idea of which principles qualify to be laws. So we all should acknowledge ourselves to be under the same laws, and we know that about each other. But it is not only that. The way that we make these laws is by asking whether we can will that everyone act on them, which amounts to the same thing as asking whether everyone can will that we should act on them. So in making these laws, we already concede authority to the point of view of others. Since the standard for these laws is that they are acceptable from everyone's point of view, Kant thinks there is an element of reciprocity built into the very idea of autonomous action. I impose the law on myself, but I can only regard it as a law if I think it acceptable from your point of view. Acknowledging that, I must acknowledge the force of a claim you make on me in the name of this law. We can make claims on each other because we regard ourselves as making the laws not just for ourselves individually but for each other, reciprocally. This is why Kant thought of us as legislating these laws for ourselves and each other, reciprocally, as something like the laws of a democracy, legislated together by rational beings in congress: the laws of a Kingdom of Ends.

But the other animals are not rational, are not autonomous, and do not participate in this reciprocal legislation. They cannot put us under obligations. Kant therefore thought that the other animals simply lie outside the boundaries of the moral community.

7.4.2 That argument is controversial, but for our purposes here the trouble is that even if it works, it is not decisive. Laws are by their very nature universal, according to Kant, and a universal law can extend its protection to someone who did not participate, and could not have participated, in its legislation. So there are actually two senses in which you can "owe a duty to someone": you can owe a duty to someone in the sense that he is the recognized authority who made the law for you, or you can owe a duty to someone in the sense that the law by its content gives him a right, which enables him to make a claim on you. Moral laws, as we have seen, give us duties to each other in the first sense, although in a distinctively democratic version of that sense. Since we are autonomous, others do not exactly have authority over us, but Kant thinks we have reciprocal authority over each other. But we could still owe things to the animals in the other sense of "owe a duty to someone": they could be covered by the content of our laws.

In his political philosophy, Kant explicitly recognized this by introducing a category of what he called "passive citizens"—including, as he supposed, women, children, apprentices, and house servants—whose rights are protected by the laws of the state even though they may not vote on those laws.[14] We are not now likely to have much patience with this category as applied to human beings, but the concept is clear enough.[15] Or indeed, even without it, we can make sense of the idea of a law protecting one who did not and could not have made it, since our most basic laws—against theft and murder, say—protect even foreigners from these violations. A "passive citizen" or a foreigner can obligate an active citizen by appealing to a law whose authority the active citizen recognizes. An animal, of course, could not actively make such a claim, but if she falls under the protection of our laws, we can recognize that she has such a claim. The fact that non-human animals cannot participate in moral legislation is insufficient to establish that they cannot obligate us in this sense. The question, then, is whether we human beings ever find it necessary, on rational reflection, to will laws whose protection extends to the other animals.

7.5 The Universalization Test and the Treatment of Animals

7.5.1 We have seen that, according to Kant, we can determine whether an action is permissible or not by formulating a "maxim" or principle, stating the reason for which an act is done, and then asking whether we could will that that principle should serve as a universal law.[16]

It would certainly make things easy for me if I could, at this point, formulate a maxim, run Kant's universal law test, show you that it establishes that we have a certain duty, and that that duty is owed to some other animal or perhaps both to the other animals and to people. But the argument is not going to be so easy, for there are notorious problems making Kant's universal law test work in any algorithmic way. Interestingly, these problems come to the fore when we try to test maxims involving the treatment of animals, for several reasons. Above I argued that to ask whether you can will a maxim as a universal law is to ask

---

[14] Kant, *Metaphysics of Morals*, 6:314–15.

[15] Some people would still place children in this category. I have already explained why I would not when I discussed the question what kind of being has moral standing (5.2.2). A child is not a type of being. Rather, childhood is a life stage. Rights holders, like the holders of moral standing, are types of being, not life stages.

[16] The material in this section previously appeared in Korsgaard, "Fellow Creatures: Kantian Ethics and Our Duties to Animals."

whether you can will the universal practice of pursuing a certain end by means of a certain kind of act without undercutting the effectiveness of that kind of act for achieving that end. For instance, to take the example I used before: Kant thinks that if making false repayment promises in order to get money was a universal law, then no one would lend you any money on the strength of a repayment promise. People, he says, would just laugh at promises to repay money as "vain pretenses."[17] Since making a false repayment promise would then not *be* a means of getting the money that you need, you could not rationally will to get the money you need by making a false promise. So you cannot will your maxim as a universal law. That is in fact only one of several ways in which people have interpreted the universal law test, but elsewhere I have argued that it is the best reading.[18]

But no interpretation of Kant's test yet devised is completely successful, if the mark of success is showing that we can derive everything we believe to be a genuine duty from the test for the right kinds of reasons. How well the test as I interpret it works depends on which of two types of act are involved in the maxim. Some act-types are purely natural, in the sense that they depend only on the laws of nature for their possibility. Walking and running, slugging and stabbing, tying up and killing—these are act-types that are made possible by the laws of nature. Other act-types depend for their possibility not merely on natural laws, but also on the existence of certain social practices, institutions, or conventions. Writing a check, taking a course for credit, and running for office are act-types of this kind: you can only perform such acts in societies with the sorts of practices and conventions that make them possible. In a society without banks, you could sign a rectangular-shaped piece of paper with your name printed on it and various numbers printed around the edges, but only in a society with banks will signing such a piece of paper turn it into money. In a society without schools, you could read things in the company of others, write papers about what you read, and perhaps even persuade someone to evaluate your work, but you could not take a course for credit.

Kant's universal law test works well for maxims that involve act-types that are supported by conventions or practices. Where a maxim involves an act-type that must be sustained by practices and conventions, and at the same time violates the rules of those practices and conventions, it is relatively easy to find the kind of problem that Kant supposed the universal law test would reveal. This is because acts that involve practices and conventions are unlikely to remain effective for

---

[17] Kant, *Groundwork of the Metaphysics of Morals*, 4:422, p. 32.
[18] See Korsgaard, "Kant's Formula of Universal Law," essay 3 in *Creating the Kingdom of Ends*, pp. 77–105, for further discussion.

achieving their ends in the face of their universal abuse. People would abandon those practices in favor of other ways of getting things done. That is what Kant thinks happens in the case of false repayment promises: if everyone abuses the convention of promising, promising ceases to work as a way of getting things done.[19] But maxims involving purely natural actions are hard to rule out by means of the test. This is why another of Kant's examples, that of committing suicide in order to escape your own misery—Kant thinks that is wrong—cannot be made to work in the same way as the false promising example.[20] Suicide is a method of escaping your own misery that depends only on the laws of nature for its effectiveness, not on any convention. No matter how universally practiced it is, it will work.

7.5.2 I think it is obvious that most of the things that human beings do to non-human animals that come up for moral scrutiny are natural acts in this sense. The relationships between human beings and the other animals are not generally governed by shared practices and conventions. Most of the things we do to non-human animals that raise moral questions are natural actions like eating them for pleasure, or experimenting on them for information, or hunting them for sport, methods that will produce the desired results no matter how universally practiced they are.[21] So the test is not going to rule them out. But since the test would fail to rule out the same sorts of actions when practiced on human beings, we should not take this as evidence that such actions are not wrong. We should only take it as signifying the inadequacy of the test.

7.5.3 This is not to say that an action involving the abuse of a convention between human beings and non-human animals is not conceivable. Imagine a vivisectionist who calls out to a former pet, "Here kitty kitty kitty...Daddy's going to give you a treat" as a way of luring the animal to the laboratory table. No matter what you think about experimenting on animals, you must be a very hard character indeed if you do not find that scenario disturbing. Yet even in this kind of case we are not likely to get the right result from the universal law test.

---

[19] Or perhaps we should say if everyone abuses the practice for some specific purpose, the practice ceases to function effectively as a way of achieving that specific purpose. I say this because we might suppose that it is only promises to repay money whose effectiveness is undercut. One of the problems with the test is a certain unclarity about the level of generality with which we should formulate the maxim in order to get a credible result.

[20] Kant, *Groundwork of the Metaphysics of Morals*, 4:421–2.

[21] Hunting or fishing a species into extinction might be an exception to this, but a universal law test that proved that would not demonstrate a duty to the animals in question. It would only demonstrate a duty to other human beings who might wish to hunt and fish. On the question whether the extinction of a species is a harm to the members of that species see 11.2 and 11.6.

Kant's argument against the universalizability of false promising depends on the thought that in a world where people in need of money regularly offered false promises, lenders would eventually *get the idea*. They would know that these promises were insincere.[22] That's why Kant thinks making such promises would cease to be a way of getting money if it were made universal law. Whether he is right or not, many non-human animals are likely to be gullible even to the most universally practiced of human tricks. But again, this appears to be an inadequacy in Kant's test, not a vindication of playing tricks on non-human animals. A similar argument could license playing tricks on gullible human beings too.

Maxims involving the treatment of non-human animals, then, have precisely the features that put Kant's universal law test under the most strain. This doesn't have to mean that there is something wrong with Kant's Formula of Universal Law, considered simply as a criterion of right and wrong. The problem may be with seeing that criterion as a kind of algorithmic test for rightness and wrongness. In other words, it may still be true that an act is wrong if we cannot will the principle behind it as a universal law. It may just be that there is no straightforward test showing when we can do that.

Usually when confronted with such problems, Kantians turn for help to the Formula of Humanity, which in any case seems to capture our ordinary moral ideas in a more intuitive way. In many cases where it seems difficult to work out whether a maxim could serve as a universal law without undercutting its own effectiveness in the required sense,[23] it seems clear and obvious that the maxim describes an action that treats someone as a mere means, or at least fails to treat her as an end in itself.[24]

---

[22] More properly speaking, potential lenders would *always already* have got the idea. Strictly speaking, Kant's test involves imagining your maxim as a law of nature (*Groundwork of the Metaphysics of Morals*, 4:421) and the laws of nature are eternal, so the effects of their universalization would always already be present.

[23] There are many problems with Kant's universalization test, and exploring them is the subject of an extensive literature. I cannot take all these issues up here, but I will mention the one that inspired the qualification "in the required sense." There is a set of problems sometimes called "coordination" problems. These are cases in which human beings have to coordinate our conduct so that we are not all trying to use the same resources at once. For instance, if you try to universalize the maxim of going to the gym early on Monday mornings so that you will have the machines all to yourself, it will fail. If everyone did that, it would not work. But obviously this is not a wrong action. I do not know of any crisp way to use the universalizability test to distinguish these cases from actions that are genuinely wrong.

[24] Not every action that, intuitively speaking, fails to treat someone as an end in itself, treats him as a *means* in any obvious sense. If I knowingly run you over in my car in my haste to escape a threat, I am not using you as a means to my escape. Your presence does not assist my escape. I simply fail to treat it as the source of a reason not to escape in that fashion.

8

A Kantian Case for Our Obligations to the Other Animals

> Even Immanuel Kant, of whom I would have expected better, has a failure of nerve at this point. Even Kant does not pursue, with regard to animals, the implications of his intuition that reason may be not the being of the universe but on the contrary merely the being of the human brain.
>
> Elizabeth Costello in John Coetzee's *The Lives of Animals*, p. 23

8.1 Introduction

8.1.1 In Chapter 7, we looked at Kant's reasons for supposing that we can have duties only to other human or rational beings.[1] Kant believes that as rational beings we reciprocally legislate the moral law for ourselves and each other, forming the moral community he calls the Kingdom of Ends. The other animals cannot participate in this reciprocal legislation, and therefore are not part of that moral community. I suggested that this argument is not decisive, even within the framework of Kant's theory, because it is possible that rational beings legislate moral laws whose protections extend to the other animals. To show this, what we have to show is that we rational beings must claim the standing of an "end-in-itself" not only for ourselves, but for the other animals as well. In this chapter, I will explain why I think we must do this, and say something about the implications of that fact for the way that we think about the Kingdom of Ends.

8.1.2 We saw in 6.1.1 that at one point in the argument leading up to the Formula of Humanity, Kant says:

Beings the existence of which rests not on our will but on nature, if they are beings without reason, have only a relative worth, as means, and are therefore called *things*,

---

[1] Some of the material in this chapter has previously appeared in Korsgaard, "Fellow Creatures: Kantian Ethics and Our Duties to Animals," "A Kantian Case for Animal Rights," "Kantian Ethics, Animals, and the Law."

whereas rational beings are called *persons* because their nature already marks them out as an end in itself, that is, as something that may not be used merely as a means.[2]

As many people read this passage, Kant is making a metaphysical claim about a certain form of value possessed by rational beings. According to this interpretation, rationality is a property that somehow confers a kind of intrinsic value on the beings who have it. They are therefore to be respected in certain ways. Lacking this property, the other animals lack this kind of value, and therefore may be used as mere means to our ends.

There are several problems with understanding Kant's argument in this way. One is that it does nothing to explain the particular *kind* of value that rational beings are supposed to have. "Value" is not a univocal notion—different things are valued in different ways, even as ends. The kind of value that Kant thinks attaches to persons is one in response to which we must respect their choices, in two senses: First, we leave people free to determine their own actions, based on their own reason, without interfering by means of coercion, force, or deception with their choice of actions and ends. Second, we regard their chosen ends (so long as they are not immoral in themselves) as things that are good and so worthy of pursuit, and, accordingly, help them to achieve those ends when they are in need. A person could certainly have some kinds of value, even some kinds of value as an end, without that implying that his choices ought to be respected and his ends ought to be pursued. A prince, or someone held by some religious tradition to be the embodiment of their god, might be valued in the way a precious object is valued, preserved and protected and cherished, without ever being allowed to do anything that he chooses.

8.2 Kant's Copernican Revolution

8.2.1 But the more important problem has to do with the wider aspirations of Kant's philosophy. In order to explain the problem, I'll have to fill in some background. The central argument of Kant's philosophy—the argument of the *Critique of Pure Reason*—is meant to establish, against certain skeptical threats, that empirical scientific knowledge has a secure foundation. In particular, Kant argued that the basic principles that lie behind scientific knowledge, such as the principle that every event has a cause, can be vindicated even though they are not empirical principles themselves.[3] But an implication of his argument (which I will

---

[2] Kant, *Groundwork of the Metaphysics of Morals*, 4:428.
[3] Contemporary physics challenges the claim that every event has a cause at the quantum level. I do not enter here into the question whether that shows that Kant was wrong about the causal

not try to summarize or expound here) is that human beings can have no knowledge of matters that are beyond the realm of experience, beyond what we can reach through ordinary empirical methods and the practice of science. Famously, Kant argued on these grounds that we cannot have *metaphysical* knowledge of such matters as whether God exists, or the will is free, or the soul is immortal. These tenets can be objects of faith, and Kant even explains how he thinks such faith can be rationally grounded, in morality itself (6.5.2), but he thinks we cannot straightforwardly *know* about such matters.

Speaking a bit roughly, Kant thinks the only claims we can make that go beyond the realm of empirical knowledge are ones that can be established as necessary presuppositions of rational activity itself.[4] The laws of logic, according to Kant, are presuppositions of the possibility of thinking in general. Unless we assume them, we are unable to think, or to understand what we are doing as thinking. The principles that ground scientific practice, such as the principle that every event has a cause, are presuppositions of constructing a theoretical understanding of the world. Unless we assume that principle, we cannot construct a theory of the world that will enable us to predict and explain events. Or, to put it another way, unless we assume it, we cannot understand what we are doing when we do science as constructing a theory of an objective world that exists outside of us, and that will enable us to predict and explain events in that objective world. The implication of this is that the laws of reason are the laws of our own minds, laws governing the rational activity of our own minds.

Kant's philosophical strategy is to identify the presuppositions of rational activity and then to try to validate those presuppositions through the method he calls "critique."[5] In the case of the principles governing scientific enquiry, this

---

principle altogether, or whether a version of his argument can be rescued. One might possibly still show that it must be true for "middle-sized" objects—the kinds of objects we ordinarily interact with. It is also worth noting that the concept of a cause is essential to our understanding of action, since when we act we undertake to make ourselves the causes of events and states of affairs in the world.

[4] Elsewhere I have argued that the principles of rationality are *constitutive* of rational activity. (See 4.2.6 and the references in note 8 to that section.) That means that what it is to be engaged in thinking, theorizing, or deliberating practically is just to follow those principles. That is a slightly stronger claim than that the principles are presupposed by the activity. It is a view about how exactly they are presupposed. I have not made that claim in this context since it is a stronger claim than I require for my purposes here.

[5] This rough description of Kant's method skates over a great many complexities and controversies in Kant interpretation. What I am calling "presuppositions" are of various kinds— constitutive principles, regulative principles, and postulates, for instance; and the arguments Kant gives to validate them are also of various kinds. The principles governing scientific theorizing get a "deduction" in Kant's special sense of the term. After Kant decided that the moral law does not need a deduction, as I go on to discuss, he instead supplied it another sort of validation he calls a

involves producing a special kind of argument he called a "deduction." Although Kant initially tried to produce this kind of argument for the principle governing practical activity, the categorical imperative, he eventually decided that it does not require a deduction. Again, putting it a bit roughly: The principles governing scientific theorizing have to be applied to the objects we find around us, and we need an argument that shows us why principles that spring from our own minds may be applied to things outside of ourselves. But the objects of practical reason—morally good objects and ends—are things that we ourselves create through the activity of our own minds, so no "deduction" is needed.[6] So our concern here will be with the presuppositions themselves.

8.2.2 Kant's denial that we have metaphysical knowledge has important implications for the practical realm, because Kant accepts something like the fact/value distinction (5.4.2). Values are not matters of fact, and we do not know *empirically* which things have value. If it were true that rational beings have an intrinsic or inherent value that non-rational beings lack, we would not learn this by, say, dissecting human and animal brains and discovering some difference between them. Since purported truths about value—purported truths such as "Rational beings are valuable as ends in themselves"—cannot be established empirically, there are only two possible ways to establish them. Either they are metaphysical propositions like "God exists" and "The soul is immortal," or they are presuppositions of practically rational activity—in particular, of rational choice and action. According to Kant's philosophy, if they were metaphysical truths like "God exists" and "The soul is immortal" they would have to be grounded in a metaphysical realm that is beyond the reach of experience, and we could not possibly know them. But Kant plainly thinks that we do have something like knowledge about value, which guides our ethical thinking. So he is committed to the view that claims about what has value must be established as presuppositions of rational choice.[7] That means he *cannot* just be claiming that rationality is a valuable property which confers intrinsic value on those who have it. Instead his task is to show us that we must presuppose that rational beings have value as ends in themselves in order to engage in practically rational activity at all.

"credential" (C2 5:48). Despite these complications, I think that the rough description of Kant's method generally fits all these cases.

[6] What I've just said is a controversial interpretation of the arguments of the *Critique of Practical Reason* at 5:29–5:50.

[7] I said above that we have "something like" knowledge, because I believe that these presuppositions, though well grounded, are purely practical commitments.

8.2.3 Let me put the same point another way: in terms of the relation between value and valuing, the activity of setting a value on something and acting accordingly. According to some philosophical theories, certain things just have value—value is a real property that those things have—and we are doing our valuing correctly when we value those things that actually have value. According to others, value depends on valuing—it is the act of valuing that has to come first, and correct valuing confers value on its object. Obviously, the worry about this kind of theory is that it makes it unclear how we determine what counts as correct valuing, and so what may correctly be valued. If it is not just a fact that some objects just are valuable and some are not, what makes it possible to value things correctly or not? How can we be correct or incorrect in our acts of valuing? Kant's answer is that there are some things that we must value if we are to value anything at all. In particular, he argues that we have to value ourselves as ends in ourselves. In that case, things can only be correctly valued if their value is consistent with our own value, and that of others relevantly like us, as ends in ourselves.

8.3 The Concept of an End in Itself

8.3.1 So how do we show that we must value ourselves as ends in ourselves? First, we must say a little more about what it means to have this kind of value. I'm going to put this in my own terms, but I hope it will be clear later on why I also attribute this view to Kant.

In Chapters 1 and 2, we looked at the difference between something's being important-to someone, or good-for someone, and something's being important absolutely, or good absolutely. I argued that "important" and "good" are tethered notions. That means that nothing can be important without being important-to someone, and nothing can be good without being good-for someone. When we say something is good absolutely, what we mean is not that it has a free-floating goodness, but that it is good-for everyone for whom things can be good, in the final sense of good, or good from everyone's point of view. To put this in a somewhat different way now, which will be helpful for the purposes of this chapter, we mean that it can be included in a universally shared or common good, one that we can all pursue together. Among other things, putting it that way will enable to us to include things that are good for someone, so long as they are not bad for anyone, among the absolute goods. So if goodness is a tethered notion, then nothing can be good or bad without being good- or bad-for someone, and to say that something is good absolutely is just to say that it is good-for us all—that is, good (or at least not bad) from every point of view, part of a universally shared or common good.

8.3.2 If we accept this sort of theory, what could it mean to say that a creature, a person or an animal, is an end in itself? First of all, if value comes from valuing, as I suggested above, then in order to have value a creature must be correctly valued by someone. The way that we value a creature for her own sake, rather than merely as a means, is by valuing what is good for her, in the final sense of good, *for its own sake,* or *just because it is good for her.* As I said in 2.1.9, we value a creature's final good from a standpoint of empathy, because when we identify a creature's final good *as* a final good, we look at the things that are functionally good for her from her own point of view, and so see them as the ends of action. This has an important implication: it means that when we say that we value a creature's final good for "its own sake," what we mean is that we value it for the *creature's* sake. Those two "sakes," so to speak, coincide.

It will help you to see what I am getting at when I say that the contrast I am looking for here is with a theory like hedonistic utilitarianism, according to which pleasure just is the good. According to such theories, caring about a creature's good "for its own sake" is not the same as caring about a creature's good "for the creature's sake." Instead, hedonistic utilitarians care about pleasure for its own sake, because they think it is good in itself. It counts as good-for the creature because it is an intrinsically good thing, and the creature has it.[8] Creatures only come into the hedonistic utilitarian story because they are, in Tom Regan's favored word, "receptacles" for the good.[9, 10] So the difference is between saying, as the utilitarians and many others do, "Certain states and things are intrinsically good, and *therefore* they are good for the creatures who have them" and saying, as I would, "Certain things are good-for creatures, and because these creatures are

---

[8] I believe that this view is incoherent. We cannot arrive at an intelligible notion of good-for from the notion of good, because we cannot identify the relevant sense of "having." See Korsgaard, "On Having a Good," especially pp. 136–40, and Korsgaard, "The Relational Nature of the Good."

[9] Singer himself uses the term in spelling out his "replaceability" view. See 9.2.3 and 11.5.

[10] Regan thinks that final goods have "intrinsic" value and creatures have "inherent" value. I do not think that final goods have intrinsic value; I think their value is relational—they are valuable-for the creatures whose final goods they are. So our accounts are different on this point. One place this difference shows up is that Regan supposes that even creatures who are not, or may not be, "subjects of a life" in his sense might serve as "receptacles" of intrinsic value. He says: "It may be that animals, for example, which, though conscious and sentient (i.e., capable of experiencing pleasure and pain), lack the ability to remember, to act purposively, or to have desires or form beliefs—can only be properly viewed as receptacles of intrinsic value, lacking any value in their own right" (*The Case for Animal Rights*, p. 246). On my way of thinking, the idea of any creature being a mere receptacle of value doesn't make any sense, because the value is either good-for that creature or not a value at all.

ends in themselves, *therefore* these things are good." (For further discussion, see 9.2.) I think that this last thought is essential to the concept of an end-in-itself, in the sense in which Kant uses the concept.

So when we value a creature's good for its own sake, at least in the sense that would imply that we regard the creature as an end in itself, we mean that we value it for the creature's sake. Creatures themselves, not pleasure or pain or intrinsic values, are the source of value. Things can be good or bad at all because they are good-for or bad-for creatures. It follows that unless we value at least some creatures as ends in themselves, we cannot see anything as good or bad in the absolute sense at all.

8.3.3 When we view creatures as ends in themselves, we do it from a standpoint of empathy with those creatures, who necessarily set a value on themselves. I say "necessarily" here, because according to the theory I laid out in Chapter 2, that's what a creature is. A creature is a substance that necessarily cares about itself, a substance whose nature it is to value itself. The creature values herself by pursuing her own functional good and the things that contribute to it as the ends of action. Valuing, according to my view, is originally an activity of *life*, a feature of a sentient creature's relationship to herself.[11]

So on my view, when we say that a creature is an end in itself, we mean that we should accord the creature the kind of value that, as a living creature, she necessarily accords to herself, and we therefore see her final good as something worth pursuing.

8.4 Valuing Ourselves as Ends in Ourselves

8.4.1 Now let's return to Kant, and his own argument that we must value ourselves as ends in ourselves.

Kant thinks that because we are rational, we cannot decide to pursue an end unless we take it to be absolutely good. As he sees it, this requirement is essentially built in to the nature of the kind of self-consciousness that grounds rational choice. As I explained in Chapter 3, a rational being is one who is conscious of the grounds on which she is tempted to believe something or to do something—in the case of action, of the motives on which she is tempted to act. Because of the way in which we are conscious of the motives for our actions, we cannot act without endorsing those motives as adequate to justify what we

---

[11] See also Korsgaard, *The Sources of Normativity*, 4.3.

propose to do. But this is just what it means to value something—to endorse our natural motives for wanting it or caring about it, and to see them as good reasons. So as rational beings, we cannot act without setting some sort of value on the ends of our actions. To say that the pursuit of an end is justified is the same as to say that the end is good. Importantly, Kant takes the judgment that the end is good to imply that there is reason for *any* rational being to promote it—that it is good absolutely. As he says in the *Critique of Practical Reason*: "What we are to call good must be an object of the faculty of desire in the judgment of every reasonable human being, and evil an object of aversion in the eyes of everyone."[12] What Kant means by this of course is not that everyone must care about the same things that I do, but rather, that if my caring about an end gives me a genuine reason for trying to make sure that I achieve it, then everyone else has a reason to value my achieving it as well, a reason not to interfere with my pursuit of it, and even a reason to help me to achieve it if I need such help. He means that it qualifies to be part of a universally shared good.

8.4.2 It is because Kant thinks that our choices in this way *create* reasons for everyone, including the agent himself, that he envisions the act of making a choice, the adoption of a maxim or principle, as a piece of legislation. To make a choice is to legislate a universal law, a law that governs both my own conduct and that of others (7.4). My choosing something is making a law in the sense that it confers absolute value on some state of affairs, a value to which every rational being must then be responsive. So when we choose something rationally, we presuppose that our getting that thing is absolutely good. The absolute goodness of our ends is a presupposition of rational action.

8.4.3 But most of the ends we actually choose are simply the objects of our own inclinations, and the objects of our own inclinations are not, considered just as such, good absolutely. As Kant puts it: "The ends that a rational being proposes at his discretion as effects of his actions . . . are all only relative; for only their . . . relation to a specially constituted faculty of desire gives them their worth."[13] The objects of your own inclinations are "relative" in the sense that they are only—or rather at most—good *for* you, that is, good relative to the "special constitution" of your nature, your "faculty of desire." I say "at most" here because, as we have seen, a badly functioning creature may want the wrong things, things that are not good for him (2.2.5), but from now on I will set that complication aside.

---

[12] Kant, *Critique of Practical Reason*, 5:61.
[13] Kant, *Groundwork of the Metaphysics of Morals*, 4:428.

It does not follow *directly* from the fact that something is good *for* someone in particular that it is good absolutely, and that anyone has reason to promote it. Since Kant supposes that a rational being pursues an end only if she thinks it is good absolutely, he does not think that we pursue the objects of our inclinations *merely* because we think those objects are good *for ourselves*. And yet we *do* pursue the objects of our inclinations. Furthermore, when we do so, we expect others not to interfere with that pursuit without some important reason for doing so, and even to help us to pursue them should the need arise. That shows that we think that our achieving our ends is good from the point of view of others and not merely good-for us.

To bring this home to yourself, don't start by thinking about big cases in which others would have to make sacrifices to help you achieve your ends. Think about the fact that you expect people not to block your way on the sidewalk, or stand in front of the lens when you are trying to take a photograph. Think about the fact that you expect people to tell you the time and directions when you ask for them, or to open doors for you when your arms are full of packages. This sort of thing suggests that we take it to be good absolutely that we should be able to act in the way that we choose to and to realize the ends that we seek, at least so long as we are not doing anything that is bad for others. But if our ends are only good relative to our own natures, or good for us, why do we suppose that their achievement is good from every point of view?

8.4.4 That is the question from which, as I read it, Kant's argument for the Formula of Humanity takes off. Kant's answer is that we take our ends to be good absolutely because we take ourselves to be ends in ourselves, or rather, that *in* taking our ends to be good absolutely we are taking ourselves to be ends in ourselves. He says: "*rational nature exists as an end in itself*. The human being necessarily represents his own existence this way; so far it is thus a *subjective* principle of human actions."[14] We "represent" ourselves as ends in ourselves by taking what is good for us to be good absolutely, by choosing our own good, that is, what is good-for us, as an end of action. It is as if whenever you make a choice, you said, "I take the things that are important to me to be important, *period*, important absolutely, because I take *myself* to be important." So by pursuing what is good for you as if it were good absolutely, you show that you regard yourself as an end in itself, or perhaps to put it in a better way, you make a *claim* to that standing.[15]

---

[14] Kant, *Groundwork of the Metaphysics of Morals*, 4:429.

[15] In a footnote at *Groundwork of the Metaphysics of Morals*, 4:429, Kant says that the principle that we are objectively ends in ourselves is just a "postulate," the argument for which cannot be

But your right to confer absolute value on *your* ends and actions is limited by everyone else's (as Kant thinks of it, every other rational being's) right to confer absolute value on *her* ends and actions in exactly the same way. So in order to count as a genuinely rational choice, the principle on which you act must be acceptable from anyone's (any rational being's) point of view—it must be consistent with the standing of others as ends in themselves. In other words, the principle on which you act must conform to the categorical imperative if your action is to be rational: you must be able to will your principle as a universal law.

8.4.5 Here is a way to think about what happens in this argument. I said earlier that Kant thinks we cannot rationally pursue an end unless we regard the end as good absolutely. Many philosophers would conclude that this implies that we can only rationally pursue an end if we think it is *in fact* intrinsically, and therefore absolutely, valuable. But as we have seen, Kant thinks we have no such knowledge. So at this point Kant reverses the argument, in a way we have looked at before. In 7.3.2, I described one way to see why you might think the categorical imperative is the correct standard for evaluating action. The argument went like this: If you do what is right, you have wronged no one, so no one has a legitimate claim against you. So it looks as if we face a problem: we have to know what is right in order to avoid being the object of a legitimate complaint. But how are we to know what is right? In fact, the formulation of the problem gives us the solution: the right thing to do *just is* the action that is acceptable to everyone, the one based on a principle to which everyone can agree. That is what the categorical imperative tells us. So it is not that everyone can agree to your performing an act because the act is right: rather, the act is right because everyone can agree to it.

Kant's move at this point is similar, or in a way, really, the same. As Kant puts it in the *Critique of Practical Reason*, his ethics involves what he calls "a paradox of method...*namely, that the concept of good and evil must not be determined before the moral law (for which, as it would seem, this concept would have to be made the basis) but only after it and by means of it.*[16] Instead of arguing that our ends must be intrinsically valuable, and therefore qualify as ends for everyone, he argues that we can rationally pursue an end only if we are able to reasonably demand that everyone treat it as having absolute value—as if it had intrinsic value, we might say. We do this by restricting our choices to things that are

completed until the third section of the book. The section referred to is his attempt to produce the "deduction" of the moral law that he later decided was not needed.

[16] Kant, *Critique of Practical Reason*, 5:63.

compatible with everyone's value as an end-in-himself or herself. The way we achieve this, in turn, is by making our choices in accordance with the moral law. The upshot of both of these arguments is this: Kant thinks that we can *make* our actions right, and our ends absolutely good, by the way that we choose them, by choosing them in accordance with the categorical imperative.

8.4.6 So, according to Kant, rationality enables us to make choices in a way that renders our actions right and our ends absolutely good. We do this by making moral choices. Kant takes this to mean that it is a rational being's capacity for *moral* choice that "marks him out" as an end in himself. He says: "Now morality is the condition under which alone a rational being can be an end in itself, since only through this is it possible to be a lawmaking member in the kingdom of ends."[17] That is why Kant thinks that rational beings, and only rational beings, are ends in themselves.

8.5 Valuing Animals as Ends in Themselves

8.5.1 Now I will explain why I think Kant is wrong about that. In fact, there are two slightly different senses of "end in itself" at work in Kant's argument, which we might think of as an active and a passive sense. I must regard you as an end in itself in the active sense if I regard you as capable of legislating for me, and so as capable of *placing* me under an obligation both to respect your choices, and to limit my own choices to things compatible with your value as an end in itself. That is what it means to see us as bound together in a system of reciprocal legislation. I must regard you as an end in itself in the passive sense if I am obligated to treat your ends, or at least the things that are *good-for* you, as good absolutely. Kant evidently thought that these two senses come to the same thing: that everyone who is an end in itself in the passive sense must be an end in itself in the active sense too. When you are just thinking about people, the two ideas do seem very close, for to demand that your end should be treated as absolutely good is just to demand that everyone should treat it as giving them reasons, and to do that is just to claim that you have the standing to make a law for others, to participate in reciprocal legislation. But when we think about animals, it becomes obvious that the two ideas are not the same. It certainly could be true that animals are ends in themselves in the sense that what is good for them is good absolutely, even if they are not capable of joining with us in reciprocal legislation.

---

[17] Kant, *Groundwork of the Metaphysics of Morals*, 4:435.

Why might Kant have thought that you can be an end in itself in the passive sense only if you are an end in itself in the active sense? One possible reason, I suppose, is that it is only rational beings who must presuppose our own value in order to engage in practical activity. This, however, would be an inadequate reason. The idea that rational choice involves a presupposition that *we* are ends in ourselves is not the same as the idea that rational choice involves a presupposition that *rational beings* are ends in themselves, for we are not merely rational beings. We are also animals—beings who have a good. Of course, the other animals don't have to presuppose anything in order to engage in practical activity, since they are not rational beings who need to be able to endorse their choices or to see them as justified. But the *content* of the presupposition behind rational choice is not automatically given by the fact that it is only rational beings who have to make it.

So the question here is: Do we presuppose our own value as ends in ourselves only in the sense that when we make a choice, we claim the standing to make a law for ourselves and others—only as autonomous legislators in the Kingdom of Ends? Or do we also presuppose our value as ends in ourselves simply as beings *for whom* things can be good or bad? In fact, Kant's argument actually shows that we must presuppose our value under both of these descriptions, as I will now explain.

8.5.2 Suppose I choose to pursue some ordinary object of inclination, something that I want. Because I want this thing, I think it is good-for me, and I make it my end. When I choose this end, I take myself to create an obligation for every other rational being—no one else is allowed to interfere with my pursuit of this thing without some very good reason, and everyone has some obligation, other things equal, to help me to pursue it if I am in need. In choosing the end, I presuppose that I have the standing to make a law for others with that content, or rather, I claim that standing. Kant thinks that in order to do this rationally, I must accord the same standing to every other rational being.

An autonomous being, however, is not just one who makes laws for everybody else. An autonomous being is also, indeed by definition, one who makes laws for herself. Kant certainly does think that whenever I make a choice I make a law for myself, as well as for other people. And this idea is not without practical content: it is the essential difference between choosing or valuing something and merely wanting it. Wanting something, which is just a passive state, does not include a commitment to continuing to want it, but valuing something, which is an active state, does include a commitment to continuing to want it, everything else equal.[18]

---

[18] This thought is common to a number of ethical theories that are like Kant's in the sense that in them ordinary values, good and bad, are constructed from natural desires, rather than being

Let me give you an example to show you what I mean. Suppose I decide to grow vegetables in my garden, knowing that this will require me to weed it on a regular basis. Then I commit myself to weeding my garden at certain intervals in the future even should it happen that I do not feel like doing so. This is not to say that I decide that I will weed my garden no matter what—though the heavens fall, as it were. But it is to say that when I take something as the object of my choice and set a value on it, it follows that any good reason I have for abandoning this object must come from other laws that I have made for myself or other commitments that I have undertaken—in other words from my other values—and not merely from a change in my desires. Having chosen to grow vegetables in my garden, I can decide not to weed it if I need to rush to the bedside of an ailing friend, for instance. But I have not really decided to grow vegetables in my garden—I have not set a value on doing so—if I leave it open that I will not weed my garden if I just do not happen to feel like it. For if *all* that I have decided when I decide I will keep my garden weeded is that I will weed it if I happen to feel like it, then I have not actually decided anything at all. On any given day when I wake up, whether I weed my garden will depend on whether I happen to feel like it, not on the supposed choice I made before. So when I choose to grow vegetables as my end, I bind my future self to a project of regular weeding by a law that is not conditional on my future self's desires. In that sense, I have legislated a kind of categorical imperative for myself. And my future self in turn also binds me, for it is essential that if she is going to do the necessary weeding, I must now buy some pads to protect her knees, and the tools for her to weed with—and I must also do *that*, whether I feel like it or not. In this simple sense, whenever I make a choice, I impose obligations on myself—I create reasons for myself. When I act on those reasons, you can say that I am respecting my own autonomy, by obeying the law that I myself have made. When someone else respects my choice, he is also governed in this way by respect for my autonomy: he takes my choice to be law.

8.5.3 But now consider my own *original* decision to set a value on some ordinary end of inclination, to treat something that is good-for me as if it were good

---

something alien to desire and possibly at war with it. (Kant, however, does not think moral values, the values of right and wrong, are derived from natural desires.) See for example Simon Blackburn, *Ruling Passions: A Theory of Practical Reason*, pp. 8–14. Blackburn argues that valuing something involves not only wanting it but being disposed to go on wanting it, thinking badly of myself if I should cease wanting it, and so on. Similarly, Harry Frankfurt says, "When we...care about something, we go beyond wanting it. We want to go on wanting it, at least until the goal has been reached...we feel it as a lapse on our part if we neglect the desire, and we are disposed to take steps to refresh the desire if it should tend to fade. The caring entails, in other words, a commitment to the desire." *Taking Ourselves Seriously and Getting It Right*, pp. 18–19. What is distinctive about Kant here is the idea that having this "commitment" is understood as making a law for yourself.

absolutely. That decision is not an act of respect for my own autonomy. After all, I cannot respect my own choices or do what is necessary to carry them out until *after* I have made them. I cannot obey the law I have made for myself until after I have made the law. So the sense in which I "represent myself" as an end in itself when I make the original choice is not captured by the idea that I respect my own standing as an autonomous lawmaker in the Kingdom of Ends. When I make the original choice, when I decide that my desire to grow vegetables is a reason for me to set a *value* on having a garden, I have no other reason for taking my end to be good absolutely, than the fact that it is good *for me*. So I am deciding to treat my ends as good absolutely, simply because I am a creature with a final good. From there all we have to do is generalize: that principle requires that we should take the ends of beings who have a final good to be absolutely valuable.

Let me try to put this another way. An act of choice has two aspects, or "moments." The first aspect is a decision I make for myself, and in a way, about myself: finding myself with a desire for something I believe is good-for me, I decide to pursue it as if it were good absolutely. The second aspect is that I embody that decision in a law that I make for everyone, including myself. While these are not really separate acts—both are embodied in the making of a law— they involve two different relationships, one in which I stand to myself, and one in which I stand to all rational beings. The relation in which I stand to myself is this: I claim standing as an end-in-itself in the sense that I take the things that are good for me to be good absolutely. The relation in which I stand to all rational beings is this: I claim standing to make a law for everyone in my capacity as an autonomous legislator in the Kingdom of Ends.

8.5.4 Of course, there are ways to challenge this conclusion. Someone might insist that when I make the original choice I still act from respect for my own autonomy, but in a different sense. I act from respect for my own autonomy not in the sense that I conform to the law I have made for myself, but in the sense that I presuppose that what is good for autonomous rational beings, and only for autonomous rational beings, should be treated as good absolutely. But that conclusion is not driven by the argument: as I said earlier, there is no reason to think that because it is only autonomous rational beings who must make the normative presupposition that we are ends in ourselves, the normative presupposition is only *about* autonomous rational beings. And in fact it seems arbitrary, because of course we also value ourselves as animate beings. This becomes especially clear when we reflect on the fact that many of the things that we take to be good-for us are not good for us in our capacity as autonomous rational beings. Food, sex, comfort, freedom from pain and fear, are all things that are good for us insofar as we are animals.

In fact, it might even be possible to make the whole argument in a stronger form. Throughout my presentation of both Kant's argument and my own version of it, I have granted Kant's view that respect for another rational being's autonomy requires us both to avoid trying to control his actions through force, coercion, or deception, and to help him to pursue his ends when he is in need. The argument Kant actually gives for the second part of that—the argument for the duty of beneficence, under the Formula of Humanity—goes like this:

Fourthly, as concerns meritorious duty to others, the natural end that all human beings have is their own happiness. Now, humanity could indeed subsist if no one contributed anything to the happiness of others while not intentionally detracting anything from it; but this is still only a negative and not positive agreement with humanity, as an end in itself, if everyone does not also try, as far as he can, to advance the ends of others. For if that representation is to have its full effect in me, the ends of a subject that is an end in itself must, as much as possible, also be my ends.[19]

Kant himself here seems to appeal to the relationship in which we stand to our own happiness: to treat others as ends in themselves in the positive sense is to take the same kind of view of their happiness as we do of our own. That view, of course, is that it is an end worth pursuing—an absolute good. So we might argue that even on Kant's own view, respect for someone's standing as an autonomous being is primarily a matter of respecting his freedom of choice and action. It is the source of our duties not to interfere with or try to control the choices of others. But it is respect for someone's standing as a being who has a good that is the source of the duties of beneficence. Beneficence requires respect for someone's animal nature, not merely for his rational nature.

8.5.5 The argument I have just given has taken some complicated twists and turns, as presentations of Kant's ideas are apt to do, but there is a way to make it simply. As rational beings, we need to justify our actions, to think there are reasons for them. That requires us to suppose that some ends are worth pursuing, are absolutely good. Without metaphysical insight into a realm of intrinsic values, all we have to go on is that some things are certainly good-for or bad-for us. That then is the starting point from which we build up our system of values—we take those things to be good or bad absolutely—and in doing that we are taking *ourselves* to be ends in ourselves. But we are not the only beings for whom things can be good or bad; the other animals are no different from us in that respect. So we are committed to regarding all animals as ends in themselves.

[19] Kant, *Groundwork of the Metaphysics of Morals*, 4:430.

8.6 Morality as Our Way of Being Animals

8.6.1 I have claimed that when we decide to our pursue our final good and require that others help us when we are in need, we presuppose our value as ends in ourselves in a sense that we share with the animals: we take the things that are good for us to be good absolutely. I have also argued that animals necessarily take themselves to be ends in themselves in this sense: that is simply animal nature, since an animal just is a being that takes its own functional good as the end of action. Each animal does this at the level of cognition or intentionality of which she is capable (3.2.4). If an animal acts in a mechanical, stimulus-response way, her final good is the evolutionary purpose of her action. More intellectually sophisticated animals who are governed by what I have called "teleological perception" (3.2.1) take the things that contribute to their functional good as their own purposes. Rational animals *think* about what is good, formulate our own conception of the good, and "legislate" it as an end both for ourselves and for others in a system of reciprocal legislation. That is the way we take ourselves to be ends.

Rational, moral choice is different from the springs of animal action, because it naturally carries us beyond ourselves to include the good of others. We know that every other sentient creature has a "center of self" in George Eliot's words, from which that creature's good appears absolutely important, as absolutely important to him or her as our own is to us. Still, there is a way in which, in moral legislation, we are just doing, at our own level of cognition and intentionality, what every animal does by its very nature: we are expressing and enacting the concern for ourselves that we necessarily have as animals. So viewed, morality is just the human way of being an animal. In moral legislation we are, in a certain way, affirming the value of animal nature itself. The claim of the other animals to the standing of ends in themselves has the same ultimate foundation as our own claim does, the same ultimate foundation as morality—the essentially self-affirming nature of life itself.

8.7 Different Moral Relations to People and Animals

8.7.1 An important feature of the conception of morality that emerges from these arguments is that our moral relationships among ourselves—by which *in this context* I mean, the moral relationships among rational beings—really are different from the moral relationships in which we stand to the other animals. I have not rejected Kant's idea that rational autonomous beings have obligations to each other that are grounded in relations of reciprocal legislation. Speaking a bit roughly, we obligate each other by making claims on each other that are reasonable because in making them we allow that others may reasonably make similar claims on us. The other animals obligate us by reminding us of what we as individuals have in common with them—that we are creatures *for* whom things can be good or bad, and that like them, although in our own special way, we each take our own good to be good absolutely when we engage in practical activity.

In 8.5.3, I argued that there are two aspects or "moments" involved in making a choice: we determine that we will treat something that is good for us as good absolutely, and we make a law to that effect that we take to be binding on ourselves and other rational beings. The first aspect or moment presupposes that being a creature for whom things can be good or bad makes you an end in yourself in the sense that it justifies you in treating your good as an absolute good. That presupposition leads to our duties to animals. It requires us to treat the good of animals as good absolutely. The second aspect or moment presupposes that being an autonomous rational being makes you an end in yourself in the sense that it justifies you in making laws for yourself and all other rational beings. That presupposition leads to our duties to all rational beings. It requires us to respect the autonomy of all rational beings. It turns out that there is an element of truth in Kant's view that our duties to animals are owed to ourselves: the animals obligate us under a law of whom each of us is, individually, the legislator: the law that obligates us to treat all beings who have a final good as ends in themselves.

8.7.2 In 5.4, I raised some worries about the usefulness of the concept of moral standing. In 5.4.3, I suggested that we should conceive moral standing to be a relational concept, not just the concept of a property. I'd like to come back to those ideas in light of the arguments that I have just made.

We can distinguish two different conceptions of what it amounts to have moral standing. On what I will call "the valuable property view," to have moral standing is to have some property that (somehow) makes what happens to you matter for its own sake. As I mentioned in 8.1.2, this is how Kant's critics understand his claims about autonomy. They think he is saying that autonomy makes human beings or rational beings uniquely valuable, and that that is why what happens to autonomous beings matters for its own sake. On a version of the valuable property view modified to accommodate the commonplace intuition that we do have some obligations to animals but not very strong ones, autonomy is a property that makes what happens to human beings matter *more* than what happens to the other animals. It is no wonder that the argument in these forms comes in for criticism from the friends of animals, who rightly protest that the fact that someone can suffer is enough to make what happens to him matter, and matter equally, if anything matters at all. If we take Kant to be making a claim about a valuable property, his argument does sound as retrograde as claiming that what happens to you matters more if you are male or white or were born in the upper classes.

What I hope to have shown in the last two chapters, however, is that Kant does not hold this conception of moral standing, which requires something like a notion of intrinsic value. Instead, Kant holds what I will call a "moral community membership" view of moral standing. On this view, moral standing is a relational property. Autonomy makes human beings or rational beings members of the moral community. This does not mean that the idea of having moral standing is not an idea about having a certain kind of value. The members of the moral community are reciprocally committed to valuing one another, in the sense of taking what happens to each other to matter. Value depends on valuing: the value of the members of moral community comes from the way they are committed to valuing themselves and each other. So we need not take Kant to be refusing moral standing to the other animals because he thinks that autonomous rational beings are absolutely or cosmically important and valuable while the other animals are not, or that autonomous rational beings are absolutely or cosmically more important and valuable than merely sentient beings are. Rather, he refuses moral standing to the other animals because he thinks that, not being autonomous, they cannot participate in reciprocal lawmaking and so cannot be members of the moral community.

And in one way, of course, he is right. We cannot enter into reciprocal relations with the other animals. If we decide we must value their good as we do our own, they are not going to return the favor. Nevertheless, each of us stands in a relation to him- or herself that is the ultimate basis of all value. That relation is that we each take the things that are good-for us to be good absolutely, rationally endorsing the natural tendency of conscious living beings, *of creatures*, to pursue their own good as if it were good absolutely. We recognize that this is a condition we share with all other creatures. Our reason for including animals in the moral community is just that: that we recognize them to be fellow creatures, with a good of their own just like ours.

8.7.3 According to the arguments I have just given, our moral relations to the other animals have a different basis and a different shape than our moral relations to other people. For myself, I take this conclusion to be a welcome one, because to me it seems intuitively correct that the sense in which we owe things to our fellow rational beings is different from the sense in which we owe things to the other animals. But it raises a question about how we are to understand how these two apparently different grounds of obligation operate in our duties to human beings.

I cannot give this complex question a full treatment here, since the answer depends on how we understand the human good. But here is a sketch of what I think. There seem to be three possibilities: (1) We have a duty both to respect the autonomy of our fellow rational beings, and to promote their good, where those are just separate matters. These two duties could then come into conflict, in which case it would be unclear which should prevail. (2) We have a duty to promote the good of other rational beings, but because rational beings function practically by making autonomous choices, the ability and opportunity to autonomously determine your own fate is part of a rational being's good. We therefore attend to the good of rational beings both by respecting their autonomy and by promoting the conditions under which autonomy flourishes. It would follow that we have duties to promote education, democracy, what Rawls called "the social bases of self-respect or self-esteem,"[20] and liberal societies conceived as those in which each citizen can pursue his or her own conception of the good. These various duties could still come into conflict with each other, or with other aspects of a rational being's good, such as, say, the duty to promote a rational being's physical or mental health. (3) It is the nature of rational beings that we determine our good autonomously, and therefore there can be no tension between respecting our autonomy and promoting our good.

Despite the intuitive attractions of the second option, I think that the third option is the correct one. Our duty to promote the good of other people, or other rational beings, is not something added to our duty to respect their autonomy, as it is on the first option. Nor is our duty to respect their autonomy a mere part of our duty to promote their good as it is on the second. Instead, our duty to promote the good of other rational beings takes the *form* of respecting their autonomy—although of course only once they are adults. In the case of rational beings, we are not confronted with two separate grounds of duty. This is not because we cannot identify things that in a general way are good for human beings apart from the lives they choose autonomously—like physical health, for instance. It is because it is up to the human beings *themselves* to decide whether to include those goods in their own conception of the good, and how to rank them against other, perhaps more idiosyncratic, goods. I think on this option we can still make the

---

[20] Rawls, *A Theory of Justice*, pp. 155–7 and part 3, chapter 7, section 67.

argument that education when young is necessary for the flourishing of beings who are to grow up autonomous. And the argument for a liberal society, in which every rational being has the opportunity to pursue his own conception of the good, is placed on an even stronger footing. It is not merely a political form that happens to be quite good for us, given our autonomous natures. It is a uniquely suitable political form for rational beings to pursue our sort of good in.

8.8 Trouble in the Kingdom of Ends

8.8.1 The arguments I have offered in this chapter, if they work, show that we are committed to the view of animals as ends in themselves, and accordingly, we should expand the boundaries of the Kingdom of Ends to include them. But it must be admitted that this inclusiveness makes three kinds of trouble for Kant's vision of the Kingdom of Ends as a sort of morally perfect world, or at least, what some will regard as trouble.

The first problem is that animals have not been admitted as our equals. They have been admitted as passive citizens, subject to the dictate of rational wills. The laws that govern our conduct towards them are laws that we make, and animals have no part in their legislation. Some will think this makes them, morally speaking, second-class citizens, and that that is objectionable. Of course, one might argue that this inequality arises not because the Kantian downplays the status of animals within the moral community, but because he has a rather exalted view of the status of people. Other moral theories do not hold that rational beings are in some sense the authors and co-legislators of moral laws.

8.8.2 The second problem is, in my view, more serious. Of course as Kant envisions the Kingdom of Ends, people do not merely make the laws together— they act on those laws, or at least it is reasonable to expect them to. But the other animals not only cannot participate in making moral laws, they also cannot be expected to act on them.

A comparison may help to show why this is a problem. In his political philosophy, John Rawls distinguished between ideal theory and non-ideal theory, and argued that, methodologically speaking, we should do ideal theory first.[21] When we do ideal theory, we determine what the principles of justice or of interaction more generally should be for an ideal community, conceived as one in

---

[21] Rawls, *A Theory of Justice*, pp. 7–8.

which everyone both can and will comply with whatever principles we choose. Only after we form that conception, and in light of it, do we develop non-ideal principles for dealing with those who either will not or cannot comply. I have myself argued that the Kantian Kingdom of Ends should be conceived as a piece of moral ideal theory, and have argued, unlike Kant himself, that we should develop special principles for dealing with evil.[22] This is one way of responding to a supposed problem with Kant's ethics, illustrated by Kant's famous argument that you must tell the truth even to a would-be murderer about whether his victim is hiding in your house.[23] The worry is that the strictness of Kantian duty leaves us helpless to respond appropriately to evil. The general idea is that we should develop principles for dealing with uncooperative agents that treat them as much as possible like cooperative ones, but without rendering ourselves the helpless tools of evil, and without foreclosing the possibility of re-entering into good moral relations.[24]

As Elizabeth Anderson and Hilary Bok have pointed out, a similar worry arises when we incorporate animals into the moral community in general, and perhaps for Kantian ethics especially. The worry is that strict duties to animals will leave us helpless in the face of the unreasonableness and amorality of the animals themselves. When we are dealing with other rational agents, we can come to an agreement on the principles that govern our interactions—that is essentially what morality is, but we can do it in more local and particularized ways as well. If we cannot find a solution that both parties are happy to agree to, we can at least negotiate and compromise. If our antagonist is too obdurate even for that, we can resort to legal force and the threat of punishment. If our antagonist is innocent, say, mentally defective, and all those measures are therefore inappropriate, we can resort to institutionalization and other forms of force. When we are dealing with animals whose behavior is threatening or intolerable to humans, it is unclear what our options are. Reasoning certainly will not work and threats are not always effective.[25] We have to deal with dogs with intractable behavior problems, rabbits and moles who damage our gardens, rats and mice

---

[22] Korsgaard, "The Right to Lie: Kant on Dealing with Evil," essay 5 in *Creating the Kingdom of Ends*.

[23] Kant, "On a Supposed Right to Lie from Philanthropy." In Kant: *Practical Philosophy*.

[24] See Korsgaard, "The Right to Lie: Kant on Dealing with Evil" and "Taking the Law into Our Own Hands: Kant on the Right to Revolution," essay 8 in *The Constitution of Agency*.

[25] In the Middle Ages, ecclesiastical law allowed for the excommunication of vermin who were destroying crops. Edmund P. Evans, in *The Criminal Prosecution and Capital Punishment of Animals*, describes how the vermin were "warned" before the sentence was carried out, as if to give them a fair chance to avoid it. See Evans, *The Criminal Prosecution and Capital Punishment of Animals*, Kindle locations 172–5.

who invade our granaries, insect pests, and coyotes that may be a threat to our children.[26] These animals are ends in themselves and they are morally innocent, but those considerations cannot leave us helpless to take action against them. As Hilary Bok writes:

If it is wrong to unilaterally harm someone who cannot understand why we impose that harm, or what she might have done to avoid it, then it is wrong to defend ourselves against nonhuman animals when they try to kill us, at least when defending ourselves involves inflicting even non-lethal harm on them. It would likewise be wrong to defend ourselves against such lesser harms as the loss of a limb or the destruction of our home. Should it turn out that termites are sentient, we might hope to lure them away from our homes by building even more enticing wooden structures for them to feast on, but it would be wrong to kill them. As [Elizabeth] Anderson writes, it cannot be reasonable to accept this kind of limitless vulnerability to non-human animals.[27]

Of course it is important to keep in mind that in cases of self-defense, we allow ourselves to treat other human beings in ways we would not allow ourselves otherwise. But the exact nature and extent of this permission is one of the more controversial questions of practical ethics, and it looks as if it might be different when we are dealing with animals.

But the fact that animals cause trouble in the Kingdom of Ends is no reason to lock them out if they otherwise belong there, as I believe they do. Problems of this kind must be acknowledged, but they only show why animal ethics, like other branches of practical ethics, is a special subject requiring principles for dealing with the special problems that it generates.

8.8.3 The third problem is, from a conceptual point of view, the hardest. I have characterized an absolute good as one that is good from every point of view, and also as one that can be included in a shared or common good which we can all pursue together. In this I have followed Kant. Kant had two ways of character-izing the Kingdom of Ends:

By a kingdom I understand a systematic union of various rational beings through common laws. Now since laws determine ends in terms of their universal validity, if we

---

[26] The omission of wild animals who prey on livestock from this list is deliberate.

[27] Bok, "Keeping Pets," in the Oxford Handbook of Animal Ethics, p. 787. She has quoted Elizabeth Anderson, who writes: "to bind oneself to respect the putative rights of creatures incapable of reciprocity threatens to subsume moral agents to intolerable conditions, slavery, or even self-immolation. As it cannot be reasonable to demand this of any autonomous agent, it cannot be reasonable to demand that they recognize such rights." Anderson, "Animal Rights and the Values of Nonhuman Life," in Animal Rights: Current Debates and New Directions, pp. 287–8. I am indebted to both Bok and Anderson for what I say in this section.

abstract from the personal differences of rational beings as well as from all the content of their private ends we shall be able to think of a whole of all ends in systematic connection (a whole both of rational beings as ends in themselves and of the ends of his own that each may set himself), that is, a kingdom of ends, which is possible in accordance with the above principles.[28]

So far I have put more emphasis on the first of those two conceptions: the Kingdom of Ends is a republic of all rational beings, whose laws are the product of reciprocal legislation. But as Kant points out here, the Kingdom of Ends can also be conceived as a whole of all good ends, every rational being as an end in himself or herself and the morally legitimate ends which each person sets for himself or herself. In the Kingdom of Ends, we pursue these together. As we saw in 6.5.2, in his religious philosophy, Kant sets before us the idea that if we conduct ourselves as citizens of the Kingdom of Ends, we may hope, at least with God's help, to produce a different kind of system of all good ends. That system is the Highest Good, in which everyone is happy in proportion to his or her virtue, and everyone has an immortal life in which he or she may achieve or approach perfect virtue, and with it the perfect happiness such virtue merits.

The details don't matter; the point is that Kant believed that through moral action we not only can make our ends good, by the way that we choose them (8.5.4), we can also, though perhaps only with God's help, achieve a situation in which everyone's good is realized. A similarly optimistic picture crowns Kant's political philosophy, although here the object of faith is the possibility that a universal peace will someday be achieved. Peace, Kant tells us, is "the highest political good."[29] Kant believed that the achievement of peace would go hand in hand with the condition in which every nation on earth is a republic, because when the people, rather than the rulers, decide whether to go to war, they will usually decide against it. Once peace is achieved, funds previously devoted to war will be devoted to education and enlightenment. Enlightenment is the condition in which people learn to think for themselves, and that leads to morality, in which people govern themselves by their own autonomously chosen laws. A Kingdom of Ends on earth is actually achieved, in which all good ends can be pursued together.

Kant may have exaggerated the extent to which all human goods can be realized together. He does not, in these discussions, have much to say about the

---

[28] Kant, *Groundwork of the Metaphysics of Morals*, 4:433.

[29] Kant, *The Metaphysics of Morals*, 6:354–5. The ideas that follow are found in "Idea for a Universal History with a Cosmopolitan Purpose," "An Answer to the Question: What Is Enlightenment?," "Perpetual Peace," and "Conjectures on the Beginning of Human History" all available in Reiss, *Kant: Political Writings*.

occasions in which someone is unhappy for the loss, or failure to obtain, some particular precious object. Morality cannot protect human beings from disease, accident, and natural disaster, as he himself pointed out (6.5.2). But I think most decent people are committed to the view that through the practice of morality and justice, we can make the world in a general way a good place for all people. In that sense we can produce a universally shared, absolute good, by the way that we make our choices. We can at least avoid destroying each other's happiness and freedom.

But once we invite the animals in to the Kingdom of Ends, that hope of making the world good for everyone is gone. The interests of animals, including now ourselves as animals, are irreparably contrary. Animals eat each other. They necessarily compete for habitat. They necessarily compete for the world's resources. These conflicts are not avoidable or occasional misfortunes, many of which could be eliminated by just institutions, but built deeply into the system of nature. Far, far more animals are born than the planet can sustain. Most of the sentient beings who are born on this planet are doomed to be eaten, or to starve, or both. Most of them will experience these misfortunes early in life, before they have had much chance at enjoying the great good of existence (2.1.8).

This problem is a conceptual one, or almost so, because of the rift it introduces in the concept of the absolute good. Consider the world from the point of view of the lion, and you will see that to her, what is good-for her is just as important as what is good-for you is to you. Consider the world from the point of view of the antelope, and you see that what is good-for him is just as important as what is good-for you is to you—and just as important to him as what is good-for the lion is to her. But it is, obviously, good-for the lion to catch and eat the antelope, and bad-for the antelope when this happens.

Nature is recalcitrant to moral standards. We can impose the form of law on our actions, but we cannot impose the form of the good on nature. This, as we will see in the coming chapters, is the source of some of the knottiest problems of animal ethics.

8.8.4 But before we look at that in more detail, let's answer our question. It is true that if we admit the other animals into the Kingdom of Ends, we cannot make the world good for everyone there. Could that be a reason for keeping them out? Kant's account is a "deontological," not a consequentialist one: we do not do what is right in order to achieve the good, but in order to treat others in a way that accords with their value. So on a Kantian account, the actual achievement of something like the highest good is a hoped-for effect of moral conduct, but not its purpose. Strictly speaking, moral conduct has no general "purpose" because when we choose an action morally, we choose the purpose or end of our action along with the act that promotes it (7.3.1). What's morally good is doing certain acts for the sake of certain ends—certain whole actions. What makes the actions morally acceptable, when they are, is that the principles on which they are based can serve as universal laws, because they treat everyone concerned as an end-in-itself.

To put it less formally, what the account calls on us to do is to treat the animals with whom we interact as ends in themselves, whose interests are absolutely important, no less than our own. In many cases, that is perfectly possible, even if a world that is good in all respects could not result from it. The fact that people like to eat meat or could learn from doing experiments on animals, for example, does not produce an *ineradicable* conflict with animals, because we can give these benefits up (see 12.3 and 12.5). The ineradicable conflicts in nature are *in general* no reason for human beings not to treat animals as ends in themselves.

8.8.5 But there certainly are cases in which the ineradicable conflicts in nature make it hard to know what it is right to do, and even make it unclear whether there is a right thing to do. These problems are confronted most directly in specific contexts. Some of them come up when the animals who live among us interfere with our own interests and become pests, although in dealing with these we may often legitimately plead self-defense. They are also confronted by people who try to manage wildlife or the animals in zoos, and by those of us who keep carnivorous pets, because of conflicts between the interests of animals. Skeptics about the moral claims of animals seize on these kinds of problems, demanding to know whether the friends of animals think we should eliminate predation altogether. Some of the friends of animals valiantly reply that we should (see 10.1). We can open the doors to the Kingdom of Ends to everyone if we can find a way, without hurting any individuals, to slowly eliminate the predators, or redirect their predatory tendencies into harmless play. Other friends of animals think the solution is that we should not try to manage wildlife, or keep carnivorous pets, or indeed any pets at all (see 10.2). In this way, attempts to confront the moral recalcitrance of nature, or perhaps to avoid confronting it, have been a driving force in the development of animal ethics.

In the last three chapters of this book I explore these practical issues. But first I want to address one last theoretical issue. In Chapter 9, I will ask how the theory I advocate, which grants moral standing to all creatures who are capable of feeling pleasure and pain, differs from a utilitarian account, and more generally what the role of pleasure and pain are in the constitution of the final good.

9

The Role of Pleasure and Pain

One might think that all men desire pleasure because they all aim at life; life is an activity, and each man is active about those things and with those faculties that he loves most . . . pleasure completes the activities, and therefore life, which they desire. But whether we choose life for the sake of pleasure or pleasure for the sake of life is a question we may dismiss for the present. For they seem to be bound up together and not to admit of separation.

Aristotle, *The Nicomachean Ethics*, 10.4 1175a 10–20

To be a living bat is to be full of being; being fully a bat is like being fully human, which is also to be full of being. Bat-being in the first case, human-being in the second, maybe; but those are secondary considerations. To be full of being is to live as a body-soul. One name for the experience of full being is *joy*.

Elizabeth Costello in J. M. Coetzee's *The Lives of Animals*, p. 32

9.1 Rapprochement with Utilitarianism?

9.1.1 Peter Singer has argued that animals have moral standing because they have interests, and that animals have interests because animals, including humans, have the capacity for pleasure and pain, especially pain. I have argued that animals have moral standing because animals, including humans, have a good in the final sense of good (8.5), and that we have a good because we have valenced responses to the things that affect the functional goodness of our own condition (2.1.7). The sense in which these responses are "valenced" is that they involve pleasure and pain. Obviously these two positions are in some ways very close. Both award moral standing on the basis of the capacity for pleasant and painful experiences, and both accord moral standing to the same creatures. Perhaps some readers are thinking that if you can reach the conclusion that animals have moral standing in virtue of their capacity for pleasure and pain from either a utilitarian or a Kantian starting point, then it must be true. If so, I would be perfectly happy with that result. Nevertheless, in this chapter I would like to say a few things about the differences between the two positions, which have both a theoretical side and some important practical implications, and about the role of pleasure and pain in the determination of the final good.

9.2 Aggregation and Its Implications

9.2.1 In Chapter 8, I described a "rift" that arises in the concept of the absolute good when nature sets the interests of creatures ineradicably at odds with each other. The absolute good is supposed to be both that which is worth pursuing for its own sake, and that which is good from every point of view. Every creature necessarily pursues what is good-for her as if it were absolutely valuable, just as we ourselves do. Having no firmer ground for doing so than they do, we should grant that every creature's final good is absolutely worth pursuing. But the goods of different creatures are in unavoidable and deep conflict with each other.

Utilitarians do not use the idea of an absolute good that is good from every point of view. Acknowledging from the start that conflicts among genuine goods are possible, they propose to resolve them by striving for an aggregate good, the maximum amount of good possible for all concerned.[1] This is a thing that they suppose is always in principle identifiable and often achievable. In the face of a conflict between different creatures' goods, they would have us maximize the good. "Don't sit around bemoaning the fact that you can't make the world good for everyone. Make it as good as possible. Do the best you can for everyone!" I think there are two problems with that response.

First of all, if, as I believe, the good is tethered, then the idea of an aggregate good does not make sense. What is good-for me plus what is good-for you is not necessarily good-for *anyone*. There is no person who is you-plus-me for whom this aggregated good is better. This may not be obvious in a case where *all* we are doing is adding more goods for different people or creatures. Suppose I have to choose between conferring a benefit on Adam, on the one hand, and conferring a benefit of the very same size on Adam together with an equal benefit on Eve, on the other. The second option seems plainly better, although we can still argue about whether there is any sense in which it is better-for everyone, or whether it is merely better-for Eve.[2] The problem becomes more obvious in a case where

---

[1] For this discussion it will not be necessary to deal with questions about whether what is maximized is the total amount of good or the average, or what exactly the unit being maximized is—pleasure, satisfied preferences, or what have you.

[2] If you think of Adam and Eve as living in the same community, you might think it is better-for both of them, because now everyone feels that everyone has been treated fairly, and each can

achieving the maximum aggregate good requires subtracting. If I can produce more total happiness by taking something away from Eve and giving it to Adam, perhaps because he wants or needs it more, this is better-for Adam, but it is worse-for Eve. There may be cases in which we should do it, say because it would be more fair, but that is not the same as doing it because the result is better, in the sense of yielding a greater aggregate. The claim that this is better-for everyone does not make any sense, since it is worse-for Eve. Tethered goods cannot be aggregated.

9.2.2 But even if you think that aggregation makes sense, the utilitarian move of resorting to an aggregate does not fix the problem—there may still be a rift in the aggregate good, depending on how we understand the goodness of the aggregate good. The only reason why the aggregate is supposed to be good is that each part of it is good, but there is a question how we are to understand the goodness of the parts. And here the utilitarian is at a crossroads.

Suppose he says, with me, that the good of each creature is good because it is good-for the creature, and we should care about all these goods because we should care about all these creatures (4.3.6–4.3.8, 8.3.2). Then even if we allow aggregation, there is still a rift in the good. The good of each creature is absolutely good, but their goods are in conflict, so they cannot all be included in the solution that gives us the greatest aggregate. The absolute goodness of the individual's good does not go away just because we took it into account when we calculated the total. Switching from the absolute good to the aggregate does not solve the problem; the rift is still there.[3]

On the other hand, the utilitarian can say—as he actually does—that the good of each creature is a good thing in itself, and not just because it is good-for the creature. In fact the only reason why the creature matters is that the creatures are the place where the good thing happens, as I will explain below. The utilitarian claim that he values all creatures "equally" is only true because he does not value creatures at all. To put it in the terms I used in Chapter 8, he does not think anyone, human or animal, is an end in itself. It is just pleasure, or whatever it is he is maximizing, that is an end.

---

enjoy the benefit without embarrassment in front of the other and so on. But when you do utilitarian calculations, all such side effects are supposed to have already been taken into account. So when you think about my example, do not be thrown by such thoughts—such things are already included in the "benefit" in question. I will discuss the question of benefits to communities in 11.6.4.

[3] See Korsgaard, *Self-Constitution*, 3.3.2.

9.2.3 These points are made vivid by Singer's attempts to argue for the view that animals who are not self-conscious are just "receptacles" for the good. The argument appears in a number of places, but to take one example: In his commentary on Coetzee's *The Lives of Animals*, Singer voices the common view that the fact that human beings anticipate and plan for the future means that human beings have "more to lose" by death than the other animals do.[4] Singer imagines his daughter protesting that death for a non-human animal—the example is their own dog Max—would mean the loss of everything *for Max*. He replies that although there would be no more good experiences for Max, they could arrange for the breeding of another dog, and then this other dog could be having good canine experiences in Max's place. In other words, what matters is not the goodness of Max's experiences *for* Max, but just that there be some good experiences going on in the world somewhere. What makes the dog matter is that his consciousness is the place where good things happen. As Singer himself puts it in an earlier paper, "It's as if sentient beings are the receptacles of something valuable and it does not matter if a receptacle gets broken, so long as there is another receptacle to which the contents can be transferred without getting any spilt."[5]

That is the problem. Utilitarians regard the subjects of experience essentially as *locations* where pleasure and pain, which they see as good and bad experiences, *happen*, rather than as beings *for whom* these experiences are good or bad. To put it another way, they think that the goodness or badness of an experience rests wholly in the character of the experience, and not in the way the experience is related to the nature of the subject who has it. So it is not essential to the goodness or badness of the experience that it is good- or bad-*for* the subject who has it (see also 12.3.4). I think that is wrong. We should not care about people and animals because they are the places where good and bad things happen in the world. We should care about people and animals because they are the sort of beings *for* whom things can be good or bad—a fate that we recognize, in our own case at least, to be of the utmost importance. It is our fellow creatures, not their experiences, to whom we should assign moral standing, and treat as ends in themselves.[6]

---

[4] Singer, in Coetzee, *The Lives of Animals*, pp. 85–91. The argument also appears in Singer, "Killing Humans and Killing Animals," and in Singer's *Practical Ethics*, chapter 5, "Taking Animal Life."

[5] Singer "Killing Humans and Killing Animals," p. 149.

[6] Singer has argued that people and self-conscious animals are not mere receptacles for value because we have a preference for our own continued existence (in "Killing Humans and Killing

9.3 The Nature of Pleasure and Pain

9.3.1 The philosophical tradition offers us two (or at least two) quite different conceptions of what pleasure and pain are. According to what I will call the Benthamite view, pleasure and pain are particular sensations, or kinds of sensations, with a definite, even measurable, intensity and duration.[7,8] This view is implausible. Certainly we can all agree that our sensations are *among* the things we often find pleasant or painful. The feeling of warmth when you pull up the covers on a cold winter night, the smell of a hyacinth, the taste of fine chocolate are among the things we find pleasant. The sting of a bee, the smell of a skunk, and the philosopher's perennial favorite, toothache, are among the things we find painful. All of these experiences involve quite particular sensations. But we also enjoy being in the company of those we like, being completely absorbed in a good book or a movie, or taking a vigorous walk in the country, and there is no reason to think that's because something like the smell of a hyacinth or the taste of chocolate is a constant accompaniment to these activities. Nor are the experiences of grief, humiliation, and regret necessarily accompanied by something like a psychological toothache, although we may keep prodding at them as we do at the tooth. In the case of pleasures like reading an absorbing novel, indeed, the sense that one is not experiencing anything but the activity itself and so that one is "lost to the world" is part of the pleasure.

9.3.2 These kinds of reflections probably inspired what I will call the Aristotelian view, according to which pleasures and pains are not sensations, but reflexive reactions to the things we experience. Specifically, they are reactions to the

---

Animals," and *Practical Ethics*, chapter 4, "What's Wrong with Killing?"). I do not think this argument works, because as long as the utilitarian thinks we can aggregate satisfied preferences across the boundaries between creatures, a person is just a receptacle for those preferences. If we kill one person, we thwart his preference for a continued existence, but we can replace him with another person whose preference for a continued existence will be satisfied so long as his existence continues. Whatever you think of that, I think it is plain that by bringing in the idea of a preference Singer is reaching for the relational character of the concept of "good-for." A preference sets up a positive relation between the one who prefers and the object of the preference.

[7] Bentham, *The Principles of Morals and Legislation*, chapter 4.

[8] The idea that there is some one thing that you feel whenever you are doing or undergoing something that you like, and some one thing that you feel whenever you are doing or undergoing something you do not like, seems out of keeping with experience, so some philosophers would prefer to make pleasure and pain each a family of sensations, with every pleasure similar to every other in respect of its pleasantness, and every pain similar to every other in respect of its painfulness. See, for just one example, Hume: "under the term pleasure, we comprehend sensations, which are very different from each other, and which have only such a distant resemblance, as is requisite to make them be express'd by the same abstract term" (*A Treatise of Human Nature*, Book 3, part 1, section 2, p. 472).

objects of experience as welcome or unwelcome, as to-be-accepted and if possible to-be-continued in the case of pleasure and as to-be-fought-off and if possible to-be-stopped in the case of pain. As the name I am giving it suggests, this view has a philosophical heritage in the views about pleasure and pain put forth by Aristotle in the *Nicomachean Ethics*.[9] There Aristotle, who sees pleasantness and painfulness primarily as properties of activities, associates pain with something like a sense of obstacle or difficulty. Pleasure, he says, is the *unimpeded* activity of a healthy faculty, or at any rate it "supervenes" on such activity.[10] Pain is the state you are in when the activity you are engaged in is too difficult, or too easy and therefore boring, or when you struggle to keep doing it although something outside is distracting you. Pain is whatever it is about the activity that makes you want to stop. Pleasure is the state you are in when you are wholly absorbed in an activity and want it to go on forever. It is an advantage of the Aristotelian view that it can explain the painfulness or pleasantness of activities and experiences that are not necessarily accompanied by any particular sensation.

9.3.3 The way that the Aristotelian view accommodates the special pains and pleasures of sensation is by focusing on the activity of experiencing them. What is particularly mesmerizing about experiencing the sensation of physical pain is that, if it is bad enough, it "impedes" pretty much every other activity you might perform by its relentless capture of your attention. But on the Aristotelian view, the painfulness of the physical sensation is not the same thing as the sensation itself. The painfulness of the sensation rests in the fact that everything in you is struggling to flee from something, in this case a sensation, which you cannot possibly flee from, because it emanates from your own nervous system. A person having a painful sensation is like someone trying to escape from her own shadow. A person having a pleasant sensation, on the other hand, wants it to go on forever. But it is not that she wants it to go on forever because it is pleasurable. Her wanting it to go on forever *is* its pleasurableness. Pleasure and pain are not so much the objects of experience, at least in the first instance, as a *form* of experience—they are the way we are conscious of our own condition, which is a fundamentally valenced way.[11] In other words, what physical pains like toothache and emotional pains like grief have in common is not that the emotional

---

[9] Aristotle, *Nicomachean Ethics*, Book 7.11–12, and Book 10.1–5.

[10] In the discussion in Book 7, Aristotle tends to identify pleasure with activity, while in the Book 10 discussion he switches (assuming the Book 10 discussion is later) to the idea that pleasure "supervenes" on activity (see 10. 4 1174b 303–33).

[11] I say "at least in the first instance" because of course we can turn the painfulness of an experience itself into an object of consciousness, by focusing our attention on it.

pains involve some sort of psychological sensation, but rather that we react to the loss of loved ones and other terrible situations the same way we react to toothache, with an overwhelming impulse of *rejection* and a desperate attempt to escape.[12, 13]

9.4 The Place of Pleasure and Pain in the Final Good

9.4.1 Aristotle says something else, in his book *On the Soul*, which is essential to understanding the role of pleasure and pain in the final good. He says:

To perceive then is like bare asserting or knowing; but when the object is pleasant or painful, the soul makes a quasi-affirmation or negation, and pursues or avoids the object. To feel pleasure or pain is to act with the sensitive mean towards what is good or bad as such.[14]

Aristotle is telling us that pleasure and pain are a kind of perception of the good, a practical perception that immediately sets the creature who experiences or anticipates it in motion to get or avoid the good or bad thing. Recall from Chapter 2 that animals, at least when they are in good condition, take pleasure in the things that promote their functional good, and in their own functionally good condition, and also are pained by things that threaten that condition, and are motivated to act accordingly. In other words, we can understand pleasure and pain as the animal's *perceptions* of the goodness or badness of his or her own condition. But that, as I am about to explain, is not all that pleasure and pain are.

9.4.2 Hedonistic utilitarians think that pleasure and the absence of pain is the final good. That is not my view. On my view, the final good for a creature is

---

[12] You might think we could turn to the sciences to settle the question which of these two views is right, but it is not so simple as that. For one thing, the science is about painful *sensations* in particular. The experience of pain begins with "nociception," the detection of injury or damage to the body. Nociception enables the creature to withdraw from the harmful stimulus quickly. Nociceptive responses, some argue, need not be conscious. It is only when the information is sent to the brain that we have conscious sensations, and only at that point that the question whether the emotional aspect of "suffering" is intrinsic to the sensations or a response to them can arise. Since the sensations are nearly always accompanied by suffering, with one exception I will mention in a moment, it is hard to tell. Since we suffer from other things besides our sensations, it seems to me that the suffering is best understood as a response to the sensations. In addition—this is the exception—there are some anesthetics, e.g. morphine, under whose influence people sometimes report that they still feel the pain but no longer mind it. My suggestion is that they still feel the sensation but since they no longer struggle against it, it is no longer painful, in the sense that it has ceased to be a source of suffering. For more on this topic, see Grahek, *Feeling Pain and Being in Pain*.

[13] See also Korsgaard, *The Sources of Normativity*, 4.3.

[14] Aristotle, *On the Soul*, 3.7 431a7–11.

conscious well-functioning, at least when the creature is in reasonably good conditions, conditions that will allow her to go on functioning well. In fact as I argued before, there is a sense in which the final good is simply conscious life itself, conscious existence itself, although that is a condition that is almost necessarily pleasant to the well-functioning animal in good circumstances (2.1.8). That may sound surprising, but if conscious life and the final good are both well-functioning, consciously experienced, then conscious life and the final good are the same thing. I realize there are obvious objections to that thought—for instance, that an animal can be alive and be functioning poorly, so let me put the point a little more carefully. Conscious life, as I argued before, is the Good-for the animal whose life it is, except when the life is in some specific way bad. If you think about it, as I said in 2.1.8, you will see that that is not a tautology. Pleasure is the awareness, the perception, of that good and of the goodness of the things that promote and constitute it, and pain is a perception of the things that tend to undermine it.

I think that the view that pleasure (and the absence of pain, but I will not keep saying that) is itself the final good is based on a mistake about the role that consciousness plays in the constitution of the final good, as I will now explain.

9.4.3 In Chapter 2, I argued that what is good for a creature must be good from that creature's own point of view. In order to have a point of view, of course you have to be conscious, so it seems clear that consciousness plays an important role in making a creature the kind of thing that has a final good. But what role exactly? The classical utilitarians, as we have seen, thought of pleasure and pain as sensations, with a certain intensity and duration. And sensations are objects or modifications of consciousness, caused in us by other external and internal events. If pleasure is itself the final good, then the role of consciousness in the construction of the final good is simply that consciousness itself *is* what can be good or bad. States of consciousness are what has value.

Against this view, a whole army of philosophers in the tradition have objected that the good cannot just be a state of consciousness. The arguments here are familiar to everyone in moral philosophy. In the service of example, Robert Nozick gave us the experience machine—a machine that delivers a steady stream of pleasant sensations and imaginary pleasant experiences directly into your brain.[15] Someone hooked up to an experience machine lives his whole life in a state of happy delusion. Most of us think that this would be bad. Similarly, most

---

[15] Nozick, *Anarchy, State, and Utopia*, pp. 42–4.

of us think it would be bad to be hated by the people whom we imagine love us and despised by the people whom we imagine admire us. Most of us think it would be bad to imagine that you are doing a great deal of good by actions that are actually causing a great deal of harm, or to spend your life carrying out some worthy but arduous project destined to collapse like a house of cards shortly after your death. Most of us think these things would be bad even if you are fated never to be cured of your delusions or to know of your failure. For, many philosophers would argue, it is not the case that it is bad to be *aware* that you are hated, or despised, or a failure, or a catastrophe to everyone around you, simply because the *consciousness* of these things is painful; rather, these conditions are themselves bad-for you, and that is *why* the consciousness of them is painful: because it is the consciousness of something that is bad.

These reflections give rise to another possible view we might take of the role that consciousness plays in the constitution of the final good. Perhaps consciousness does not make *any* real difference to what constitutes your final good: perhaps it simply enables you to be aware of whether you are achieving your final good or not.

But of course that does not seem right either. The arguments against utilitarianism that I just mentioned work by driving a wedge between an agreeable consciousness and a bad reality; but we can also construct arguments that drive a wedge between a disagreeable consciousness and a good reality. Perhaps the people whom you suppose despise you actually love and admire you deeply. Perhaps efforts of your own that seem fruitless to you are actually doing a great deal of good in the world. Are we to say of someone who suffers permanently from these negative illusions that he is having a good life, in the final sense of good, but fails to know it? In Frank Capra's movie *It's a Wonderful Life*, the Jimmy Stewart character, George Bailey, contemplates committing suicide in the belief that it would have been better for everyone else if he had never been born, though in fact, as the movie shows us, he is a great force for good in his community.[16] Suppose that he had actually done it? If his life had ended in suicide committed out of despair, would it still have *been* such a wonderful life? Could Capra have made a movie about that life, perhaps called *It Was a Wonderful Life. Too Bad He Didn't Know It*?

9.4.4 Now let me apply these reflections to my own view. In Chapter 2, I distinguished between the idea of something's being good-for a creature in the functional sense and something's being good-for a creature in the final sense.

---

[16] Directed by Frank Capra, RKO, 1946.

I also argued that it is only creatures who are capable of being pleased and pained by things that are good- or bad-for them in the functional sense who have a final good. If we accept the idea that consciousness must either be the whole of the final good or something that is not part of the final good at all but only makes us aware of it, you might think that I am caught in a dilemma. If I agree with the utilitarian that states of consciousness constitute the final good, then I must say that pleasure is the final good and the most that your functional good can be is a cause of that pleasure. Either that, or I must say that your functional good itself really is the whole of your final good, and all that consciousness does is make you aware of it: pleasurable states of consciousness are just an awareness of a final good that exists completely independently of them.

But this just shows that these are not the only options. What it leaves out is that for an animal, enjoying well-functioning and the things that promote it is partly *constitutive* of well-functioning itself. Pleasurable consciousness is neither a mere effect of well-functioning nor a mere awareness of it. It is a perception of the good, but that is not all that it is. For a conscious animal, taking pleasure in your own well-functioning and the things that promote it is part of what it *is* to be well-functioning. It follows from this that conscious well-functioning is itself a condition that is *necessarily* pleasant to the well-functioning animal in reasonably good circumstances. That is why Aristotle says, in the passage I have made one of the epigraphs of this chapter: "But whether we choose life for the sake of pleasure or pleasure for the sake of life is a question we may dismiss for the present. For they seem to be bound up together and not to admit of separation."[17]

There is no way to say it without a slight air of paradox: an animal who is otherwise well-functioning and in conditions liable to promote her well-functioning but who is not enjoying herself cannot be well-functioning after all. So George Bailey, the character in *It's a Wonderful Life*, does not exactly *realize* that he has had a wonderful life, since his life is not wonderful (or anyway is not quite as wonderful), *until* he realizes it. Pleasure is both a perception of the good and an essential part of the good, because an animal who is well-functioning must perceive that she is well-functioning—that is an essential part of the way that she functions.

9.4.5 In 2.3.1, I argued that there is something essentially reflexive about the nature of the self—you cannot have a self without being to some extent aware

----

[17] Aristotle, *Nicomachean Ethics*, 10.4 1175a 18–21.

of yourself. The self is not something completely objective of which self-consciousness just happens to make us cognizant: since having a self is having a point of view, some degree of self-consciousness is partly constitutive of having a self. What I am saying now is really the same thing, but with an emphasis on the valenced character of that self-consciousness. We do not have to choose between the self being wholly constituted by self-consciousness, and the self being something completely independent of consciousness of which consciousness only makes us aware. The same is true of the final good. In fact this is why I said earlier that pleasure and pain are *forms* of self-consciousness (2.3.2). Pleasure and pain are just the valences of conscious life's essential awareness of itself.

9.5 Matters of Life and Death

9.5.1 If a conscious animal necessarily takes pleasure in her own well-functioning and the things that promote it, and if well-functioning just is living, then to feel pleasure is simply to feel yourself living. But there's a complication about pain. If feeling pleasure is feeling yourself living, then it might seem that feeling pain is feeling yourself dying. In one way that is right, for to feel pain is to be aware of the features of your condition or of assaults on your condition that will kill you if they go on unhindered. But of course in another way to feel pain is to feel yourself living, for to feel pain is to feel the life forces in you struggling against causes of death. Being pained by the things that threaten well-functioning is as much a part of what it is to be well-functioning as taking pleasure in well-functioning and the things that promote it. So pain is just as essential to well-functioning as pleasure. Does this threaten the plausibility of the claim that conscious life is the good for the creature whose life it is?

I do not think so. Pain can be healthy, to be sure, but if the healthy pain continues, it must be because the things that threaten well-functioning continue, and then soon you will not be well-functioning after all. Pain is in the business of putting itself out of business. Pleasure, like conscious life itself, is in the business of keeping itself in business. This, as we have already seen, is the essence of Aristotle's view of what these two conditions are. Of course there are exceptions: there are pains that last forever, or at least about which we can say that we are functioning *better* if they do. Grief, remorse, and regret, in certain cases, could be examples. It is no accident that these are all cases of "psychological" pain. Physically, a creature cannot remain at war with her environment forever, but psychologically, we can be in a permanent state of war with the tragic facts of our lives. In these cases, we must admit that pain is part of the good. It is better, not just morally, but better-for you, to be a person who grieves for your lost loved ones forever than to be a person who simply ceases to care much about them after a while.

9.5.2 If conscious life is itself the good, what counts as the bad? Is it death? You might be tempted to think that if, as I have claimed, everything that is good must be good-for someone, death cannot be the bad, since there is no one around for death to be bad for. The received philosophical answer to that sort of conundrum is that the badness of death is the badness of loss, the loss to the creature who has died of whatever good things would have come in her way if she had lived longer. I have already endorsed the view that the badness of death is the badness of loss, and explained why I think there is an atemporal creature who suffers that loss (5.3.3). I do not quite agree that what the creature loses is "the good things that might have come in her way," because I do not agree with the picture of life as a kind of open space within which things that are good and bad independently of life itself make their appearance (2.1.8). In my view, the good things in life are all ways of living life well—modes of well-functioning. Health is physical well-functioning, and to be curious and understand things is to be intellectually well-functioning, to appreciate beauty is to be perceptually well-functioning, to love and be loved is to be socially well-functioning. This is another way of putting a view I argued for earlier, that the good for a creature is relative to her capacities (4.4.3).

Death is the depravation of these goods, but of course we can be deprived of them in life as well, and that is painful. Are they bad because they are painful or because they are forms of ill-functioning? You will want to say that not everything that can be bad about life is some sort of depravation, a mere failure to function well. You may fail to be loved, but you may also be hated. You may not be very healthy, but that is not the same as suffering torments. If you undertake some great endeavor and fail, you are not in the same position as if you had never tried. These seem to be positive evils, not mere failures to function well. But in fact, all evils of which we are conscious are positive evils. This is one of the strange effects of consciousness itself: it makes privative states into positive ones. Darkness is only the depravation of light, but a conscious creature can see, and fear, the dark.

9.6 Kantian Naturalism

9.6.1 In Chapter 8, I argued that Kant should not be interpreted as claiming that rationality is a property that simply confers intrinsic value on us. To claim that, we would have to have metaphysical insight into a realm of intrinsic values, and we do not have such insight. For the same reason, I think that the utilitarians cannot just claim that pleasure and the absence of pain is the good. Of course they have various arguments for that conclusion, and I am not going to review them here. But in the end I think they are laying claim to a kind of metaphysical insight that human beings do not have, and that is not there to be had.

The position I have been laying out is intended to be, in a certain philosophical sense, naturalistic. I do not think that utilitarianism is. I have not been able to explain why I think that animals have moral standing without at the same time explaining some of my views on a much larger question—why there is such a thing as value in the world at all. The story I have told is not naturalistic in the reductive sense—I have not argued that value is reducible to any natural condition or fact, such as pleasure and pain. Rather, the story is naturalistic in the sense that it explains the existence of value in terms of valuing, and it explains the existence of valuing as something that is inherent in a sentient creature's relation to herself. Value is a perspectival notion that arises within the point of view of two forms of conscious life (4.5.1). First of all, there is the point of view of sentient animals, who are led to pursue their own good by responding favorably to the things that are functionally good for them and aversively to the things that are functionally bad for them, and so become the bearers of a good in the final sense of good. And second, there is the point of view of rational animals, who are conscious of all this, endorse what is good-for ourselves as good absolutely, and in this way confer the value of an end in itself on ourselves and on animals in general. To understand why there is such a thing as value, we need only understand the connection between value and conscious life itself.

9.6.2 People are sometimes startled when I describe Kant's philosophy as naturalistic, but in the sense I have just described, it is: Kant explains the things that look metaphysical and mysterious in terms of the way our cognitive powers work, in terms of the presuppositions of rational activity. So although Kant himself did not endorse the idea that we have obligations to animals, I think there is nothing surprising in the fact that a case for the standing of animals can be made in his philosophical terms. Kant's epistemic modesty—his dictum that we cannot have any knowledge beyond the scientific—is an acknowledgment of the human place in nature, of our limitations as well as our special status. Kant denied that human beings have an insight into the nature of things as they are in themselves. I think he believed that it would really only make sense to ascribe that kind of insight to ourselves if we knew that the world was created by a god in whose image our own minds were created. At the same time, Kant believed that as rational beings we can bring intelligibility and reason into the world, both through our powers of theoretical understanding and our capacity for moral action. I have argued that nature imposes a limit on the extent to which we can do this in practice (8.8.3). Given that on Kant's view, moral laws are our laws, the laws of human reason, not laws written into the nature of things, it is not surprising that it should be so. In any case, on a Kantian conception, what is special about human beings is not that we are the universe's darlings, whose fate is absolutely more important than the fates of the other creatures who like us experience their own existence. It is exactly the opposite: What is special about us is the empathy that enables us to grasp that other creatures are important to themselves in just the way we are important to ourselves, and the reason that enables us to draw the conclusion that follows: that every animal must be regarded as an end in herself, whose fate matters, and matters absolutely, if anything matters at all.

PART III

Consequences

10

The Animal Antinomy, Part 1
Creation Ethics

Assume a human being who honors the moral law, and who allows himself to think (as he can hardly avoid doing) what sort of a world he would *create*, were this in his power, under the guidance of practical reason.

Immanuel Kant, *Religion within the Boundaries of Mere Reason*, 6:5

10.1 Eliminating Predation

10.1.1 One of the most vexing questions in animal ethics is whether human beings ought to try to eliminate predation. I do not now mean the question whether we should try to eliminate the predation we ourselves practice—whether we should stop eating meat, and using animal products that require us to kill animals or make them suffer (see 12.3 for that question). I mean the question whether we ought to try to prevent predation among the other animals, or rather, whether that would be a good thing to do if we had any idea how to do it. Predation, after all, is the cause of great suffering. Whatever the adults may have assured you when you were a child, it is not always a quick bite to the neck followed immediately by death or a merciful unconsciousness due to shock. Bears and wolves will sometimes start eating an animal who is still alive and conscious. Hyenas disembowel their living prey. Pythons squeeze their prey to death. Shrews paralyze their prey with venom, so that they can eat them alive and fresh at their leisure. Orcas will chase mother whales with calves until the mother collapses from exhaustion, so that she can no longer protect her calf, whose tongue they like to eat. Chimpanzees tear live monkeys and bushbabies apart. Crocodiles dismember their prey while rotating them underwater in a "death roll." Tapeworms starve their hosts to death. And of course some animals who manage to escape from their predators nevertheless suffer painful and debilitating injuries in the process. Fearfulness pervades the lives of many animals who are at risk from predators every day.

These facts are horrifying, although perhaps none of these methods of predation is as brutal as our own most recent method, raising animals on factory farms, where the animal's whole life, not just her final scene, is filled with suffering (12.3.1). In fact, death by predation in the wild is probably not as brutal as the protracted descent into ever increasing suffering and ever more terrifying dementia that so many human beings are forced to undergo as we die nowadays. But they are horrifying enough to inspire the thought that the world would be a better place if predation could be prevented.

But better for whom? I have argued that everything that is good must be good-for someone in particular. At first glance, one feels tempted to say, better for the members of prey species, at least in the short run, perhaps, but worse for the members of predator species, who would then starve to death. So not better absolutely, anyway not just like that.

10.1.2 In 2010 Jeff McMahan wrote an editorial for the *New York Times* called "The Meat Eaters."[1] In it he suggested that it would be a good thing if we could "arrange for the gradual extinction of carnivorous species, replacing them with new herbivorous ones" or perhaps "intervene genetically, so that currently carnivorous species would gradually evolve into herbivorous ones." McMahan thinks this would, if we could do it, make the world a better place. "If I had been in a position to design and create a world," McMahan muses, "I would have tried to arrange for all conscious individuals to be able to survive without tormenting and killing other conscious individuals. I hope most other people would have done the same." As things are, we are stuck with the existence of real individual predators, whose claim on our benevolence is just as good as that of the real individual prey animals, and McMahan's idea is meant to accommodate that fact—to slowly recreate the natural world in order to eliminate predation in such a way that no existing individual, not even a predator, need be harmed.

Of course McMahan is not proposing that we actually attempt this. Notoriously, human attempts to meddle with the delicate balance of nature do not always go well. As McMahan himself points out, the result might be to:

create a Malthusian dystopia in the animal world, with higher birth rates[2] among herbivores, overcrowding, and insufficient resources to sustain the larger populations. Instead of being killed quickly by predators, the members of species that were once prey would die slowly, painfully, and in greater numbers from starvation and disease.

---

[1] McMahan, "The Meat Eaters," *New York Times*, September 19, 2010.
[2] I believe he means rates of survival beyond infancy.

Although McMahan does not suggest this himself in the editorial, it is easy enough to imagine someone who shares his temptation to recreate the natural world going one step further. Presumably if we were in a position to intervene genetically with predator species, we would be in a position to intervene with prey species as well. So why not use birth control to prevent the "Malthusian dystopia" by simply keeping the herbivores' numbers down to sustainable levels? Perhaps this would cause unhappiness in some animals, who have a strong urge to be parents, or who would be bored if they did not have to feed, protect, and raise any chicks, cubs, or pups. After all, that is what non-human animals *do*, it is what their lives consist in: they get food for themselves and they produce offspring, and if they are like most birds and mammals, they spend much of their lives begetting, feeding, protecting, and raising those offspring. So we would be depriving them of the substance of their lives. But that is no worse than what we do to our pets when we get them "fixed." In fact, perhaps we could alleviate the animal's boredom by giving them toys.[3]

10.2 Abolitionism

10.2.1 But is treating animals as pets acceptable? Some defenders of animals, especially those who take a broadly Kantian line, call themselves "abolitionists." They take their name from opponents of slavery before the Civil War in America, implying that animals who now live among us do so as our slaves. Abolitionists believe that we should abolish all human uses of the other animals whatever.[4] Gary Francione focuses on the legal side of the question, urging that we can only use the other animals for our purposes if their legal status is that of our property, and that no sentient being should ever be the property of another being.[5] Tom

---

[3] Alternatively, we could eliminate the suffering involved in predation, although not the death, by killing prey animals painlessly and then feeding them to the predators. But then the predators would be the ones who might feel boredom. Martha Nussbaum points out that in the Bronx Zoo, tigers who appeared to be frustrated by their inability to engage in hunting behaviors were given large balls on ropes whose resistance and weight "symbolize" a gazelle, large versions of the toy mice we give our house cats for the same reason. She reports that a tiger given such a toy "seems satisfied" (*Frontiers of Justice*, pp. 370–1).

[4] Abolitionists characteristically also have a view that is at once a moral view and a view about political strategy: they oppose making incremental improvements in the way we treat animals, on the grounds that it gives the public a false sense of moral reassurance. They believe what we do to the animals is so plainly wrong that the only morally acceptable response is to stop it immediately, and also that as long as incremental improvements salve the public's conscience, we will never do that. I am not here concerned with that side of the abolitionist view.

[5] Gary Francione, "Animals: Property or Persons?," in Sunstein and Nussbaum, *Animal Rights: Current Debates and New Directions*.

Regan argues that no other animal should be used as a resource for human beings. He says:

What's wrong—fundamentally wrong—with the way animals are treated isn't the details that vary from case to case. It's the whole system. The forlornness of the veal calf is pathetic, heart-wrenching; the pulsing pain of the chimp with electrodes planted deep in her brain is repulsive; the slow, tortuous (sic.) death of the raccoon caught in the leg-hold trap is agonizing. But what is wrong isn't the pain, isn't the suffering, isn't the deprivation. These compound what's wrong. Sometimes—often—they make it much, much worse. But they are not the fundamental wrong.

The fundamental wrong is the system that allows us to view animals as *our resources*, here for *us*—to be eaten, or surgically manipulated, or exploited for sport or money.[6]

As Regan emphasizes here, the fundamental objection is to *use*, to treating animals as means to our ends, not to suffering. And pretty much all interaction counts as use. Regan's objection applies to all of the ways in which we make animals work, including work that we might think is compatible with a good life for the animals in question, or could be made so. Among the things abolitionists urge us to abolish is the work of seeing eye dogs, search and rescue dogs, capuchin monkeys who help the handicapped, and animals who act in the movies and on television. Even what we might think of as the most benign and egalitarian form of interaction between people and animals—sharing our homes with companion animals, keeping pets, counts as use. As Francione insists, pets are a kind of property, and to treat a sentient being as property is wrong.

10.2.2 The abolitionist objection can be put more formally in terms of Kantian ethics. As we have seen, Kant's ethics requires us to treat every human being, every rational being, as an end in itself, and never merely as a means to our ends. In Chapter 8, I argued that we should treat every sentient animal as an end-in-itself too. Kant's principle does not imply that you can never employ another person in the service of your ends, but it puts a restriction on your doing so. You must act in such a way that it is possible for her to consent to the way you are treating her. Then you are treating her as an end and not a *mere* means, because she can still determine her own actions.

Obviously, this does not mean merely that the other person can say "yes" to whatever transaction you are engaging her in. To avoid using someone as a mere means, we have to make sure that her consent is free, informed, and uncoerced. But in some situations, there are problems about making sure that someone's

---

[6] Regan, "The Case for Animal Rights," in *In Defense of Animals*, pp. 13–14. Regan probably meant "torturous." I owe the point to Byron Davies.

consent really is like this, and in many situations, it is not feasible to get explicit consent at all. Fortunately, Kant thought we can identify the *kind* of action to which consent is possible. As I have argued elsewhere, Kant intends the "possible consent" criterion in a literal way: there are types of actions to which it is literally impossible to consent.[7] Someone cannot possibly consent to the way she is being treated if the *nature* of the action prevents her from having any *opportunity* to consent to it. Most obviously, this way of understanding the consent condition rules out all actions that involve force and coercion: people who are forced to do something have no opportunity to refuse to do it.[8] Kant thought his criterion rules out deception as well. If you lie to someone, she cannot consent to the way you are treating her because she does not know that you are lying, and so does not know what you are really doing to her. For instance, in the false promising case that we looked at before (7.3.1), the person to whom you offer the false promise thinks you are seeking the temporary use of her money, when in fact you are seeking to take it away from her permanently. She has no opportunity to consent to that, since your real end is hidden from her.

The general idea is that knowledge of what is going on and some power over the proceedings are the conditions of possible consent. Any action that by its very nature robs the person to whom it is done of knowledge of what is going on or power over the proceedings violates those conditions. So actions that intrinsically involve force, coercion, and deception are ruled out. To avoid treating others as mere means to our ends, we must avoid such actions.

But animals cannot give their free, unforced, and informed consent to what we do to them. Even when they go along with us willingly, they often cannot foresee or understand the consequences of what they do. Nor can we interact with them as ends in themselves by avoiding force, coercion, and deception—or in any case we don't. Even the most benign of human/animal relations is pervaded with force. I take my cats to the veterinarian for their own good, but when it comes time to do so, I lure them to come to me with an offer of treats, and then I shove them into little crates and lock the doors, in the teeth of their heartfelt struggles and protests. I then turn them over to a terrifying stranger who pokes and prods them, sticks needles into their bodies, who may put them under anesthetics that completely deprive them of any control over the proceedings, and who may one day kill them at my request.

---

[7] Korsgaard, "The Right to Lie: Kant on Dealing with Evil," essay 5 in *Creating the Kingdom of Ends*, pp. 137–40.

[8] That is, the criterion rules out all coercive actions except those undertaken to protect freedom of action more generally, such as the actions of the political state.

But if it is impossible to interact with animals in a way that respects them as ends in themselves (and I will come back to the question whether this is really so in 12.2.1), then the abolitionists think it is better if we keep them at a distance and, as far as possible, do not interact with them at all.

10.2.3 Abolitionists and animal rights theorists distinguish themselves from animal welfarists, whose primary concern is with the suffering we inflict on animals. But even animal welfarists may believe that all of the ways that we include animals in our lives should be abolished, including keeping pets, on the grounds of the suffering we cause animals when we use them. On the website of People for the Ethical Treatment of Animals (PETA), we find this:

We at PETA very much love the animal companions who share our homes, but we believe that it would have been in the animals' best interests if the institution of "pet keeping"— i.e., breeding animals to be kept and regarded as "pets"—never existed. The international pastime of domesticating animals has created an overpopulation crisis; as a result, millions of unwanted animals are destroyed every year as "surplus."

This selfish desire to possess animals and receive love from them causes immeasurable suffering, which results from manipulating their breeding, selling or giving them away casually, and depriving them of the opportunity to engage in their natural behavior. They are restricted to human homes, where they must obey commands and can only eat, drink, and even urinate when humans allow them to.

Because domesticated animals retain many of their basic instincts and drives but are not able to survive on their own in the wild, dogs, cats, or birds, whose strongest desire is to be free, must be confined to houses, yards, or cages for their own safety.

This is a best-case scenario. Millions of dogs spend their lives outdoors on heavy chains in all weather extremes or are kept locked up in tiny chain-link pens from which they can only watch the world go by. Millions more are confined to filthy wire cages in puppy mills, forced to churn out litter after litter until they wear out, at which time they are killed or dumped at the local animal shelter. Even in "good" homes, cats must relieve themselves in dirty litterboxes and often have the tips of their toes amputated through declawing. Dogs often have to drink water that has been sitting around for days, are hurried along on their walks, if they even get walked, and are yelled at to get off the furniture or be quiet.

Most compassionate people never imagine that anyone could throw a litter of kittens out the window of a moving car, and they would certainly be shocked by PETA's inches-thick files on cases of dogs and cats who have been shot with arrows, blown up with firecrackers, doused in gasoline and set on fire, cooked in microwave ovens, used as bait in dogfights, tortured in satanic rituals, beaten with baseball bats by bored kids, dragged behind cars to "teach them a lesson" for running away, or bound in duct tape to silence their barking. Abuses such as these occur every day.[9]

---

[9] PETA website: "Animal Rights Uncompromised: Pets," <http://www.peta.org/about-peta/why-peta/pets/>, as of April 16, 2017.

According to PETA, the lives of pets are unnatural at best, and utterly miserable at worst. Pets are forbidden to act on their natural instincts. They are completely vulnerable to abusive owners. Large numbers of cats and dogs are doomed to die prematurely because breeders and irresponsible owners produce more animals than the market will bear. Because there are now so many homeless cats and dogs out there, who will suffer or be killed prematurely if they are not adopted, PETA urges compassionate people to adopt those animals as pets. But as another document on their website tells us, "It is important, also, to keep our companion animals from reproducing, which perpetuates a class of animals who are forced to rely on humans to survive."[10] Keeping pets is allowable and even worthy *now*, given that the pet trade has produced all these surplus dependent animals. But the children of the future will not, if the abolitionists have their way, have cats and dogs. Pet-keeping, like all uses of animals, they think, should be phased out.

10.2.4 The message of the abolitionists is clear. From a principled point of view, we should not use animals for our own purposes because they are not ours to use. They are not mere means, but ends in themselves. Such beings cannot decently be treated as property. When you are dealing with a human being, you can make use of him without treating him as a mere means by getting his free and informed consent, or by making sure that your action is consistent with his possible consent, by avoiding all forms of deception, coercion, and force. But we cannot get the informed consent of animals, and even our most benign uses of animals may involve deception and force.

So in this case, abolitionism leads to apartheid: humans and animals must be separate but equal, and live on the opposite sides of a great divide.[11]

---

[10] PETA Website: "Doing What's Best for Our Companion Animals," https://www.peta.org/issues/companion-animal-issues/companion-animals-factsheets/whats-best-companion-animals/, as of July 27, 2017.

[11] Of course this could not happen literally in a geographical sense. In their book *Zoopolis*, Sue Donaldson and Will Kymlicka bring out forcefully that much of the animal rights literature ignores what they call the "liminal" animals, wild animals who live around human beings and who may occupy niches that human activity makes available: the birds, squirrels, pigeons, and rats who eat our garbage or nest on the structures we build. They remark "the traditional ART [Animal Rights Theory] view ignores the dense patterns of interaction that inevitably link humans and animals. It rests implicitly on a picture in which humans live in urban or other human-altered environments, assumed to be largely devoid of animals (except for unjustly domesticated and captured ones), while animals live out in the wild, in spaces that humans can and should vacate or leave alone" (p. 8). We can't just decide not to interact with the animals who live among us. We must find ethical ways to deal with them when they become nuisances to us, and we also may owe them assistance in certain circumstances, say when they are injured because of our actions or in especially cold winters or droughts.

10.3 The Animal Antinomy

10.3.1 Some people will be inclined to make fun of the two extreme positions I have just described. I am not. I think both sets of arguments are plausible. What I want to draw your attention to now, however, is simply the following striking result.

After laying out McMahan's argument, I imagined an interlocutor carrying it along one further step: to avoid the "Malthusian dystopia" we control the herbivores' tendency to overbreed by giving them birth control. In effect this would make all animals domestic, not necessarily in the sense of "tame," but in the sense they would be dependent upon us to control their breeding and their food supplies, and in general for the good or bad condition of their lives.[12] In that sense, *all animals would be domestic.*

On the other hand, if the abolitionist program were carried out, eventually there would be no more domestic animals—not even dogs—for we would no longer breed animals for food, make them work for us, or make them members of our families. Essentially dependent animals, animals who have become tame through breeding, would be allowed to go extinct. *All animals would be wild.*

10.3.2 Kant gave an important role in his theoretical philosophy to a kind of problem he called an "antinomy," a close cousin of Zeno's famous paradoxes. You face an antinomy when, starting from the same premise, you can make two perfectly reasonable-sounding arguments to two diametrically opposite conclusions. For example, suppose we start from the premise that each part of a substance has some size. Then we can argue:

1) Substances must be infinitely divisible, because each part of a substance has some size, and if it has some size, then we can cut it in half.
2) Substances cannot be infinitely divisible, because each part would have to have some size, but an infinite number of parts each with some size would add up to something infinitely large.

Or suppose you start from the premise that there must be a complete causal explanation for every event. Then we can argue:

1) We must be able to trace every event to a first cause, which set off the series of events leading to the one we are trying to explain, since if we can keep

---

[12] Clare Palmer provides a useful rundown of the different things meant by "wild" in *Animal Ethics in Context*, chapter 4, and in "The Moral Relevance of the Distinction between Domesticated and Wild Animals," in *The Oxford Handbook of Animal Ethics*, pp. 702–3.

tracing the causes of an event back forever, we will never reach a *complete* causal explanation of that event.

2)   We cannot trace any event to a first cause, which set off the series of events leading to the one we are trying to explain, since if there is a first cause, there is no causal explanation of that first cause, and therefore no *complete* causal explanation of the events that it set off.

We here seem to have come upon a practical antinomy. We start off from the premise that we have duties to animals, where we take that to imply both that we must not wrong or harm them ourselves, and that we must protect them from natural evils if we can. That, after all, is what we owe to people. And then we get the two conflicting arguments:

1)   It is our duty to make all animals domestic, since we cannot protect wild animals from natural evils.

2)   It is our duty to make all animals wild, since we cannot avoid wronging domestic animals ourselves.

10.3.3 Kant thought of the antinomies as serious threats to our faith in reason itself. He thought that if we could not resolve them, skepticism about the power of reason to guide us to the truth would be justified. Extreme conclusions of the sort I have been describing do seem to play a role in driving some people to skepticism about whether we have duties to animals, or any duty more extensive than the duty not to hurt them "unnecessarily." In particular, as Lori Gruen points out, the idea that anyone committed to treating animals as having the same kind of moral standing as people must be committed to preventing predation is often offered as a *reductio ad absurdum* of the position.[13]

So we need to look a little more closely at both sets of arguments. In the rest of this chapter and the next I raise some doubts—although perhaps not decisive ones—about the argument that we should make all animals domestic in order to eliminate natural evils like predation. I call this position "creation ethics" since it involves the idea that we should, as far as possible, take on the role of a creator with respect to the natural world. This will lead us, in Chapter 11, to a consideration of the role that the preservation of species should play in our ethical thought. In Chapter 12, I will consider the abolitionist arguments against the various ways that we use animals for our own ends.

---

[13] Gruen, *Ethics and Animals*, p. 179.

10.4 Creation Ethics

10.4.1 As against proposals like McMahan's, many people have a powerful intuition that, to the limited extent that it is still possible, human beings should leave wild animals alone. We should not harm them, but beyond that their lives are not our business. So long as we think that our duties to animals should parallel our duties to people, however, this intuition can seem hard to justify. Tom Regan proposes that we need not intervene between predator and prey because the predators, not being moral animals, are doing no injustice.[14] But a crocodile, or for that matter, a seriously insane person, who attempts to kill a human being is doing no injustice, and yet we certainly have a duty to protect their human victims if we can.

Clare Palmer argues that we do not in fact have a duty to protect wild animals from natural evils.[15] We have a duty to protect all animals from harms inflicted by ourselves, and to repair the damage if we cannot avoid inflicting harm, but it may be argued that a positive right to assistance or protection only kicks in as a result of certain forms of interaction. Domestic animals have a positive right to our aid and protection, because they serve us, and are dependent on us, and above all because we control their breeding. We bring them into existence in order to serve us, and in doing so we have made them vulnerable in certain ways.[16] But we are not responsible for the plight of wild animals. So it is not that the wild animals are doing no injustice, as Regan would have it, but that we are doing no injustice in staying out of their affairs. I think there is a great deal of plausibility in Palmer's position. But her position does not necessarily imply that we would be doing anything *wrong* if we did attempt to aid the wild animals, so McMahan might still argue that his proposal for getting rid of the predators altogether would be a good thing to do if we could.[17]

Rosalind Hursthouse, however, goes for the stronger position. She argues that "the lives of most wild animals are red in tooth and claw" and that we have a duty of respect for animals which "entails leaving them to live their own form of life,

---

[14]   Regan, *The Case for Animal Rights*, pp. 284–5.

[15]   Palmer, *Animal Ethics in Context*, and "On the Moral Relevance of the Distinction between Domesticated and Wild Animals," in *The Oxford Handbook of Animal Ethics*.

[16]   As Palmer points out, dependence by itself is not enough to establish a duty of aid. Urban rats are dependent on humans, but that does not seem to lead to duties of positive aid. See "On the Moral Relevance of the Distinction between Domesticated and Wild Animals," in *The Oxford Handbook of Animal Ethics*, pp. 720–1.

[17]   In her book *Animal Ethics in Context*, Palmer canvasses both the position that we need not assist wild animals and that we ought not. McMahan considers a position like Palmer's in his essay, and argues that even if we do not have a duty to eliminate the predators, we have a moral reason to do so.

not one that we, playing God, create for them." This makes it sound vaguely as if trying to impose our own moral standards on animals would be a kind of cultural hegemony, like colonial missionaries forcing native peoples to wear more modest clothes. We might reply that it is only the predators who are red in tooth and claw, and that if we did intervene, it would be in the interests of protecting the prey animals, not in the interests of making the predators lead a more virtuous form of life.

McMahan himself addresses the idea that eliminating predation would be "playing God" in his editorial, pointing out that the charge has frequently been brought by "devotees of one religion or another...to obstruct attempts to mitigate human suffering by, for example, introducing new medicines or medical practices, permitting and even facilitating suicide, legalizing a constrained practice of euthanasia, and so on." Arguably, we are at least as much "playing God" when we decide for other people that they may *not* be allowed to choose the moment and manner of their death as when we decide that people may choose these things for themselves.[18] McMahan also replies that "there is no deity whose prerogatives we might usurp. To the extent that these matters are up to anyone, they are up to us alone." As he points out, we are already causing extinctions, and to that extent we are already determining the shape of the natural world. So he thinks that "we ought to guide and control the effects of our action to the greatest extent we can in order bring out the morally best, or least bad, outcomes that we can." What's wrong with playing God, if we can make things better?

10.4.2 This brings me back to the question I asked at the end of 10.1.1. If we eliminated predation, for whom would the resulting future world be better?

I have argued that everything that is good must be good-for someone. If that is so, then everything that is better must be better-for someone too. One implication of this view is that if you compare two different scenarios with entirely different creatures in them, neither can be better than the other.

I know that this claim seems startling. In fact, while it might seem reasonable to claim that everything that is good must be good-for someone, this implication is one of the main obstacles to people's accepting it. Many people believe, for instance, that a world full of happy people and animals is better than a world full

---

[18] This is not exactly McMahan's example. The options he describes as equally "playing God" are "administering a lethal injection to a patient at her own request" and giving her "a largely ineffective analgesic only to mitigate the agony, though knowing it will kill her as a side effect." His target is the distinction some philosophers make between killing and letting die, or between "doing" and "allowing" more generally. I have changed the example because it seems to me that an important point that has nothing to do with that debate is available and relevant here.

of miserable ones, *even if* the two worlds we are comparing contain entirely different inhabitants.

But, you may ask, isn't there anybody for whom the happier world is better? Isn't it better if the world is full of happy people and animals, because it is better *for* the people and animals *in it*? The trouble with that claim is that the alternative, unhappy world would not be worse for *those* people and animals, since in the alternative world they would not exist at all. If we are comparing two worlds containing the *same* inhabitants, in one of which those inhabitants are miserable and in one of which they are happy, the second world is clearly better for *them*. But suppose we are not comparing two worlds with the same inhabitants. If you are miserable, would it better *for you* if you were replaced by someone who is not?

The proposal that we eliminate predation by intervening in the evolutionary process is a proposal that we replace the animals who would otherwise exist with different animals. For whom, then, would we be making things better? For us, maybe, since we would not have to worry about all that predation going on. But in what sense would it be better for the animals themselves?

10.4.3 This is not a rhetorical question: I think there *is* a sense in which it would be better for "the animals," but I think we need to be clear about what that sense is. There are several issues at work here, and I need to untangle them to make it clear why I think there is a real question.

First of all, I obviously do not want to say that anything that is better must be better for some presently existing creature, or we could not talk intelligibly about making the distant future better or worse for anyone at all.[19]

Second, the argument against McMahan's proposal that I have just suggested is a version of an argument we have looked at before, the argument from non-identity (5.3.5). Just to remind you, the argument from non-identity appeals to the fact that if we, say, fail to control climate change, or seriously pollute the environment, we are not harming any particular future individuals, since if we do take measures to control climate change or pollution, it is likely that different individuals will be born. No individual will be in a position to say to us "you made the world worse for me, by failing to control climate change," because we could justifiably retort that if we had controlled climate change, he most likely would never have been born at all. The proposed argument against McMahan's proposal is a version of this. It says that the world without predators is not better-for the

---

[19] Unless perhaps we adopt the position that Aristotle vaguely flirts with—that someone is made better or worse off by the fate of his or her descendants into the indefinite future. But I don't think this is what we want here. See note 14, 5.3.3.

animals who live in it because they are different animals than the ones who would otherwise have existed.

I don't think the argument from non-identity works, at least not if it is intended to show that there is no one to whom we owe a better future. As I suggested earlier (5.3.5), I think that sometimes the individuals to whom we owe a duty are picked out by the relationships in which we stand to them rather than by their individual genome. In particular, this happens when these relationships are the ground of the duty. So you can have a duty to make things as good as possible for "the members of future generations," or "your children," or "your neighbors," or "your employees," whoever they turn out to be. It is in their capacity as the occupants of those roles that they have a complaint against you if you fail to do what you can to prevent climate change, or to save money for their education, or to keep your property in good order, or to make your factory safe for workers, or whatever it might be. I also argued that this is not to say you do not owe these duties to any real particular individuals (with particular genomes), because once those to whom you owe this duty are born (or otherwise come to occupy the roles in question), they are atemporal beings who have claims and rights against you that extend back through time. So the reason for creating the better world (or better conditions for your children, or better conditions for your workers) is not simply that it is a better state of affairs, but because you have a duty to whoever occupies those roles to make things as good for them as you can.

But even if this is a good response to the argument from non-identity in the cases of climate change or having children, it is not obviously available in the case of changing the nature of the predators. The difficulty here is this: in order for my objection to the argument from non-identity to work, there must be future creatures to whom we stand in a relationship that gives us a duty to make things as good as possible for them. But McMahan's proposal is not exactly based on the idea that we actually stand in such a relationship to the animals of the future. It is based on the idea that we could take that relationship *on*. Perhaps that is why, in the editorial, McMahan emphasizes that we are already causing extinctions, and therefore changing the shape of the animal population. To that extent, we do already stand in the relation of a creator to future animals. But I think that some people would argue that we should eliminate predation even if we did not.

10.4.4 I want to be clear here that I completely agree with McMahan's thought that, were I in the position of the creator, I would not have created a world in which conscious, sentient creatures can only live by tormenting and killing other conscious, sentient creatures. I believe that if you are going to create conscious, sentient creatures, you have a duty to make conditions as good as you possibly can for them. That is a duty you owe to your creatures, in your capacity as their creator, and in their capacity as your creatures, whoever they might turn out to be. That is why we have a duty not to have children until we can afford to give them a good education and a good life, even if this means that genetically different children will be born. If nature itself had an omnipotent creator, creating the world from scratch, that creator would have been free to design his creatures however he liked, and as far as we can see, that creator could have designed creatures who do not have to live at each other's expense.

But this is not the relation in which we stand to the other animals. We are not their creators, and we are not creating a world from scratch. We are the inhabitants of a world we already share with the other animals, and the question we are asking is what we owe to *them*. There is an important difference between simply comparing two worlds populated with different inhabitants, and asking which is better, and asking what sort of a world, or a family, you should create if you are starting from scratch. It follows that there is also an important difference between substituting one state of affairs for another, and creating a state of affairs from scratch.

To see this, consider gentrification. When a neighborhood is gentrified, new housing and other institutions that attract more affluent residents are introduced, and as a result what once was a slum may get cleaned up. Now it's a "better" neighborhood. But for whom is it better? Superficially we can say that the neighborhood is a better place for "its residents." But it is not better for the original slum residents if they simply can no longer afford to live there and have to move to some other slum somewhere else. So the sense in which someone who decides to gentrify a neighborhood is making it better for "its residents" is not one that directly supports the idea that gentrification actually does any anyone any good. Call that the problem of gentrification. I will return to it later on (11.7.1).

10.4.5 Part of my worry here—and it is controversial—is that eliminating predation would involve *radically* changing the nature of animals—not just the predators but all of them. For one thing, domestic animals are different in systematic ways from wild ones. They tend to be smaller, have smaller brains and teeth, and to have certain juvenile characteristics. It is also important to grasp that predation is not an incidental fact of animal life. It is not just a way of dying. It is the condition that determines the activities, the whole lives, of animals. Animals have offspring as often as they do because it is necessary for them to do so in order to keep their numbers somewhat stable in the face of predation, and similar threats. Many mammals and birds breed on a yearly basis, and have more than one or two offspring at a time. The vast majority of these offspring die early in life, many of them as a result of predation. Most of the creatures who are born into this world are fated to be someone else's dinner, and get to do little else. Nature itself is a kind of gigantic factory farm, producing billions of miserable short-lived creatures just to feed a very few others.[20] From a moral point of view, it is a horror. But nevertheless, these facts determine the content, the substance, of animal life. What animals do is eat, hunt, forage, and produce and often feed and raise their offspring. If they didn't have to do those things, it is not clear what their lives would consist in. Of course, they could still eat. The herbivores could still forage—assuming the plants survived the change. (Since plants are fertilized and the soil enriched by decomposing animal bodies, we cannot take it for granted that we could radically reduce the number of animals who are born and die, without radically changing plant life as well.) But it seems fair to say that animal life would change radically in the absence of predation.

10.4.6 The claim that we would have to radically change the nature of animals if we got rid of predation is disputable, to be sure, but suppose there is something in it. In Chapter 4, I argued that the good for an animal is relative to its nature (4.4.3; see also 9.5.2). If I am right about that, there are limits to the extent to which you can do an animal any good by changing its nature. As I admitted there, it can be hard to identify exactly where that limit is—where the line is between changing a creature and replacing him—but it looks as if the boundary is roughly in the neighborhood of species membership. Changing a creature's species is not doing him any good, but rather killing him in order to make something else with his organic parts. To see why this matters, forget the future for a moment, and suppose we are just talking about an existing generation of animals. Each species of animal has its own sort of good, but as I noted before, there are common elements. All animals, for instance, can suffer from illnesses. Suppose that we discovered that rabbits have more resistance to disease than foxes. Could we do the foxes any good by turning them into rabbits? How would that be any different from killing all the foxes and replacing them with rabbits?

10.4.7 But of course, the defender of McMahan's proposal may reply that our relationship to future animals is not like that. We can take up a position that is more like that of a creator with respect to future generations of animals. We are not proposing to change any existing individual's nature but simply to produce new animals with improved natures. We might, for instance, be able to breed

[20] I was almost afraid to write this sentence, lest some careless reader conclude that factory farming can be justified because it is "natural."

more disease-resistant foxes, and it seems plausible to say that we would have done "the foxes" some good.[21] Certainly when we do undertake to control the breeding of animals, we have a duty to breed them in ways that favor their chances of having a good life. That is why human beings have been wrong to breed dogs selectively for traits that make them more susceptible to various physical problems, merely because we have a use for those traits or consider them aesthetically pleasing. Bulldogs have chronic breathing problems because they are bred for flat faces, and may have difficulty giving birth without cesarean section because we like them to have big heads and narrow hips. Very small dogs are more likely to have knee and heart problems; very large dogs have problems with their hips and are prone to heat prostration. Wolfhounds, Great Danes, and Golden Retrievers are susceptible to bone cancer because of their large size. The Chinese Shar-Pei is bred for skin folds that make it susceptible to painful skin infections. The genes that give Dalmatians their spots also make them susceptible to urinary blockages. These animals all have problems that we bred into them, and I think in doing that we have done them a wrong.[22] It is not a good answer to reply that they have no complaint, because if we had not bred them that way they would not have existed at all. We created these animals, and creators have a duty to make things as good as possible for those they create.

So we have duties to breed animals in ways that make their lives as good as possible *if* we undertake to control their breeding at all. We would be in a position more like that of a creator if we chose to take that position up. It is important to ask, though, why we should think we have a duty to take that position up. To whom would we owe that? As I pointed out in 5.3.5, we are not generally obliged to have children just because we could give them a good life. So why should we be obliged to create new species of animals just because they would be better off than the ones who would otherwise be here?

10.5 Individuals, Groups, and Species

10.5.1 I have suggested that you are not changing an individual creature but replacing him if you change his species, and that you cannot do any good to an

---

[21] The reason for the scare quotes will be explained in 10.5.2. There is a question about whether a species of animals is the kind of group which you can do some good. I discuss the question whether a species has a good in 11.4 and 11.6.

[22] See *Nature* website: "Dogs that Changed the World: Selective Breeding Problems," September 16, 2010, <http://www.pbs.org/wnet/nature/dogs-that-changed-the-world-selective-breeding-problems/1281/> and Claire Maldarelli "Although Purebred Dogs Can Be Best in Show, Are They Worst in Health?," February 21, 2014, Scientific American website, <https://www.scientificamerican.com/article/although-purebred-dogs-can-be-best-in-show-are-they-worst-in-health/>.

individual animal by replacing him. This may give you the impression that I intend my argument simply to generalize to cover species as well as individual animals—we cannot do future animals any good by replacing them with different species of animals. It may also give you the impression that I think we ought to preserve the present array of species, because we otherwise we would be substituting different animals rather than benefitting the ones that are here. But those would be bad arguments, and I am not making them. Evolution is constantly changing the array of species anyway, and as McMahan points out, we are already having an influence on evolution, by driving many species to extinction. We are determining which kinds of animals exist. The animals of the future will be different animals and different kinds of animals no matter what we do. McMahan is only urging that if we could, we should nudge evolution in ways that will bring it about that future animals will not be subject to a certain kind of harm, the harm of predation. And predation is not a species-specific kind of harm, but one to which all animals are subject, at least when they are young. So isn't there a clear sense in which getting rid of it makes things better for the animals of the future?

10.5.2 I have argued that individual animals have a good, and that because of that we have duties towards them. But we also freely throw around phrases like "good for X" and "better for X" and "we owe it to X" where the X in question may be a group of things or a type of thing. These uses often bring ethical questions in their wake. Consider, for example, the hard problem of reparations, of who might owe them to whom. People wonder about things like these: might Americans or white Americans owe black Americans reparations because of the terrible legacy of slavery, and the harms that followed in its wake? Do the groups in question include Americans or white Americans or black Americans whose families arrived in America long after slavery had been abolished? Does the group who might owe reparations include Americans who cannot be said to benefit from the disadvantages black people suffer from as a result of the legacy of slavery because they are themselves disadvantaged in some systematic way? For instance, are the native Americans, who were pushed aside by the same European colonists who brought the slaves over, among the Americans who might owe these reparations to the descendants of slaves?

Behind these familiar dilemmas is a more general question. What exactly makes a group or a type a morally relevant entity, a moral agent or a moral patient? What makes you a member of such a group? Is a species such a group? Do all of the animals collectively (or all of them except us) form such a group? Is this a group to whom we might owe it to rid them of the evils of predation, or for

11

Species, Communities, and Habitat Loss

Look around the world: Contemplate the whole and every part of it: You will find it to be nothing but one great machine, subdivided into an infinite number of lesser machines, which again admit of subdivisions to a degree beyond what human senses can trace and explain. All these various machines...are adjusted to each other with an accuracy which ravishes into admiration all men who have ever contemplated them. The curious adaptation of means to ends, throughout all nature, resembles exactly, though it much exceeds, the productions of human contrivance.

Cleanthes, in Hume's *Dialogues Concerning Natural Religion*, p. 15

Look round this universe. What an immense profusion of beings, animated and organized, sensible and active! You admire this prodigious variety and fecundity. But inspect a little more narrowly these living existences, the only beings worth regarding. How hostile and destructive to each other! How insufficient all of them for their own happiness! How contemptible or odious to the spectator! The whole presents nothing but the idea of a blind nature, impregnated by a great vivifying principle, and pouring forth from her lap, without discernment or parental care, her maimed and abortive children!

Philo, in Hume's *Dialogues Concerning Natural Religion*, p. 74

11.1 The Value of Species

11.1.1 It is a puzzling fact that so many people seem to care about species so much more than they care about the animals themselves. Many people who eat meat from factory farms with equanimity are outraged when someone kills an animal whose species is endangered. We are now in the sixth mass extinction in earth's history, and the first one in which the cause of the extinctions is a species itself—*homo sapiens*. Pretty much everyone agrees that this is a terrible thing. But many people regard the extinction of *any* species as a tragic event. What is not clear is why exactly this second thing should be so.

Biologists teach us that biodiversity is a good and even a necessary thing, keeping the ecosystem healthy and well-functioning. Mass extinctions are a threat to biodiversity. But considered in itself, biodiversity does not require any particular array of species, or that any particular species should continue to exist. It unbalances things if too many species go extinct at once, and that is what is happening now. But that does not show that the extinction of any given species is somehow regrettable. Indeed, some species are more necessary to the health of an ecosystem than others—apex predators, for instance, and natural ecosystem managers like beavers—so from the point of view of ecology some extinctions are more worrisome than others, at least in local time and place. Some may not matter ecologically at all, if the vacated niche is easily filled.

Of course, human beings also worry about extinction when the particular species that is endangered is one that we find interesting or aesthetically appealing or in some other way compelling. The last tigers living in the wild will probably disappear in our lifetimes, and it is hard to contemplate that fact without dismay. But that is considering the animals' value for us, not for themselves.

11.1.2 In the two quotations that I have made the epigraphs of this chapter, Hume's characters, Cleanthes and Philo, in the *Dialogues Concerning Natural Religion*, are disagreeing about the Argument from Design: about whether nature really gives us evidence that it was designed by an omnipotent and beneficent god. But they could equally well be taken to represent the opposed positions of "holistic" environmental philosophers who believe that ecosystems and species have intrinsic value, on the one hand, and animal ethicists, who look at the world from the perspective of the individual animal and a concern for the individual animal's good, on the other.[1] Cleanthes, taking the ecological view, finds his imagination "ravished into admiration" by the way everything in nature fits together and depends on everything else. But Philo, who considers the individual animals as "the only beings worth regarding," bemoans the hapless cruelty of a natural world into which too many creatures are born and doomed to suffer and die.

11.1.3 Holistic environmental philosophers, among others, claim that species have "intrinsic value." Some also think that ecosystems, and even the whole biosphere, nature itself, have intrinsic value, and that the value of a species

---

[1] The holistic environmental philosophy is exemplified by Aldo Leopold, "The Land Ethic," in *A Sand County Almanac*, J. Baird Callicott, *In Defense of the Land Ethic: Essays in Environmental Philosophy*, and Holmes Rolston, III, *Environmental Ethics: Duties and Values in the Natural World*.

consists in its contribution to those. There is some tension between these views. A thing is supposed to be intrinsically valuable if it is valuable in virtue of its own intrinsic nature, in virtue of what it is, rather than because of the way it is related to something else.[2] A species might, as it happens, have both intrinsic and contributory value, but those two ways of being valuable cannot be the same thing. Another problem with appealing to the concept of intrinsic value in general is that there are no particular rules for applying it. It is a matter of "intuition" which things have intrinsic value, at least according to G. E. Moore, the philosopher who has given us the most systematic account of the concept of intrinsic value.[3] Many utilitarians think that pleasure is intrinsically good and suffering is intrinsically bad, and you can tell that just by thinking about them. One can make that sort of claim about species or ecosystems or the whole of nature as well. But it is not clear how to proceed when people's "intuitions" disagree.

G. E. Moore thought that there is a way, not to avoid the use of intuition, but to focus it. He thought that we could identify intrinsic value by a test of isolation: something is intrinsically good if you think it is good when you consider it all by itself, apart from its relation to anything else.[4] One problem with using the test in this context is determining the level at which we are supposed to apply the test when we think about the value of species. When you think of the species "elephant" apart from anything else, does it seem good to you? How about "African elephant" and "Indian elephant"? Are both intrinsically valuable, and as an entirely separate matter? If we could not preserve the African elephants, would there be any special reason, so far as intrinsic value is concerned, to preserve the Indian ones? As for the biosphere, or the whole of nature, it is a little odd to apply Moore's test of isolation in that case. The test of isolation asks us to think of the object as it is in itself, independently of its relations to anything else, but that is the only way we *can* think of the whole of nature.

11.1.4 The philosophers who favor the view that species have intrinsic value may reply that they are not using the term in Moore's sense, but rather in the sense Kantians have in mind when we describe rational beings or animals as "ends in themselves."[5] In Chapter 8, I argued that there are actually two slightly different

---

[2] See Korsgaard, "Two Distinctions in Goodness," essay 9 in *Creating the Kingdom of Ends*.

[3] Moore, *Principia Ethica*, and "The Conception of Intrinsic Value" in Moore, *Philosophical Studies*.

[4] Moore, *Principia Ethica*, pp. 53 and 112.

[5] I myself more or less equated Moore's notion with Kant's in some of my early papers, most notably "Two Distinctions in Goodness" (essay 9 in Korsgaard, *Creating the Kingdom of Ends*).

senses of that idea, although in the case of people they come together: someone is an end in himself if he is capable of putting you under an obligation through reciprocal moral lawmaking, and someone is an end in himself if what is good for him is good absolutely. It's the second sense that matters here. If we take that kind of value to be "intrinsic value," as the name "end-in-itself" seems to imply, then it might seem as if anything that has a good that matters has intrinsic value. If it then seems as if things can be good for a species, or an ecosystem, then we might be tempted to conclude those things have the value of "ends in themselves" too. I will take up the question whether and how things can be good for a species in 11.4.

If you accept the idea that everything that is good must be good for someone, for some creature, then you must deny that it makes sense to say that species or ecosystems have intrinsic value. According to the view I have been advocating, it is plain that the health of an ecosystem matters because it matters to the creatures who depend upon it, and the extinction of a species matters when it threatens the biodiversity and so the health of the ecosystem and with it the welfare of its members. The only question then is whether the existence of a species or its good, if it has one, also matters in some other way.

11.2 The Good of a Species and the Good of Its Members

11.2.1 Before I turn to that question, I want to mention another attitude we might find puzzling. I believe that some people think that caring about species and whether they go extinct is a way of caring about the animals. I do not mean just caring about the other animals in the ecosystem who depend in one way or another on the existence of that species of animal, but caring about the members of the species itself. Is the extinction of a species bad for its members?

It is obvious that the animals who are members of a species are likely to suffer *while* it is going extinct. If a species of animal is going extinct, something bad is happening to the members of that species. They are probably dying prematurely, and in unpleasant ways. Climate change is destroying their fitness for the environment in which they live; or an epidemic of a disease for which they have no immunity is wiping them out; or members of an invasive species against whom they have evolved no defenses are eating them or outcompeting them for whatever food they eat; or sheer loss of habitat is leaving them no place where they can live and raise their young; or humans are hunting and killing them for food or for their horns or tusks or their pelts or whatever. So the events that are causing the extinction are also, independently, bad for the individual animals.

But they would be bad for the individual animals even if they were not causing the extinction.

Another, perhaps more direct way in which the process of extinction can be bad for the animals themselves is that they might be unable to find suitable mates and companions. The members of a species need each other. Lonesome George, a tortoise who was discovered on the Galápagos Island of Pinta, was the last (known) living member of his subspecies for at least forty years. The scientists taking care of him tried to mate him with females of closely related subspecies, not, of course, to cure his lonesomeness, but in hopes of preserving his genes. But no viable eggs were produced. I will come back to this sort of consideration later on.

11.2.2 But the process of extinction is not extinction itself. Is extinction bad for the animals whose species go extinct? Of course you might be tempted to say that extinction cannot be bad for the animals in the extinct species, since those animals no longer exist. But in Chapter 5, I argued that creatures can be both harmed and wronged after their deaths. Death itself—the condition, not the process—can be a harm to an animal, namely the harm of loss. So perhaps extinction could be some sort of harm to the animals whose species go extinct. Indeed, people tend to think of extinction itself as if it were a kind of death, the death of the species.

I think there's a problem with that way of thinking about extinction, and I'll come back to that point (11.5), but in the meantime let me mention two reasons for doubting that caring about the survival of a species amounts to caring about the animals themselves. First of all, and most obviously, things that are "good-for" the species are not always good-for the individual animals who are its members. I've put the scare quotes around "good-for" a species (although it is a notion to which I appealed myself in 2.2.4), because we should be prepared to ask whether a species is the sort of thing that has a good, and if so, what kind. I will do that shortly, but for now, let's assume that the things that keep a species from going extinct are good-for it. Then predation can be good for a species, if it prevents a drastic increase in population that would lead to extinction itself. If an overpopulation in a species is destroying the food resources of those very animals faster than the food resources can renew themselves, then bringing in an apex predator will be good for the species. Or if it would take too long for that to work, then the population might need to be culled by human wildlife managers to save the species as well as to maintain the balance of the ecosystem more generally. But it is certainly bad for an individual animal to be killed.

The second reason has to do with one of the human differences I described in Chapter 3 (3.4). Human beings, as I noted there, are characterized by "species-being": we think of ourselves as members of our species, and our species as having a shared narrative history, and even as carrying out some collective projects—exploring the universe, coming to a better understanding of nature, curing poverty and illiteracy and illness—projects that carry beyond our own individual lives. Our own lives get meaning and value from the thought that we are contributing in some way to those collective projects. As Samuel Scheffler has argued, this gives us a stake in the future of our own species.[6] Many of our own activities would make little sense to us if we expected the human species to go extinct in the near term. But none of this is true of the other animals. Their concerns are even more local. They have no stake in the long-term survival of the species of which they are members. The process of going extinct is bad for them. But extinction—the fact, not the process—itself is not, anyway not for that kind of reason.

11.3 What Is a Species?

11.3.1 Before we can ask whether a species has a good, we need to ask what a species is. This turns out to be a complicated metaphysical issue on which biologists and philosophers of biology have interesting debates.[7] A central question is whether a species is more like a type or more like a particular population. If being a member of a species is being the bearer of a type, we need to ask what the defining or perhaps even essential features of the type are. Presumably they will include the features that explain how the members of the species function as living things: the specific ways in which they characteristically get their food, reproduce, and defend themselves. Similarly, if being a member of a species is being a member of a particular population, we need to ask what unifies that population. Two popular choices nowadays, very roughly described here, are that (i) the population is united by having the ability and tendency to interbreed,[8] and that (ii) the population is a particular lineage on the "tree of life," a group that starts to exist when it "branches off" from another group and ceases to exist when another group branches off from it.[9] A slightly oversimplified story holds that

---

[6] Scheffler, *Death and the Afterlife.*

[7] For help with this discussion I am indebted to Peter Godfrey-Smith, *Philosophy of Biology,* chapter 7, and personal correspondence.

[8] I say "the tendency" to interbreed rather than the ability, because there are animals whom we think of as members of different species who can interbreed successfully but who just don't, at least in the wild. Canids—wolves, foxes, coyotes, dogs—can all interbreed. Lions and tigers can interbreed in captivity.

[9] Peter Godfrey-Smith points out that an odd implication of this view is that a species counts as going extinct whenever another species branches off from it, even if organisms which are typologically just like its members continue to be produced from the original lineage. So for example if

until Darwin taught us the theory of evolution everyone thought of species as the bearers of types characterized by essential properties, while the theory of evolution taught us that a species must be a population with variation in it for natural selection to work on.

An odd thing about this debate is that you might think that even if we define a species as a unified population, there must be at least a rough type corresponding to it, even if we do not want to think of this type as an essence that does not admit of variation.[10] After all, an organism is a material object and, in principle, material objects can be copied. Suppose a species is a population whose members have the capacity and the tendency to interbreed successfully. In principle, we could *make* an organism that has whatever features make that capacity and tendency possible. (Imagine we have some sort of very advanced body-scanning technology that we can use to make exact copies of organic bodies.) If we then let it loose among the population, it would function just like one of its more ordinarily produced members. Would it then be a member of the species? A little oddly, it looks as if on the view that defines a species as a population whose members have the ability and inclination to interbreed, the replicant would be a member of the species, while on the view that defines a species as a lineage, the replicant would be an imposter.[11]

11.3.2 Sometimes we think of species more as types, sometimes more as interbreeding communities or lineages. When I criticized the marginal cases argument in 5.2.3, and when I argued that the good for a thing is relative to its nature in 4.4.3, I was thinking of the members of a species as characterized by a type of functional unity. But if a species really were *just* a type, it could not have a good, because a type is not the kind of thing that has a good. Its members would all have the same type of good, but that would not amount to the type's having a good. It

---

purple lilacs evolved from white ones, but white ones also continue to produce white ones, the white ones count as going extinct or turning into a new species at the moment the purple ones branch off. Proponents of the theory agree that this is a problem. However it is solved, this implication might make this conception of what a species is a particularly unhelpful one for thinking about what, if anything, is regrettable about extinction.

[10] The type might be genetic rather than one of outward appearance or behavior. There are species where sex differences or functional roles make some of the members look and act quite different from others. Peter Godfrey-Smith, who drew my attention to this, used the example of the angler fish, in which the male is extremely tiny and attaches himself for life to the female's body, living the rest of his life as a sort of sperm-producing organ. Or think of the difference between the queen bee and the workers.

[11] You might think we could meet the objection thus formulated by interpreting the copying mechanism as an odd form of reproduction; one step out from cloning, so to speak. But that does not really help, because in principle a copying mechanism could also make a good copy of a member of a species completely by accident.

also could not exactly go extinct, since that is not the sort of thing types do either.[12] There would be nothing in the world that bears the type, but the type itself would not be extinct.[13] On the other hand, if the members of a population did not have *anything* in common (this is impossible to imagine, since *something* has to unify them into a population)—if there were no common type the members bear—it's hard to see how anything could be tragic about its extinction. What has to be tragic about extinction, if anything is, must have something to do with the fact that its type is no longer realized in the world. So for the purposes of this discussion, I am going to suppose that we need to think of a species both as populations and as types, without trying to sort out the hard question of how those two ideas are related.

11.4 Does a Species Have a Good?

11.4.1 Does a species have a good? Is its own extinction bad for it? That last question may seem surprising, since we are inclined to assume that anything that tends to keep a thing in existence is "good-for" that thing. Strictly speaking, this is not always true. Fireworks, musical notes, and disposable hand wipes perform their functions better if they remain in existence only as long as they are needed. But it is usually good-for us if the artifacts we use remain in existence, since it is expensive and time-consuming to replace them. Since the function of artifacts is in general to be good-for us, I suppose we can say that it is good for them to last, in the functional sense—it enables them to perform their function well. But I think the main reason we tend to think it is better for things to last is that we make a kind of animistic analogy between artifacts and living things. What shows this is that when we are thinking about what extends the duration of an artifact, we refer to its duration as its "life." "Using good gasoline will extend the life of your car." That sort of thing.

11.4.2 One reason that we think that extinction is bad for a species is that we tend to think of species as if they were living things, and of extinction as a kind of dying. The way an animal stays alive—by eating—and the way a species keeps itself in existence—through its members reproducing—can seem analogous. In Aristotle's terms, both processes impose the species' form on organic matter. Because a species has a tendency to maintain itself that is similar to an organism's

---

[12] I owe the point to Russell Powell, "On the Nature of Species and the Moral Relevance of Their Extinction," in the *Oxford Handbook of Animal Ethics*, p. 607.

[13] There is nothing in the world that bears the type "unicorn" but that does not show that unicorns are extinct.

tendency to maintain itself, it seems natural to think of it as having a functional organization rather in the same way that an organism does. We might say that it keeps itself in existence through its genes, which instill its members with the drive and ability to reproduce. If it has a functional organization, then it has a functional good: events and conditions are good-for it that enable it to keep on existing, to stay "alive." Similarly, some philosophers think that events that render the members of a species more fit are good-for it, since a species whose members are fit is less likely to go extinct. These events may include the death of less fit individuals, which is one reason why what's good-for a species isn't necessarily good-for its members.

11.4.3 Granting all this, still, I think it is a bit fanciful to think of a species as having a functional good like an organism, for two reasons. First of all, in Chapter 2, I argued that *ultimately* what justifies us in thinking of animals as functionally organized is that they have a point of view, from which the things that contribute to their self-maintenance and reproduction appear as final goods (2.2.5). Although final good is functional good taken as an end of action, functional good itself only exists within, or relative to, the point of view of the creatures who care about the things that conduce to their own existence and reproduction. But a species is not conscious and has no point of view, so it cannot have a final good in my sense. If something must have a final good in order to have a functional good, species do not have a functional good either.

Perhaps one species could be said to have a point of view—our own. This is because language and communication gives us a kind of collective or overlapping consciousness in which we all, at least potentially, share. When Carl Sagan famously said "We are a way for the cosmos to know itself" he used "we" as the pronoun for that collective consciousness.[14] But the other species—I am talking about the species now, not their members—are not conscious entities, and have no final good, and to that extent it is odd to regard them as having a functional good. A species has no point of view from which the things that help it to continue in existence could be viewed as good.

11.4.4 I said there are two reasons why it is fanciful to think of a species as a kind of living thing. Before I can explain the second, it will be instructive to compare the good of a species to the good of a plant.

First, a positive point. I mentioned before (2.2.3) that even if a plant does not have a final good in the sense of something to aim at, the good of a plant is "final" in a different sense. The good of a plant is "final" in the sense that the explanation

---

[14] Sagan, *Cosmos: A Personal Voyage*, episode 1: The Shores of the Cosmic Ocean.

of why things are good-for it ends with the plant. The contrast here is with artifacts. We think of artifacts as having a functional good, even if it turns out this way of thinking is a bit animistic, but the explanation of why things are good-for them ultimately refers to us and the uses we have for them. It does not end with the artifacts themselves, so in that sense they do not really have even a functional good of their own. But plants do seem to have a functional good of their own. We might think of the good of a species as being like that of a plant in this respect: when we explain why certain conditions are good for the species, the explanation ends with the species. The functional good of a species would not be a final good in my sense. But it would be a good of its own.

But now the problem. Just now I pointed out that even the notion of functional good is relative to a point of view. When we speak of plants as having a functional good, we are regarding them rather as if they were animals—as if, like animals, they had selves and took the things that conduce to the survival of those selves as final goods. That might seem fanciful in the same way that thinking of a species as having a good seems fanciful, since as far as we know plants are not conscious. But plants have so much in common with animals that it is natural for us to think of them that way. And there is a good reason to do so. A plant's adaptive tropic responses and an animal's ability to be guided instinctively by perception to the things that are good for her *are* analogous. Think of a plant's roots reaching deeper into the soil when the moisture is further down, and an animal's going to get a drink of water when she is thirsty. The difference between the plant's tropic responses and the animal's action might even, ultimately, be a matter of degree (2.2.3). In that case, plants would be, in a very elementary sense, agents, and so might be said to have a final good.

But can a species be considered a kind of agent, even in the sense that a plant is? At most, it acts when its members do. Part of the difficulty here rests in the fact that we think of species both as a population and as a type. If we think of a species as a population, it is more natural to think of it as acting when its members do, than if we think of it more as a type. As I've already mentioned, we think of a species as maintaining itself when its members reproduce. We may also be tempted to think of the species as "responding adaptively" when its members do. Suppose the members of some species change the balance of their diet in response to a shortage in one of its components, or move to a new area to avoid an increase in competition. Here again we are tempted to say that the species has responded adaptively through the action of its members—that it has saved itself, like the thirsty plant or animal who finds water. But many cases of adaptation are not like this: they do not involve the members of the species doing something, but just involve the members who have become more fit because of some change in the environment reproducing more and the ones who have become less fit dying off. In these cases the adaptation does not really come "from within" in the same sense that an animal's action or a plant's tropic response does. The species "adapts" as a result of the forces of natural selection working *on them*, not as a result of something it or its members "do." So the sense in which a species can be seen as an agent is quite limited.

11.4.5 My point in making these remarks is just to show that the analogy between the way a species maintains itself and the way an organism does is limited. That means that the sense in which a species has a functional good is also limited. But talk of what is and is not "good for" a species is almost inevitable when we are thinking about the natural world. I am not suggesting that we could do without it. But I think a lot of the time people simply fail to distinguish among the ideas that I have been trying to separate here. We tend first of all to exaggerate the sense in which a species even has a functional good, and we fail to distinguish between the idea that a species has a functional good and the idea that a species is something like an organism with a final good.

I also think that one of the things behind this conceptual squishiness is a tendency in our thought which is pernicious: the view of a species as a kind of generic living thing.

11.5 Species as Generic Organisms

11.5.1 Peter Singer quotes Leslie Stephen as saying: "Of all the arguments for Vegetarianism none is so weak as the argument from humanity. The pig has a stronger interest than anyone in the demand for bacon. If all the world were Jewish, there would be no pigs at all."[15] Singer interprets Stephen's remarks in terms of a view we looked at earlier (9.2.3), the view that non-self-conscious creatures are "receptacles" for the good:

Stephen views animals as if they were replaceable, and with this those who accept the total view [total utilitarianism] must agree. The total version of utilitarianism regards sentient beings as valuable only in so far as they make possible the existence of intrinsically valuable experiences like pleasure. It is as if sentient beings are receptacles of something valuable and it does not matter if a receptacle gets broken, so long as there is another receptacle to which the contents can be transferred without any getting spilt. Although meat-eaters are responsible for the death of the animal they eat and for the loss of pleasure experienced by that animal, they are also responsible for the creation of more animals,

---

[15] Leslie Stephen quoted in Singer, "Killing Humans and Killing Animals," p. 149.

since if no one ate meat there would be no more animals bred for fattening. The loss meat-eaters inflict on one animal is thus balanced, on the total view, by the benefit they confer on the next. We may call this the "replaceability" argument.[16]

The total utilitarian thinks we should maximize the amount of pleasure in the universe, regardless of how it is distributed among creatures. This means that it is permissible to kill a creature as long as you put another in its place, to reproduce the pleasure that would otherwise be lost. Singer understands Stephen to be saying something similar.

But even if Singer is right in his interpretation of Stephen's view, it does not quite explain what Stephen says. Who is "the pig" who supposedly has a particular interest in the demand for bacon? No actual particular pig has a (positive) interest in the demand for bacon. The demand for bacon is going to get her killed. Even if the pig does owe her life to the demand for bacon, and in that sense we think of her as having benefitted from it, she would still be better off if everyone became a vegetarian during her lifetime.[17] On the other hand, no merely possible pig, who might get born, has an interest in the demand for bacon, since no merely possible pig has an interest in anything. Leslie Stephen seems to be thinking that there is some generic, archetypical animal called "The Pig" who is benefitted in a general way from the practice of eating bacon, because this practice brings pigs into existence. This generic animal serves as a kind of abstract representative of the species "pig." The supposed benefit to "The Pig" is that if people did not eat bacon, the species would go extinct. Then we think that because the species is represented by this generic archetypical pig, the species can be benefitted and harmed in something like the way a real animal can.

11.5.2 We do it all the time. We refer to species as "the" followed by the same word we use when we are talking about an individual animal. The wolf has gone extinct in England. The wolf is hungry. The wolf is injured. The wolf is endangered. The wolf (that one, the one I have been watching through my binoculars for months now) is thriving. The wolf (the species) is thriving. Here's one possible reason why we talk this way. Michael Thompson has pointed out that we use a particular grammatical form, usually called the generic, to describe facts

---

[16] Singer, "Killing Humans and Killing Animals," p. 149.

[17] Singer, at least at the time he wrote the paper, might have denied this. He accepted the replaceability view, for animals although not for people, but his acceptance depends on another premise. He argued that non-human animals lack any conception of themselves as beings with temporally extended identities, and therefore lack any interest in the continuation of their lives into the future. Later he argued the replaceability argument works only for animals that do lack such a conception.

about the characteristic "life form" of an organism.[18] Generics are not universal truths or mere statistical generalizations. For instance, we might say "Wolves have litters in the spring." We do not mean either that every wolf has a litter every spring or merely that most wolves do, but that this is what wolves characteristically do, that it is what their life cycle involves. Because of this, it can seem especially apt to use the construction "The X . . . " in the generics that describe the life form of a species. The generic sentence gets a generic subject. "The monarch butterfly migrates south every winter." "The mountain goat is a sure-footed climber." "The grey wolf mates for life." Perhaps that way of talking bleeds over into our talk about the threat of extinction. But "The wolf is endangered" or "the wolf is extinct" could not be one of Thompson's life-form generics. It is not part of the characteristic life-form of any organism to be endangered or extinct.

11.5.3 However natural it is to use expressions like "the wolf is a pack hunter" to describe the characteristic ways in which wolves get their food, the use of expressions like "The wolf is endangered" to refer to the species has pernicious consequences. The trouble comes from both directions. On the one hand, it makes us think that caring about a species is a way of caring about the animals in it, even though what is "good-for" the species is not necessarily good-for the animals in it. On the other hand, it allows us to regard the animals themselves, the real particular animals, as if each of them were merely a kind of abstract representative of his or her species. We come to think of animals as interchangeable and replaceable, not just, as Singer says, because one of them is just as good a receptacle for pleasure as another, but because their individual identity does not matter at all. To use a bit of popular philosophical jargon, it's as if each pig were just a token of the type "Pig" *and nothing more.* Holmes Rolston, who argues that it is a good thing when animals are killed if it improves the species, puts it this way: "The individual is a receptacle of the form, and the receptacles are broken while the form survives, but the form cannot otherwise survive."[19] When you view animals this way, it can seem as if their lives are only individually valuable if they are the receptacles of an especially valuable form. Being rare or endangered would be one way of having that special value.

---

[18] Michael Thompson, part 1, "The Representation of Life," section 4 "The Representation of the Life-Form Itself," in Thompson, *Life and Action*, pp. 63–82.

[19] Rolston, *Environmental Ethics*, p. 148. Notice that the very idea that increased fitness "improves the species" can mean either that it makes the species better able to survive or, if we don't think of species as agents, simply that it makes it more likely that it will survive. In the first place it is like acquiring a skill; in the second it is like getting a protective coating. Note also that, as I have already pointed out, a type, or "form" as Rolston puts it here, cannot, strictly speaking, fail to survive (11.3.2). All that can happen is that there are no more tokens of the type.

That way of thinking causes us to forget what matters. Every sentient animal is a real individual with a center of subjectivity of her own, with experiences that matter to her. Every sentient animal's life—his or her individual life—is valuable, at least to the extent that it is valuable to the animal herself. Every animal's death is a loss to the animal herself, unless she is in such bad condition—or living in such bad conditions—that it is no longer worth living for her. It does not matter if the members of a species are commonplace or if they are all alike. Your own life and experiences would be just as important to you if there were lots of other people who were essentially just like you. If you take what is good for you to be good absolutely, you take yourself to be an end in yourself. We do take ourselves to be ends in ourselves, and we have no more grounds for doing so than any other animal. All of the particular wolves and the particular pigs have that kind of value. "The Wolf" and "The Pig," where those phrases are used to name the species, do not. Thinking of species as generic organisms with a final good of their own is pernicious, because it causes us to lose track of the real final goods and evils of their members.

11.6 How to Care about Species

11.6.1 Does this mean that we should care about endangered species only for the sake of biodiversity and the benefits it brings to us and to other creatures? Does it mean that when we ourselves put a species in danger of extinction, we are doing no wrong to its members? No. I have already pointed out one reason: animals whose species is going extinct are surely being harmed individually. But that is not the only reason.

At the end of Chapter 10, I raised the question what makes a group or a collective normatively significant, what makes it an agent, or a moral agent who can do right or wrong, or a moral patient who can be treated rightly or wrongly. I have already suggested some reasons for thinking it makes only limited sense to regard a species as an agent. But we can still ask whether a species is a moral patient, something we might wrong. So now I want to look more directly at the question what makes a collection of creatures a morally significant group.

11.6.2 The most obvious way in which a collection of creatures becomes a morally significant group is illustrated by political units like the state. When people form a political state, they adopt a set of procedures for making decisions together, and when those procedures are followed, the resulting decision counts as an action of the group as a whole. A state's laws, passed by its legislative body, are its collective decisions, and their enforcement is a collective action. The political state is therefore an agent. In fact political states are rational and moral agents, because the agents who occupy the roles in them are rational and moral agents. States can also do things to each other that individual people cannot, like making treaties and going to war.

Once a group of creatures is an agent, it is also a moral patient. States can wrong each other, by violating treaties or waging unjust wars. Other organizations that have organized decision-making structures also count as collective agents, and therefore as patients. That's why corporations, companies, clubs, foundations, and other such entities can do things and have things done to them, and why we can make laws that govern their actions.

More informally, and more fuzzily, people act collectively as a culture when they (or large numbers of them) share attitudes and values, and know that they do that because they have language in which those attitudes and values get expressed and affirmed. When they act on those shared attitudes, knowing that they do so, they function as a group. Then they can also be patients, acted on by other agents. A state or another culture or a corporation can wrong them, say by refusing to respect their right to live by their values, or destroying their monuments or their works of art.

11.6.3 Can a group of animals be a collective agent? Certainly social animals do things together. They hunt in packs. A group of animals forages together. They gang up on another animal who has intruded into their territory. How exactly they manage to coordinate their activities without either formal decision-making structures or language is a fascinating question. Plainly, the process involves things that are like formal decision-making structures and language. They have leaders who determine what the group is going to do, for instance. They stay within range of each other as they forage by communicating through signals, or simply by watching each other's behavior. That enables them to warn each other of predators, or to gather together to rest in the heat of the day. If we count living as an activity, then living is something that animals do together, not just social animals now, but all animals who reproduce sexually. Insofar as a group of animals is a collective agent, it can be a collective patient too. You can do things to a group of animals that do not just amount to doing things to each of the animals. You can prevent their shared activities as such. You can break up the group.

11.6.4 There are different ways in which things can be good or bad for a group. Sometimes something is good for a group only because it is good, individually, for its members. But sometimes a thing is good for a group because it makes group activities and other shared goods possible. In this kind of case, the way in which the thing is good for any one animal depends on its being good in a similar way for the others. Consider, for example, a public park. If the reason you value the park is so that you will have a place to go and commune with nature in relative solitude, the park is good for you as an individual. It might be good for other individuals for the same reason, or for other individual reasons—as a place to go running, perhaps. But given your reason for valuing it, it would be good for you even if no one else had any use for it. But if you value the park because it has a baseball diamond, or a stage for open-air theater, the way it is good for you depends on its also being good in a similar way for others. You value it because it makes shared activities and experiences possible, because it makes it possible for you and those around you to function together as a community. If I value the park for communing with nature and you value it as a place to go running, it is a sort of shared good, but its sharedness is accidental. But if we value the park because it has a baseball diamond, or a stage for open-air theater, it is an *essentially* shared good.

Habitat is like that. It is an essentially shared good for the members of a species who live in a given area. It is not good merely because it provides each of the members of the species with food, air, and water. It is good because it enables them to function together in all kinds of ways—to hunt together or forage together or rest together in the heat of the day. It is good because it enables them to find reproductive partners (remember Lonesome George in 11.2.1). When an animal reproduces, the way in which her habitat is good for her depends upon its also being good in a similar way for her offspring. That is why the point I am making now applies to non-social animals as well as social ones, although it is more obvious in the case of social animals.

The point I am trying to make here is an extremely simple one. The members of a species in a given area form a community, and that community has a shared good of its own.[20] You cannot care about the welfare of animals without caring about the welfare of those communities. An existing community of animals is like an existing species, in that caring about the community carries our concern for presently existing animals a certain distance into the future. But a community of animals with a shared good is something more obviously worth caring about for the sake of the individual animals themselves than the bare existence of the species as a type.

---

[20] In ecology, "community" is often used to refer to organisms of *different* types who have ecologically significant interactions. I am not using the term that way here: I am using the term to talk about organisms of the *same* type who live together.

11.6.5 When a species of animals becomes extinct in a given area because of human activities, it is a sure sign that we have been harmful to the point of fatal to those animals' communities. To the extent that we think of a species as a population, we can say something even stronger, for when we think of a species as a population, each community of animals is a *part* of the species. In that sense, when we are harmful to the community, we are harmful to the species itself. In fact, our talk about extinction often is actually talk about communities. Sometimes we say things like, "The X is extinct in Y" where X is a kind of animal and Y is a region. Sometimes X is a distinct subspecies, once found only in that region, and now gone forever, but sometimes not even that: sometimes X is a once-common species whose range is contracting. Because a group of interbreeding animals who are geographically separated from others are bound to evolve some distinctive attributes over time, the distinction between a community and a subspecies is bound to blur. In all of these ways, caring about communities and caring about species or subspecies amounts to almost the same thing. In any case, the members of species are also members of communities for whom habitat is a shared good, essential to both the group and the individuals. When we threaten the existence of a community of animals by destroying or reducing its habitat, or of course in other ways, we are threatening the species in a way that is bad for its members.

So what I am suggesting is that we might owe it to the animals in these communities not to disrupt their shared lives by robbing them of their territories. Why? For the same reason that we owe it to future generations not to pollute or overheat the planet. It is not ours, but belongs to all of its creatures.[21] Of course we should care about biodiversity, and for that reason alone we should stop destroying habitat—I will say more about how below (11.8.4). But we should also preserve habitat for the sake of the communities of animals that are so important to the individual animals themselves.

11.6.6 Trying to preserve communities of animals would give us reasons to do a lot of the same things that trying to preserve species does, but not all. Notably, it would not provide a justification for putting members of endangered species in zoos, since that is not a way of preserving their communities. Biodiversity might provide a reason for putting members of endangered species in zoos, but even that would only make sense if we had a genuine plan to re-establish their habitat in the near-term future, perhaps near-term enough so that those individual animals would benefit. We should not make animals live in zoos just to preserve

---

[21] For a theoretical defense of this claim—that we are not the sole owners of the planet—based on Kant's theory of property rights, see Korsgaard, "The Claims of Animals and the Needs of Strangers: Two Cases of Imperfect Right."

the type. Dale Jamieson writes, "Is it really better to confine a few hapless Mountain Gorillas in a zoo than to permit the species to become extinct? To most environmentalists the answer is obvious: the species must be preserved at all costs. But this smacks of sacrificing the lower-case gorilla for the upper-case Gorilla."[22] The upper-case Gorilla is another of those generic animals, like Leslie Stephen's Pig: an abstract representative of a species whose members are not conceived as having real individual lives at all.

11.7 Eliminating Predation Again

11.7.1 Now I am ready to finish off the unfinished argument from Chapter 10. In 10.5.2, I asserted that "the animals" form a normatively significant group. I can now explain that that is true because, and to the extent that, animals have overlapping or shared interests—for instance, their interest in the planet's being suitable to sustain life. We are wronging "the animals" (including ourselves) if we put that in danger. I also agreed that there is a sense in which we could make "the animals of the future," the members of this group who will exist later on, better off if we eliminated predation, although as I pointed out before it is a little unclear what their lives would then consist in. But "the animals of the future" are not the only normatively significant group we have to contend with. Communities of lions and leopards and sharks are also normatively significant groups, to whom we have obligations, including obligations to support or at least not to undermine the continuing existence of their communities. We should preserve these communities for the sake of the individual animals in them. Now it becomes important that we have an obligation to improve things for "the animals of the future" by putting an end to predation *only if we take on the role of the creator with regard to them*, and that we have no obligation to do that (10.4.4, 10.4.7). But we do have obligations to support or at least not to undermine existing animal communities even if we *don't* take on the role of the creator. Arguably, we would violate those obligations *by* taking on the role of creator with respect to the world's future animals, if this leads us to do things to undermine existing animal communities. To that extent, and very much to my own surprise, I think the charge that this would be "playing God" in a bad sense is justified. It seems to me that we would be undermining existing animal communities, especially those of the

---

[22] Dale Jamieson, *Morality's Progress: Essays on Humans, Other Animals, and the Rest of Nature*, p. 173.

predators, if we started genetically manipulating the predators or phasing them out of existence. In a general way, we would be wronging the existing inhabitants of the planet in order to put a different class of inhabitants in their place. So the proposal that we phase out the predators does have what in Chapter 10 I called the problem of gentrification (10.4.4) after all.

11.8 Restoring Habitat

11.8.1 Some environmentalists seem to reason this way: Habitat loss is bad because the members of a species need a place to live, and if they don't have a place to live, the species will go extinct. And that's bad, because every species is intrinsically valuable.

Short as it is, this piece of reasoning has way too many steps. Habitat loss is bad because animals need a place to live, period.

11.8.2 An obvious way to restore habitat is to give wild animals some land. It is not the only way, because it can be just as important to, say, provide land bridges over highways to keep migration routes open and things of that kind. But still it is essential. But how much land? I said before that the planet is not ours, but how much of it is, or should be, and how much should we give back? Half, says the biologist E. O. Wilson, although his concern is more with preserving biodiversity than with the wrong we are doing to animal communities. He explains:

A biogeographic scan of Earth's principal habitats shows that a full representation of its ecosystems and the vast majority of its species can be saved within half the planet's surface. At one-half and above, life on Earth enters the safe zone. Within half, existing calculations from existing ecosystems indicate that more than 80 percent of the species would be stabilized.[23]

11.8.3 If the only species whose members mattered were human beings, perhaps we could (vaguely, in principle) figure out how best to populate the planet. We could decide what counts as the ideal lifestyle for a human being, determine what resources that lifestyle requires, then see how many of us the planet can support, making sure that we take into account the need for biodiversity and the need to preserve the environment for human beings in the future. But there are two problems with this.[24]

---

[23] Wilson, *Half-Earth: Our Planet's Fight for Life*, p. 4.

[24] Actually, there are more than two problems. For one, I have ignored the problem of how we would allow for technological changes that would change our idea of what the best lifestyle is and what the resources needed to support it are.

First of all, human beings are not the only species whose members matter. But even if we knew what the ideal lives for members of the other species are and what resources they required, we could not make the relevant calculations without first deciding which species are going to exist, and in what proportions. In different geological eras, different groups of animals have "dominated" the planet. So different ways of proportioning the planet to species are possible. How could we possibly decide how to proportion the planet to different types of animals, if one type of animal is no more important than any other?

The second problem is more practical. In 2012, science writer Tim De Chant calculated that if everyone now living in the world were to have the lifestyle of the average American, it would take the resources of 4.1 planets like earth to support it. Even if everyone were to have the lifestyle of an average French person, it would take 2.5 planets like earth.[25] So unless you think that the ideal life for a human being is something that requires much less in the way of resources than the life of a present-day American or European, we are already way, way, over the limit. If I have not convinced you that people are no more important than animals, you might wonder how we can even contemplate giving land back to the animals, when we have got all those already-existing people to support?

11.8.4 But in one way at least, it is easier than it looks. According to the United Nations Food and Agriculture Organization, 26 percent of the earth's terrestrial surface is used for livestock grazing, and one third of the planet's arable land is used to grow livestock feed.[26] Using land to grow vegetables to feed people is much more efficient, would feed more people and free up lots of land. So never mind the exact numbers or proportions—if we want to free up some land for the other animals, and return some of the land to the wild, all we have to do is stop eating meat.

If we did this some domestic species would go extinct, but as it stands most of the animals in these species lead short miserable lives on factory farms. Although they live together, indeed, crowded together, they do not live in communities that make shared activities possible. They just live side by side. Even the sense in which they count as "species" is a little challenged in some cases. Recall the definition of a species as an interbreeding population. The domestic turkey has to be bred by artificial insemination, because the male actually grows too big to

---

[25] Tim De Chant, "If the World's Population Lived Like..." as of August 8, 2012, <https://persquaremile.com/2012/08/08/if-the-worlds-population-lived-like/>.

[26] These figures are from Alastair Bland, "Is the Livestock Industry Destroying the Planet?," Smithsonian.com, August 1, 2012, <http://www.smithsonianmag.com/travel/is-the-livestock-industry-destroying-the-planet-11308007/>.

mount the female. When animals cannot engage in shared activities or even breed naturally, there is little left of the species besides the type. Is anyone tempted to think that the extinction of those species or the disappearance of those types would be a tragedy, either for us or for the animals themselves? If we do all give up eating meat, should we carefully preserve some of those non-reproducing turkeys in zoos?

The practice of eating meat and using animal products is not only bad for the domestic animals who get abused and eaten. As we'll see later on, it is bad for the climate (12.3.2) and a disaster for biodiversity. It is also bad for the wild animals, whose communities are being crowded off the planet so that the members of an already unsustainably large population of human beings can all eat lots of meat.

11.9 Should Humans Go Extinct?

11.9.1 Let's talk about that unsustainably large population of human beings. In Chapter 10 I quoted some of the arguments against pet-keeping offered by PETA (10.2.3). It is a fact worthy of serious consideration that many of PETA's arguments against the practice of keeping pets, and some other arguments against pet-keeping as well, seem to apply equally well to a practice I will call "reproductive freedom." Reproductive freedom obtains when adult human beings are permitted to have as many children as they choose, and to keep those children under their control unless the adults are caught doing something specifically wrong. Consider these comparisons:

1. The practice of pet-keeping is wrong because it generates extra animals who are killed prematurely because no one who is fit to care for them wants them. Reproductive freedom generates extra children who languish in orphanages or are neglected or abused in foster homes because no one who is fit to care for them wants them.

2. The practice of pet-keeping is wrong because it places many animals almost completely at the mercy of people who are brutal and ruthless. Since the brutality takes place in private homes, it is often only by luck that it is discovered and the animals are taken away. Reproductive freedom also places many children almost completely at the mercy of adults who are brutal and ruthless. Since the brutality takes place in private homes, it is often only by luck that it is discovered and the children are taken away.

3. The practice of pet-keeping is wrong because even if the owners are not brutal and ruthless, it puts animals in the care of people who cannot provide

the animals with a reasonably good life. But reproductive freedom also places many, many children in the homes of people who are unable to provide them with a reasonably good life.

4.   I'll add one more: many people criticize keeping cats, in particular, at least if they are allowed outdoors, because of the effects of outdoor cats and feral cats on other species. Cats, after all, are superb hunters. Human beings have brought cats all over the world, including many places in which they are an invasive species, against whom local prey animals have little defense. In 2013, the BBC reported a study, "The Impact of Free-Ranging Domestic Cats on the Wildlife of the United States,"[27] by Scott R. Loss, Tom Will, and Peter P. Marra of the Smithsonian Conservation Biology Institute.[28] They reported that cats are responsible for the deaths of between 1.4 and 3.7 billion birds and between 6.9 and 20.7 billion mammals annually. The article mentioned that cats had been blamed for the global extinction of 33 species.

But reproductive freedom and the enormous and uncontrolled increase in the human population which it has created has made the human species the cause of the sixth great extinction event on the planet, not to mention climate change.[29]

The BBC quoted one of the authors of the study as saying "Our study suggests that they [cats] are the top threat to US Wildlife." Really? Apparently, it is hard even for a *scientist* to think of *homo sapiens* as just another species (3.5.2).

11.9.2 So there's another possible solution to the problem of the current great extinction event. We human beings could decide to go extinct.

When I first started looking at the literature on animal ethics, I was a little surprised to find that the friends of animals were not more inclined to advocate this. After all, both the animal ethics literature and the environmental ethics literature endlessly detail the ways in which human beings are the cause of enormous suffering to the other animals, systematically violate their rights, upset the balance of nature and destroy the climate, and so on. We have crowded out the wild animals and filled the world with domestic animals, most of whom

---

[27] Rebecca Morelle, "Cats Killing Billions of Animals in the US," BBC News Science and Environment, January 29, 2013, <http://www.bbc.com/news/science-environment-21236690>.

[28] Scott R. Loss, Tom Will, and Peter Marra, "The Impact of Free-Ranging Domestic Cats on Wildlife of the United States," *Nature Communications*, January 29, 2013, <https://www.nature.com/articles/ncomms2380>.

[29] I do not in the least intend these remarks to serve as a *reductio* of PETA's arguments against pet-keeping. I think human reproductive freedom is a very questionable value, for all of the reasons mentioned in the text.

are being raised for food and whose short miserable lives are not worth living. It seems especially puzzling that utilitarian authors, who want to maximize happiness and who regard animals as our equals, do not suggest that the members of the species who are knowingly causing all of this misery might have a duty to bow out.[30] But it's the opposite. Singer at one point suggested that on a total utilitarian view, it would be good for the planet to contain as many human beings as it can hold.[31] It is also puzzling that environmental "holists" do not advocate human extinction. Aldo Leopold tells us that "A thing is right when it tends to preserve the integrity, stability, and beauty of the biotic community. It is wrong when it tends otherwise."[32] But nothing has ever been as bad for the biotic community as unhindered human reproduction. Shouldn't it follow that it is wrong for humans to reproduce, and right for us to stop reproducing and let ourselves go extinct?[33]

Are these philosophers in bad faith? Is it that they just don't really mean it when they say that all animals are equal, or that the biotic community is sacrosanct? Or do they just somehow overlook the possibility that we could go extinct, like someone who counts the people in the room and forgets to include himself? When you look at the world locked rigidly into your own point of view, you do not appear as one of the things in it. That's how people can say things like, "It is necessary to eradicate invasive species when they are driving the native ones to extinction" without blinking.[34]

Actually, at least some of the philosophers I have in mind could justify dismissing the human extinction option, if they did consider it, in their own terms. They would appeal to one of the two forms of human superiority I undertook to debunk in Chapter 4. Peter Singer's thought about filling the world with people is, he tells us, based on the idea that people are better happiness producers than the other animals.[35] Holmes Rolston, an environmental holist, defends human superiority in the other sense: he thinks we are

---

[30] Perhaps we should go extinct only after we have made sure that species of domestic animals who are dependent on us and unlikely to survive in the wild have gone extinct, so that we do not leave them in the lurch.

[31] Singer, "Killing Humans and Killing Animals," p. 149.

[32] Aldo Leopold, "The Land Ethic," in *A Sand County Almanac*, p. 217.

[33] I owe the point to Lori Gruen, who, commenting on Holmes Rolston's view that predation is good when it improves a species, remarks, "if a whole species was disrupting the integrity, stability, and beauty of an ecosystem, then the holists should support killing off that species, much as they support the wolf's killing the elk" (*Ethics and Animals*, p. 171).

[34] In her book *The Invaders*, Pat Shipman points out that there are two lists of invasive species on the internet, one listing the 100 worst invasive species, the other attempting to list all of them. Neither of them mentions *homo sapiens*, native to Africa and causing extinctions all over the planet.

[35] Singer, "Killing Humans and Killing Animals," p. 155, n. 9.

evaluatively superior to the other animals because of our supposedly superior capacities.[36] In different ways, these philosophers and many others assume that the world is a better place with human beings in it, and that is why they think we should not go extinct.

11.9.3 I don't accept these claims of human superiority. I also think that if you claim the world is better with human beings in it, you must answer the question, "Better for whom?" A world with human beings in it may in some sense be better for human beings, but it is certainly worse for most of the other animals. So am I committed to the view that human beings should decide to go extinct?

In 3.4, and again in 11.2.2, I pointed out that human beings have a different kind of stake in the future of our own species than the other animals do. The value and meaningfulness of our own lives and many of our own activities depends on situating our lives in the ongoing human story. Although the value of communities gives the other animals some sort of stake in the near-term future of their species, we have a stake in the longer-term survival of our species. We treat that, along with the other things that are good for us, as something that is good absolutely. But morality also commits us to making our good as shareable as possible, given the limits imposed by nature, with the good of other creatures (8.8.3), who like us are ends in themselves. I think we have a sort of right to try to secure the long-term future of our species. But on the Kantian view I advocate, it is the kind of right we can forfeit—we can fail to deserve it—if we continue to abuse the individual animals and the animal communities with whom we share the world (6.5.1).

[36] Rolston, *Environmental Ethics*, chapter 2, section 2, "Human Dominion over Animals."

12

The Animal Antinomy, Part 2
Abolition and Apartheid

How will we teach the children to speak when all the animals are gone? Because animals are what they went to talk about first. Yes, and buses and food and Mama and Dada. But animals are what they break their silence for.

Martin Amis, *London Fields*, p. 97

12.1 Reorganizing Nature

12.1.1 In 10.3.1, I suggested that work on animal ethics has produced a kind of Kantian antinomy, a case where the same premise appears to yield opposite conclusions. Supposing that we have a duty not to harm animals, and to protect them from harm if we can, those who advocate what I have called "creation ethics" argue that in order to protect animals from natural evils we must make them all domestic, while abolitionists argue that in order to protect animals from our own abuses we must make them all wild.

Antinomies reflect deep disturbances in our thought. The disturbance in this case comes from a conflict between our moral standards and the way that nature works. The natural world staunchly resists moral reorganization. As a result, we are unable to treat all animals in the way that morality demands, that is, as ends in themselves who have a claim to be treated in a way that is consistent with their good. Many people try to deal with the resulting problems by telling themselves that animals are so dimwitted that they cannot really suffer very much, or so unimportant that their suffering does not matter. The friends of animals, knowing that these things are not true, think that we have to reorganize the population of the natural world, so that all animals are either domestic and under our protection, or wild animals with whom we do not interact at all.

Using both reason and intelligence (3.2.2–3.2.3), we human beings have managed to exempt ourselves from many natural evils and to minimize others. The fortunate among us have shelter from the elements. We have medical care that prevents many physical evils, and eases those which our own animal nature makes inevitable. We do not have to worry every day about whether we will have enough food and other resources to get by. At least in the Western industrialized world, we have nearly conquered infant mortality, so that we no longer have to give birth over and over again, only to see most of our offspring die, like most of the other animals do. We have so thoroughly conquered it that our population is out of control. If we did get it under control, we could create a more equitable world in which all human beings enjoyed a high quality of life. As I argued in 8.8.3, morality teaches us how to construct a world that is, to a large extent anyway, good for all of us, governed by standards to which all of us can agree.

But we cannot extend these benefits to all of the animals, in part because the system of predator and prey, and the competition for natural resources, sets them inevitably against each other. There is a limited amount of space, time, and organic matter available to living things, and we all compete for it. We human beings are ourselves no longer prey, except to the occasional crocodile, unless you count viruses and bacteria and marketers as predators. We need not be predators, although in one respect that is just lucky—if we were obligate carnivores like cats, we would have to eat meat. On the other hand, in recent years, scientists have discovered a number of features of plant behavior that suggest that they have something at least analogous to sentience, so perhaps we are out of luck after all.[1]

12.1.2 Another problem is size. It is pretty hard to avoid harming things that are not somewhere in the same general size range as you are. But the world is teeming with organisms, most of them tiny by our standards. Some of these creatures may, for all we know, be sentient.

Consider the dust mite. The dust mite is a microscopic relative of the spider who lives in bedding, carpets, and curtains. Dust mites feed on discarded flakes of the skin of people and other animals. Unless your pillow is brand new or has recently been laundered, there are about 40,000 of them living in it right now, and they and their excrement make up about 10 percent of its weight. Although no one is sure, there is evidence that insects and spiders feel pain. Thomas Eisner, a distinguished chemical ecologist who studied the chemical defenses of insects, describes the result of one of his experiments this way:

What hurt us, evidently, caused spiders to react as if it hurt them as well. In more formal terms, one could say that the sensing mechanism by which spiders detect injected harmful chemicals such as venoms may be fundamentally similar to the one in humans that is

---

[1] Actually, apparently we are not out of luck. Daniel Chamovich, in *What a Plant Knows: A Field Guide to the Senses*, argues that plants do not feel emotion or pain. See p. 6, p. 172.

responsible for the perception of pain...we came to the conclusion that invertebrates perceive pain, and that their sensory basis for doing so may not be much different from our own. There is therefore good reason for treating invertebrates humanely.[2]

Since the dust mite is an arachnid, a relative of the spider, it seems possible that dust mites can feel pain. Many people are allergic to dust mites, and try to keep their bedding clear of them, so on the internet you can find advice like this:

There are six different ways to kill house dust mites (HDM). You can freeze, boil, poison or microwave them on high for 5 minutes, dry them up like a raisin, or put them in a hot tumble dryer for 20 minutes.[3]

It is no wonder that people who care about animals end up wanting to change the population of the world to make it more morally tractable. Maybe in addition to making all animals domestic, or making all animals wild, we should make them all large.[4]

12.1.3 Kant thought that the antinomies he discussed could be resolved if we accepted his distinction between the world as it appears to us and the world as it is in itself.[5] I believe that the animal antinomy can be resolved if we accept that there is a distinction between what we ought to do and what we can do. To put it more properly, we must reject the widely accepted principle that "ought implies can." According to this principle, we cannot have a duty to do something that we are unable to do. There are two different ways to reason from the principle that "ought implies can." One way, exemplified in Kant's central use of the principle in the *Critique of Practical Reason*, is to infer that you can do something—in particular that you can bring yourself to do it, that you can find the motivation— from the fact that you ought to.[6] The other way is to reason from the fact that you cannot do something to the conclusion that you do not have to. It is this second kind of reasoning that is at work here. That is why some people like to grill vegetarians with questions designed to expose inconsistency. "Do you feed your cats meat?" "What would you do if you found out plants are sentient too?" They

---

[2] Eisner, *For Love of Insects*, p. 253. The experiment is reported scientifically in Thomas Eisner and Scott Camazine, "Spider Leg Autotomy Induced by Prey Venom Injection."

[3] HouseDustMite.com, "Dust Mite Questions and Answers: How to Get Rid of Dust Mites," <http://housedustmite.com/questions/>.

[4] Earlier I argued that "moral standing" is a relational concept. I suppose it would be possible to argue that if something is so different from us in size that we cannot interact with it on moral terms at all, it does not have standing in relation to us. I think that would be going too far though. My intuition says at least that if dust mites are sentient, and we had a humane way to kill them, we should prefer that.

[5] Explaining how Kant's antinomies are resolved would take us too far afield.

[6] Kant, *Critique of Practical Reason*, 5:30.

hope to conclude that we cannot have duties to animals, because we could not possibly fulfill them if we did.

There are two problems with this. The first is that, at least on a Kantian account, our duty is not to achieve the good, but to treat individuals in a way that accords with their value as ends in themselves (8.8.4). Those duties are owed not just to abstract representatives of the group "animals" but to the particular animals with whom we ourselves interact. They are owed not to all of the animals, but to each of the animals, one by one, as individuals. There are plenty of animals whom we can treat as we ought.

The other problem is that the principle that "ought implies can" is not true. It is true that we cannot blame people for failing to do what they ought to if they could not do it, and also that when we find ourselves in circumstances like that, we should not blame ourselves. But that is a different point altogether. Thinking that "ought implies can" means thinking that there must be some guarantee that morality and nature are going to fit together somehow. Without some sort of theological underpinning (6.5.2), there is simply no reason to believe that that's true.

12.1.4 In the last two chapters, I hope I made it clear why I think what we might call a "preservation ethic" is superior to a creation ethic from a moral point of view, as well as from the point of view of our concern for biodiversity.[7] Rather than trying to create new and more morally tractable species of animals, I think we should do what we can to interact with the existing animals and the ongoing animal communities that already exist, in a way that respects the absolute value of their good.

Abolitionists, like creationists, want to change the nature of animals in a way that they think would make it easier for us to treat them well, or rather, to stop mistreating them. Instead of wanting to make all animals domestic, they want to make all animals wild. But in one way their position is stronger than that of the creationists. I argued before that although one world cannot be better than another if they have different inhabitants, the creator of a world has a duty to make things as good as possible for whoever she creates (10.4.3–10.4.4). As I have tried to emphasize, part of the problem with creation ethics is that it invites us to *take up* the position of the creator with respect to wild animals, and it is not clear why we should do that, or if we would have the right to even if we could. But we

---

[7] Of course, in the short term, this harmony of concerns will not stop environmentalists and animal ethicists from coming into conflict over matters of policy, over issues like how to treat animal overpopulation and invasive species. As I suggested in 8.8.5, there are genuinely intractable moral conflicts as a result of nature's clash with morality.

are *already* in the position of the creator towards domestic animals, so the claim that we might have a duty to stop creating them is more plausible. Most of us believe that you have a duty not to create a creature whose life, you can foresee, would not be worth living. At least if the lives of domestic animals are not worth living, we have a duty to stop bringing them into being. So in the rest of this chapter I will consider the abolitionists' claims, by taking at least a glancing view of some of the practical issues that arise in animal ethics.

12.2 How to Treat Animals as Ends in Themselves

12.2.1 In 8.5, I argued that there are two senses in which we take ourselves to be "ends in ourselves." We take what is good for us to be good absolutely, and we take ourselves to have the authority to make laws for ourselves and each other through our choices. It is because rational beings are ends in themselves in the second sense that others must treat us in ways to which, as I explained in 10.2.2, it is possible for us to consent. Since we stand in a relation of reciprocal lawmaking with rational beings, other rational beings get to "vote" on the transactions in which we engage them, so they must be in a position to consent. Animals are ends in themselves in the first sense, but not the second. Their wills are not governed by laws they make for themselves or each other but by nature. So I do not myself accept the argument I offered in support of the abolitionists in 10.2.2, to the effect that since we cannot get the consent of animals, we should not interact with them at all. I think that our duty to them is to treat them in ways that are consistent with their good.

In "Interacting with Animals," I suggested that we ought to treat animals in ways to which they would consent if they could.[8] I now think that was not a good way to express my view. There is no reason to treat the other animals in a way that tries to mimic the particular kind of respect we owe to autonomous beings, because the other animals are not autonomous. It is not clear that treating animals in ways to which they would consent if they could would be any different from treating them in ways that are consistent with their good, anyway. But if the two criteria are different, the consent-mimicking criterion might give us results which seem intuitively wrong anyway. Perhaps, for example, our pets would never consent to being euthanized no matter how much they are suffering.[9] Their instinct for life might be too strong. There are people in whom the love of life works that way.

---

[8] Korsgaard, "Interacting with Animals," in *The Oxford Handbook of Animal Ethics*, p. 110.
[9] I owe the example to Jonathan Vogel.

Recall Tom Regan's remark, quoted in 10.2.1, that "What's wrong—fundamentally wrong—with the way animals are treated isn't the details that vary from case to case. It's the whole system. The fundamental wrong is the system that allows us to view animals as *our resources*, here for *us*." Since I think we are treating animals as ends in themselves in the sense that they are ends in themselves if we treat them in ways that are compatible with their good, I do think we need to think about "the details that vary from case to case."

12.3 Eating Animals

12.3.1 So let's start with the easy case: factory farms. In previous references to factory farming in this book, I've assumed the reader knows the main facts. If you do not, you should read the description in Peter Singer's book *Animal Liberation*. In case you need a reminder, here is a summary from the website of PETA:

The factory farming industry strives to maximize output while minimizing costs—always at the animals' expense. The giant corporations that run most factory farms have found that they can make more money by squeezing as many animals as possible into tiny spaces, even though many of the animals die from disease or infection.

Animals on factory farms endure constant fear and torment: They're often given so little space that they can't even turn around or lie down comfortably. Egg-laying hens are kept in small cages, chickens and pigs are kept in jam-packed sheds, and cows are kept on crowded, filthy feedlots.

Antibiotics are used to make animals grow faster and to keep them alive in the unsanitary conditions. Research shows that factory farms' widespread use of antibiotics can lead to antibiotic-resistant bacteria that threaten human health.

Most factory-farmed animals have been genetically manipulated to grow larger or to produce more milk or eggs than they naturally would. Some chickens grow so unnaturally large that their legs cannot support their outsized bodies, and they suffer from starvation or dehydration when they can't walk to reach food and water.

When they've grown large enough to slaughter or their bodies have been worn out from producing milk or eggs, animals raised for food are crowded onto trucks and transported for miles through all weather extremes, typically without food or water. At the slaughterhouse, those who survived the transport will have their throats slit, often while they're still conscious. Many remain conscious when they're plunged into the scalding-hot water of the defeathering or hair-removal tanks or while their bodies are being skinned or hacked apart.[10]

Actually this summary fails to mention a few other relevant facts. Because of the overcrowded conditions, the animals on factory farms often engage in agonistic

---

[10] PETA website: "Factory Farming: Misery for Animals," <http://www.peta.org/issues/animals-used-for-food/factory-farming/>.

behavior towards each other. To prevent them from damaging each other, the beaks of the birds are trimmed, and the tails of the pigs are clipped, without anesthetics. Since the number of people who take "care" of the animals is kept minimal, animals who are injured can go unnoticed for long periods of time. There are also well-documented cases of sadistic behavior on the part of these people, perhaps a way of coping with the moral horror they are confronted with daily. It goes on and on.

As I said before, a strength of the abolitionist case is the plausible principle that you should not bring a creature into existence if you know in advance that the creature's life will not be worth living. That is of course exactly what factory farmers do, in numbers that are staggering. To quote David J. Wolfson and Mariann Sullivan:

It is almost impossible to imagine the number of farmed animals. Approximately 9.5 billion animals die annually in food production in the United States. This compares with some 218 million killed by hunters and trappers and in animal shelters, biomedical research, product testing, dissection, and fur farms, combined. Approximately 23 million chickens and some 268,000 pigs are slaughtered every 24 hours in the United States. That's 266 chickens per second, 24 hours a day, 365 days a year. From a statistician's point of view, since farmed animals represent 98 percent of all animals (even including companion animals and animals in zoos and circuses) with whom humans interact in the United States, all animals are farmed animals; the number that are not is statistically insignificant.[11]

12.3.2 It is always a question whether piling on different kinds of arguments will undercut the main one you want to make or add to its force. There is a certain danger to leaving the high ground behind. For example, suppose I am trying to convince you not to kill your rich uncle for his money, and I carefully explain to you why every life is sacrosanct, or some such thing, and then I add, "and if you get caught, you might go to prison for a really long time." It is not really clear that I've strengthened my case, is it?

But in this case, it is irresistible to pile on the arguments. So let me remind you: factory farming is not only responsible for the misery of the animals it produces. As I have already pointed out, factory farming, and animal farming more generally, is responsible for the loss of biodiversity, because a third of the world's arable land is used to grow livestock feed, and over a fourth of all of the world's land is used for livestock grazing. This means that factory farming is also cruel to

---

[11] Wolfson and Sullivan, "Foxes in the Henhouse: Animals, Agribusiness, and the Law: A Modern American Fable," in Sunstein and Nussbaum (eds), *Animal Rights: Current Debates and New Directions*, p. 206.

wild animals, because it leaves them with no place to live. Finally, as Christopher Hyner tells us:

A multitude of environmental problems our planet faces share a common instigator: animal agriculture and our reliance on meat and dairy products. According to the United States Department of Agriculture (USDA), global agriculture—dominated by livestock production and the grains grown to support it—accounts for 30% of greenhouse gas emissions.[1] A 2006 study by the United Nation's Food and Agriculture Organization (FAO) finds that 18% of global greenhouse gas emissions is directly attributable to livestock production, which is more than the emissions attributable to the entire transportation sector.[2] Whichever number is relied upon, agricultural emissions are only going to increase as rising incomes and urbanization drive a global dietary transition towards increased consumption of meat and dairy products.[3] The growing demand for animal agriculture is expected to be a major contributor to a roughly 80% increase in global greenhouse gas emissions from the agricultural sector.[4][12]

As Hyner observes in a footnote, the numbers he has just reviewed may well be an underestimate, since "a more recent and comprehensive study published by Worldwatch Institute, however, finds that livestock and their byproducts actually account for 51 percent of worldwide human-related greenhouse gas emissions annually." So besides being cruel to domestic and wild animals, factory farming is a major cause, perhaps the major cause, of both the loss of biodiversity and climate change. How many arguments do we need?[13]

12.3.3 Even if these arguments show that factory farming is a terrible thing all around and should be abolished, both for the sake of animals and people, you might wonder whether they show that you should become a vegetarian or a vegan. After all, unless a lot of other people do likewise, your refusal to buy the products of factory farms is not going to put them out of business. In fact, maybe you could do more good to the animals themselves (leaving aside the effects on the climate and biodiversity) by continuing to eat meat but pressuring, say, fast

---

[12] Christopher Hyner, "A Leading Cause of Everything: One Industry that Is Destroying Our Planet and Our Ability to Thrive on It."
The references are as follows: [1] USDA, USDA Climate Change Science Plan 4 (2010), available at <http://www.usda.gov/oce/climate_change/science_plan2010/USDA_CCSPlan_120810.pdf>.
[2] Henning Steinfeld et al., FAO, Livestock's Long Shadow: Environmental Issues and Options (2006), available at <http://www.fao.org/docrep/010/a0701e/a0701e00.htm>. Robert Goodland and Jeff Anhang, Livestock and Climate Change, *World Watch Magazine*, November/December 2009, at 11.
[3] and [4] David Tilman and Michael Clark, Global Diets Link Environmental Sustainability and Human Health, *Nature*, 515, 518, 520 (2014).
[13] Although fishermen who fish in open waters don't bring their victims into existence, a similar panoply of arguments applies to intensive fishing. If fish are sentient, its methods are unbelievably cruel, as well as damaging to the marine environment. See Jonathan Balcombe, *What a Fish Knows: The Inner Lives of Our Underwater Cousins*.

food chains to insist that the animals from whom they get their products be treated more humanely.

I will say more about humane farming below. But first, let's get back to the high ground. The question is not about just numbers and consequences. It is about you and a particular animal, an individual creature with a life of her own, a creature for whom things can be good or bad. It is about how you are related to that particular creature when you eat her, or use products that have been extracted from her in ways that are incompatible with her good. You are treating her as a mere means to your own ends, and that is wrong.

12.3.4 Faced with the horrors of the factory farm, some people turn to the possibility of "humane farming," a system in which the animals are not abused or made to suffer but treated well during their lives. So far as meat production is concerned, this option may be tempting for those who believe that while suffering is an evil for non-human animals, death is not, or anyway, not as much as it is for people.

One reason why some philosophers believe this is that they think that because (some) animals do not have any sense or conception of themselves as extended in time, they do not really have selves that are extended in time—they exist in the moment. As we saw before, Peter Singer has argued that animals who are conscious but not self-conscious may be regarded as "receptacles" for pleasure and pain (9.2.3; 11.5.1). Singer argues that such animals are in a sense "impersonal" and their pleasures and pains have only an impersonal value.[14] Their pleasures and pains are good or bad things, but they are not really good- or bad-for anyone. A utilitarian should have no objection to killing such a creature even if she is having a pleasant life so long as you replace her with another creature who will have an equally pleasant life, so that you are not reducing the total amount of pleasure in the world. Singer thinks that the question whether a given species of farm animal is in this category is an empirical one, and there may be reason to doubt that many of them are, but suppose they were. Then, Singer thinks, you could justify humane farming, since the animals who were killed would presumably be replaced.

I should say that I am not sure Singer would completely agree with my way of putting his argument. He seems to think that pleasures and pains *are* good- or bad-for the conscious animal as long as she is alive, for he says an animal has an interest in the quality of her experiences during her life. But if the animal is just a place where the experiences are happening, it is not clear that they are good-for

---

[14] Singer, "Killing Humans and Killing Animals," p. 151, *Practical Ethics*, p. 111.

or bad-for her. I have already suggested that all sentient animals are in a sense self-conscious (2.3.2) and that they do have identities over time, although to varying degrees (2.3.3). Even if I am wrong about those things, I do not think it makes any sense to regard pleasures and pains as things with impersonal value. Pleasures and pains are good-for and bad-for the animal who undergoes them. The goods that an animal would have experienced had she lived longer are therefore a loss to the animal who is killed.[15] As I argued in 2.1.8 (see also 9.4.2), life itself is good-for the sentient animal, unless it is for some specific reason bad. To eat an animal, you obviously have to kill her and deprive her of that good.

Jeff McMahan agrees that the goods that an animal would have experienced if she had remained alive are a loss to her. He thinks, however, that the comparative badness of suffering and death for animals is often different for animals than it is for people, because animals are less psychologically connected over time than people.[16] I will not try to rehearse his complex argument here, but it has some plausible consequences. Suppose a person is facing a serious illness; the treatment will be excruciatingly painful and debilitating, but there is a high probability that she will eventually recover and be able to resume the activities that give value to her life. Now suppose a dog is in the same position. When we ask whether it is worth it for the person to go through all that suffering, we characteristically think that it is, while it is not so clear that it is worth it for the dog to go through all that suffering, just so he can someday resume chasing squirrels and enjoying his owner's company. The present dog is presumably less psychologically connected to the future dog than the present person is to the future person, because the dog is not connected to his past by episodic memory or to his future by anticipation. So it is more like we are making the present dog suffer for the sake of some other dog.[17]

I think many people share the intuition that the comparative badness of suffering and death is different for people and animals. The relevance of this to

---

[15] There are controversies about how to measure this loss, of course, which I am passing over when I say "had she lived longer." How long? Forever? As long as the fullest or average lifetime of members of her species? As long as she personally would have lived if it had not been for this particular event, if we can even calculate that?

[16] McMahan, *The Ethics of Killing: Problems at the Margins of Life*, especially pp. 189–203, and pp. 487–93; and "The Comparative Badness for Animals of Suffering and Death," in Višak and Garner (eds), *The Ethics of Killing Animals*.

[17] McMahan also thinks it is less worth making the dog suffer because he thinks the person's activities are likely to be more valuable than the dog's. I have already explained why I disagree with that in 4.4.

the justifiability of humane farming, however, depends on your moral theory. McMahan thinks it is relevant because it makes it a *little* more likely that utilitarian or consequentialist calculations will come out in favor of humane farming. The value of the enjoyment people get from eating meat is not enough to outweigh the disvalue of the animal suffering and death caused by factory farming, but it might outweigh the disvalue of animal death alone, supposing that is all we have to worry about with humane farming. However, if you reject the idea of aggregating creatures' interests in this way, as I did in 9.2, all this shows is what we knew anyway: humane farms are not as bad as factory farms, but that does not mean they are justifiable. Death is not consistent with the good of the animals.

Of course, you may think humane farmers could let animals live out their natural term of life. But there is one feature of factory farming that, for economic reasons, humane farms would probably share. The lives of the animals grown for meat are very short, because there's no profit in keeping them around, eating their heads off at your expense, once they have reached the right size and stage of development to be someone's dinner.[18] When we think about the animals who live on factory farms, this thought perhaps provides some consolation. At least their horrible lives are short. As Peter Singer says, "Perhaps those who die early are the lucky ones, since their hardier companions have nothing in store for them except another few months of crowded discomfort."[19] Actually, if Singer's "replaceability" argument did apply to farm animals, and if I'm right about the implications of that argument, this would not be true. If animals really lived in the moment, and a longer stretch of good experience was not better for them, a longer stretch of bad experience would not be worse for them either. It would be a worse *thing*, by utilitarian criteria, but it would not be worse *for* the particular animals who underwent, or rather housed, it. But that just shows how implausible the replaceability argument is. In any case, when we think about animals living on a humane farm, the fact that their lives would be short certainly offers us no consolation.

---

[18] A chicken can live for about seven years. On a factory farm, a chicken raised for food is killed at about seven weeks, and one raised for eggs is killed at about one year. A male chick of an egg-laying hen is killed immediately. A pig can live for about fifteen years; one raised for food is killed at six months, while a breeding sow is killed at three or four years. A cow can live for twenty years; a dairy cow is killed at five or six years; a beef cow at about one year, and a veal calf at sixteen weeks.

[19] Singer, *Animal Liberation*, p. 118.

12.4 Working Animals and Animals in the Military

12.4.1 In theory, at least, there is a more interesting question about whether dairy products and eggs could be produced humanely or not. I am not going to go into this question here, because answering it requires hard knowledge both about the needs and desires of the animals involved and the conditions that are actually required to extract the products from them. The same point applies to many kinds of working animals: seeing-eye dogs, search-and-rescue dogs, police dogs, animal actors, and so on. Since I think that treating an animal as an end in itself only requires treating the animal in a way that is consistent with her good, I think it is in principle possible that it could be permissible for us to use animals in these ways. This is not to say that the way we use these animals at present necessarily meets the required standard. There are many cases in which it is obvious that we abuse working animals. The use of wild animals as circus performers comes to mind; neither the living conditions nor the training methods are, to say the least, compatible with the good of these animals. But in other cases, we need detailed knowledge both about the demands of the work and the needs of the animals in order to sort these questions.

12.4.2 You might think it is an objection to what I have been saying that we do not always treat *people* in ways that are consistent with their good. Sometimes we ask people to make sacrifices, in return for benefits they have received in the past, or for the sake of causes that are worth it. Could we also reasonably ask that of animals? This question is brought into sharpest focus by the use of animals in the military, although it is also relevant to the use of dogs in search-and-rescue missions, or for police work, when those kinds of work are dangerous.

In the past, horses were the most salient case of the military use of animals, at least in the Western world, but these days it is dogs. Dogs apparently make excellent soldiers.[20] They are fierce, loyal, capable of being trained to fight, and frightening to the enemy. They have special skills no human being has, like the ability to sniff out explosives. They can provide protection and help as well as comfort to human beings who are in harm's way for the sake of their countries. But do we have the right to ask it of them? Why should dogs suffer and die just because we human beings cannot find a less idiotic way to work out our differences?

Obviously, the question whether we can ask dogs to serve in the military is tangled up with the difficult question what makes it all right for a government to

---

[20] The dogs in the US military actually are soldiers. They have ranks, in accordance with which they must be treated, for instance.

ask its people to go to war. But just for starters: In a democracy, in theory anyway, the people who go to war have played a role in the decision-making process that led to the war, even if they were drafted. (Dog soldiers have to be drafted. They cannot volunteer. Contrary to what you have read in the press, we do not have an all-volunteer military now.) The people who go to war at least voted for the officials who made the decision to go to war. But the dogs can have no voice in that decision. Even in countries that are not democracies, the people who go to war live under the protection of the laws of their countries and benefit from its institutions, including its military. But as things stand, the dogs usually do not benefit much from those. If the war is just, the people who go to war are among those who stand to lose if the war is lost. It is not so clear about the dogs.[21] At least in some countries, people who object to war on principled grounds have the option of conscientious objection. Dogs could not have that.

But suppose, contrary to fact, that we treated domestic animals not as property, but as something more like a subordinate population, and that we made laws that actually effectively protected their interests and their rights.[22] Although I admit to being very uncertain, it does not seem to me totally crazy to suggest that under those circumstances we would have the right to draft dogs to serve in a genuinely just war.

But then another question arises. Starting in the Vietnam War, the United States Navy has used dolphins and sea lions for military purposes. These animals have been trained to detect lost or enemy swimmers or to locate underwater mines. The dolphins' use of sonar, like the dogs' ability to sniff out explosives, gives them a valuable asset for underwater work that human beings lack. But dolphins and sea lions are wild animals. Such laws as protect wild animals are generally aimed at the conservation of species, not at protecting the individual animals, and in any case, dolphins and sea lions do not live in any particular nation, but in the open seas. Is there a moral difference between drafting domestic animals for military purposes and drafting wild ones? If my proposal that the military use of dogs in a society that actually protected their rights and interests might be justified has any plausibility, then there would be a difference. Even in our own society as it stands, it seems to me that the use of wild animals for military purposes is morally worse than the use of domestic ones.

---

[21] It could be true, if the enemy is a would-be conqueror from a culture that treats its dogs even worse than the country in question does.

[22] I make a case for treating animals as a subordinate population rather than as property in "The Claims of Animals and the Needs of Strangers: Two Cases of Imperfect Right."

12.5 The Use of Animals in Scientific Experiments

12.5.1 Like the abolitionists, I believe that the use of animals in laboratory research and experiments that are painful, invasive, or fatal is unjustifiable, and even barbaric. It is an obvious case of treating animals as mere means to our ends, as well as being immeasurably cruel. We do not have the right to use our fellow creatures in these ways. I have found that this is a feature of views like mine that generates a lot of resistance, even from people who are otherwise friendly to the idea that we ought to treat animals much better than we do.[23] I admit that this is a hard issue, at least psychologically. When we learn of the things that actually go on in research laboratories, we are filled with horror. But when we think of the benefits that scientific research on animals might bring us, we cannot bear to give them up. Like St. Augustine, we hope that God will give us mercy and compassion—but not yet.[24]

Still, to check that your moral intuitions are really what you think they are, try to imagine that we live in a world where no one has *ever* used animals in research before, and someone proposes it *for the very first time*. "I know how we could find out if that stuff is toxic. We could drop it into a live rabbit's eye! I know how we can study withdrawal symptoms. We can get a bunch of dogs addicted, and then take away the drugs! I know how we can find out if that substance causes cancer. We can give it to a bunch of monkeys, and see if they get cancer! After all, these creatures are completely at our mercy, so why not?" Do you really think you would have responded, "Oh, right, there's the solution! Let's do that"? Don't you think you might have said, "That's out of the question"?

12.5.2 In 4.3, I suggested that there is a sense in which continued life might be more important to a human being than to another animal, and so, if you had to choose between saving a human being and saving the other animal, that might be a reason for saving the human being. (I also suggested some reasons for hesitating

---

[23] In their book *Zoopolis* Sue Donaldson and Will Kymlicka also comment on this point and mention a number of defenders of animals who argue, with regret, that it would be too great a sacrifice to give up all research on animals. They remark "But to view this as a sacrifice is already to misunderstand the moral situation. After all, there are countless medical technologies and medical advances that don't exist today because we refuse to use human subjects for invasive experiments. It is hard to overestimate the advances that medical science could have made by now if researchers had been able to use human subjects, rather than imperfect animal stand-ins. Yet we do not view this as a sacrifice" (p. 43). I am very sympathetic to the spirit of these remarks, but I am not sure their last comment is true of everyone. One of my students reported to me that his instructor in a biology course once remarked, "Of course it would be *much* better if we could do these experiments on humans. But that would raise ethical problems."

[24] In his *Confessions*, Augustine reports praying "Give me chastity and continence, but not yet," p. 169.

about the view, in 4.3.6–4.3.8.) Tom Regan made a similar point in *The Case for Animal Rights*, appealing to a case in which there are four human beings and one dog on a lifeboat, and one of them must be thrown off if any of them are to survive. Regan argued that because death is a greater harm to people than to animals, the dog should be the one who is sacrificed. In fact Regan argued that we should be willing to throw any number of dogs off the lifeboat to save the human beings.[25] In an early review, Peter Singer called on Regan "to explain the apparent discrepancy between his readiness to throw a million dogs out of a lifeboat in order to save one human being, and his refusal to allow even one dog to be used in a lethal—but painless—experiment to save one or more human beings."[26] Part of their dispute is about whether the numbers of animals involved matter, and I'll come back to that part below, but the point I want to emphasize now is different. Regan, in his reply, emphasized that there is a difference between choosing between two creatures who are already in harm's way, and deliberately putting one creature in harm's way just to benefit another (or any number of others).[27] It is only in the first kind of case, when both the dog and the human are already under threat and we can save only one of them, that we should weigh the amount of harm done to one against the amount done to the other. Certainly, if you ask yourself "Would I be using the dog as a mere means to human ends if I did that?" the answer is clearly "Yes" when we use animals in experiments, and to me at least it seems to be "No" in Regan's lifeboat case.

But, some will say, the use of animals in medical testing and experiments saves human lives, by curing fatal illnesses. Doesn't that mean we have to choose in this case? Isn't it permissible to kill someone in order to save yourself or your loved ones if you or they are in mortal danger? Can't we kill in self-defense, sometimes even in cases where the person who is posing a threat to us is innocent? (Imagine an insane person, not responsible for his actions, has got hold of a gun.) When do we get to say, "I had to do it: I had to kill him: it was him or me," or "I had to kill him: it was him or my child"?

That can be a hard question, and there may well be cases in which we are not sure whether it is appropriate to say "It was him or me" or not. But plainly, the answer is not "whenever I could benefit from hurting him" or even "whenever I could save my own life or that of a loved one by sacrificing him." If a madman has got hold of a gun and is threatening to shoot your child, many of us think you

---

[25] Regan, *The Case for Animal Rights*, pp. 324–5.

[26] Singer, "Ten Years of Animal Liberation," *New York Review of Books*, January 17, 1985.

[27] Regan and Singer, "The Dog in the Lifeboat: An Exchange." *New York Review of Books*, April 25, 1985.

may shoot the madman if it is the only way to save your child. But you may not steal the madman's organs even if your child will die without a transplant.

12.5.3 We are often told that the use of animals in research saves lives. There is a problem with this claim. I am not talking now about the empirical question whether we have really learned as much from animal testing as its proponents claim. The problem is with the concept of "saving lives."

I feel tempted to put my point like this: "Lives are never saved. They are only extended. Everybody dies in the end." That is not exactly the right way to put, so here is another way. The concept of "saving a life" can only appropriately be applied in certain circumstances, and specific features of the context matter. (1) Suppose you are about to be hit by a truck, and I pull you out of the way. I have saved your life. (2) Now suppose you are about to be hit by a truck, I pull you out of the way, but you stubbornly return to the place you were standing, and get hit by the truck after all. I have tried to save your life and failed. (3) Now suppose you are about to get hit by the truck, I pull you out of the way, and four years later you return to the exact same spot, where you get hit by a truck. Should we say that I tried to save your life and failed? Why not? The only obvious difference between (2) and (3) is the time interval between my action and your return to the spot.

When the appropriateness of applying a concept depends on specific features of the context in this way, there is something wrong about incorporating it into a statistical or general claim. When we are thinking statistically, I now feel like saying, if research on animals really does any good, it is by extending human lives, not by saving them. Now you might reply that that is not quite right either, because if the research produces a drug that cures a fatal disease, it enables doctors to "save lives" in the more contextual sense. Suppose someone comes down with the disease, and a doctor whips out the drug, and the person who would have died right then instead lives enough more years for our concept of "saving a life" to apply. Then the drug has enabled the doctor to save a life. But that response only applies when the medicine or treatment discovered is addressed to directly fatal conditions. It does not seem to apply to research aimed to finding medicines or treatments for conditions that wear you down eventually, like high blood pressure or type 2 diabetes.

I am not saying this to denigrate the achievements of science. I think life itself is the good, so of course I think that extending life is nothing to sneeze at. But I still think it gives the question a different feel. Don't ask yourself whether you think it is worth it to torture and kill animals to save human lives. Ask yourself whether you think it is worth it to torture and kill animals to extend human lives.

How many animals are you willing to consign to lives of torment and premature death so that you can live for three more years or ten more years?

12.5.4 A commonly accepted philosophical justification for animal medical research is a utilitarian one. The justification invokes the picture of a certain kind of case. Experiments are done on a finite and hopefully small number of animals, and maybe they do suffer quite badly or die early as a result of the experiments, but the result is a medication which cures many human beings of some horrible or fatal human disease. It looks like a straight case of cost/benefit analysis, though all the costs are to the animals and all the benefits to people.

The case of the discovery of insulin, which is *always* invoked in these arguments, seems to fit the picture pretty well. Before insulin was discovered in the early twentieth century, a diagnosis of type 1 diabetes was basically a death sentence. People with diabetes could be kept alive for a little while on diets with almost no sugar, but not for long, so the disease was essentially fatal. Experiments on dogs in the 1880s in Germany had showed that if a dog's pancreas was removed, the dog would get diabetes. So people knew there was a connection of some kind there.

Following up on this insight, two researchers working together in 1921, Banting and Best, experimented on more dogs. They started with ten, removing the pancreases from some so that they would get diabetes, and performing a procedure on others that was designed to enable the researchers to extract secretions from their pancreases that the researchers believed would cure diabetes. By the end of two weeks, seven of the ten dogs were dead, most of them accidently from the surgery or an infection resulting from it. But in very short order—within months—they were able to lower the blood sugar of a dog they had given diabetes with a chemical extracted from another dog's pancreas. There was more work to be done, and more experiments involving dogs, cats, and cattle, but not two years after they started, in 1922, they tried the extracted substance—insulin—on 14-year-old Leonard Thompson, who was on the brink of death, and who revived, and lived to be 27. After this success, insulin extracted from the pancreases of cows and pigs was used to keep people with diabetes alive until we learned how to produce the substance artificially. Many people who were on the brink of death were suddenly saved.[28]

This story has all the elements of the standard justification: the number of animals used, at least for the immediate initial discovery of the drug, appears to be finite and even small. Since we eventually learned to produce insulin

---

[28] See Michael Bliss, *The Discovery of Insulin*.

artificially, the killing of animals to get the product did not have to go on indefinitely. The disease was no longer fatal, and the drug made it possible for diabetics to lead pretty normal lives. So it looks as if you can count the cost—including the cost in animal suffering—and by a utilitarian calculation it was "worth it" in terms of almost indefinite gains to human beings.

Above all, both because diabetes was fatal, and because there was a boy immediately involved who would have died otherwise, we can apply our contextual notion of "saving lives" in this case. The drug enables doctors to "save lives" in the contextual sense, and as for Leonard Thompson—he lived another thirteen years, and thirteen years is enough of an interval to allow for the concept of "saving lives" to apply to his case too.

But the features of this case that make it seem to fit both the standard justification and the concept of saving lives are quite special. The connection between hurting and killing animals and "saving" human lives is not usually this immediate and direct.

12.5.5 Earlier I promised to say something about the question whether the number of animals who suffer matters. I think that the standard utilitarian justification is a little misleading on this point, which is why I have been saying that the insulin story "seems" to fit the standard justification. I began my account of the insulin story by noticing that experiments on dogs in Germany in the 1880s established the connection between the pancreas and diabetes. How many dogs were involved in those experiments? What were the prior experiments that prompted the scientists to engage in them? Did those prior experiments involve animals? The trouble here is that medical knowledge is cumulative, and human beings have been dissecting animals to learn about the body at least since ancient Roman times. So we cannot really ever say, "Only 100 animals suffered to produce this result." Maybe there is a fact of the matter about the number of animals who have suffered or died prematurely to produce the result, but nobody knows what it is.

Of course, there is nothing we can do about the animals who have already suffered or died prematurely. That suffering and death is, in economists' jargon, a kind of moral sunk cost. Economists tell us that it is irrational to factor sunk costs into a decision. So presumably they would tell us that the *practical* question at any given moment isn't "How many animals will have suffered to produce this drug?" which we cannot really answer. Rather, in a practical case, we should ask, "Given what we already know, do we have good reason to believe we could find out how to cure this disease by making only a certain number of more animals suffer, few enough that the benefits of the results to people outweigh the harms to the animals?"

But it is worth noting that even if we decide to permit animal experimentation only in cases in which we could honestly say "Yes" to this question, the suffering of animals in laboratories will go on indefinitely, so long as human beings continue to exist, unless we cure all human diseases, or eventually decide we have *nothing* more to learn by experimenting on animals. Experimenting on animals is a practice, not a one-time event, and if we license the practice, the amount of animal suffering we are licensing is always indefinitely large. The only way to avoid licensing an indefinite amount of future animal suffering at our hands, even if we limit ourselves to using animals in experiments only in what a utilitarian would regard as a justified case, is to find alternatives to animal testing.

Since we've got to return to the high ground if this is ever going to end, why not go there now? The air is better up there.

12.6 Companion Animals

12.6.1 Finally there is the question of keeping companion animals. I think many people are astonished to learn that anyone thinks this is wrong, and with some reason. When we live with pets, they share with us in many of the benefits of civilized life: shelter from the elements, medical care, longevity, freedom from predators, regular food. These are benefits from the point of view of any animal. In 10.2.3, we looked at PETA's arguments against pet-keeping. It is true, as PETA points out, that animals living in human homes aren't allowed to urinate when-ever and wherever they please, and they get yelled at for making too much noise. But those are prices we *all* pay for the benefits of civilized life.

But are these benefits sufficient to make living in human homes worth it to the animals? The lives of animals in their natural state consist mainly of getting food for themselves and their offspring, and reproducing. According to my own theory that life is itself the good, that means that that's basically what their good is too: carrying on the activities of feeding themselves and reproducing successfully, in their own characteristic ways, under conditions that make that possible. But these central activities are exactly the activities of which the best owners deprive their pets, by getting them spayed and neutered and supplying them with food. In 10.4.5, I suggested that because of this, the creationist proposal that we get rid of predation in the wild would involve our radically changing the very nature of animals and the substance of their lives. But that's exactly what we do with pets. So there's a real question here. If we are going to keep animals as pets in ways that are consistent with their good, we have to provide them with conditions and activities that at least are effective substitutes for the conditions and activities that are naturally good for them. Can we do that?

12.6.2 Another important set of moral issues arises from the fact that, at least as things stand, pets are completely dependent on, and completely in the power of, the particular person or family who owns them. When you die, your adult human companions will (hopefully) mourn you, but they will also learn to live without you. If you have dependent children, and it is not already obvious who should take over their care, the courts and social services will figure something out. Since pets must be dependent on someone, if you have made no arrangements for this eventuality, your pets are just out of luck. As things stand, they go into shelters, where they may eventually be killed if no one wants them. A similar point holds about animals who develop behavior problems that make it difficult or impossible for people to live with them (8.8.2).[29] When people develop problems that make them intolerable to live with or impossible to take care of, we have (ideally anyway) social institutions designed to take over their care. We do not just kill them to get them out of the way. But there are few institutions designed to take over the care of animals in this position, and they are not among our public institutions. Even if the best option is to kill the animal with behavior problems, it is not clear that the decision should be left to the individual owner. As things stand, people can ask veterinarians to kill their pets for quite frivolous reasons. No individual should have this kind of power over another.[30] A society that decides it is going to allow pet-keeping should have some kind of social infra-structure dedicated to ensuring their welfare, some sort of social services for pets. This is not as crazy as it might sound. It is the kind of work that private animal welfare organizations already do in cooperation with law enforcement, but expanded and made into a more formal institution of our society.

12.6.3 All of this shows that the institution of pet-keeping is morally more problematic than you might think at first glance. It is not easy to meet the needs of animals and to provide them with the protections they should have. But does it show that pet-keeping should be abolished once the supply of excess animals has run out?

PETA's list of objections to pet-keeping contains two different kinds of complaints: those based on the idea that it is impossible to control abuses of

---

[29] This is brought out forcefully by Hilary Bok in "Keeping Pets," in Beauchamp and Frey (eds), *The Oxford Handbook of Animal Ethics.*

[30] A particularly poignant example of both of these problems is given by parrots, whose life spans are comparable to ours and so who may outlive their owners. They bond strongly with their owners and suffer seriously from the loss. People also can find them difficult to live with: as highly intelligent and highly social animals, they need a lot of attention, and they can be very aggressive. Many of them, after losing their owners, being given up by owners who find them hard to deal with, or being caged for long periods of time without much social interaction, end up mentally ill in sanctuaries. See Mira Tweti, *Of Parrots and People: The Sometimes Funny, Always Fascinating, and Often Catastrophic Collision of Two Intelligent Species.*

the practice, and those based on the idea that even with the best will in the world, we cannot give animals a good life as our companions. Here, I am (rather optimistically) going to set aside the objections based on the inevitability of abuse, and (also optimistically) going to assume that the needed social services could be provided. I want to focus on the claim that it is impossible for us to give animals a good life.

A clear case can be made that we have kept animals as pets that we should not have, and kept them under conditions that we should not. We cannot possibly give wild animals a good life in our homes, especially large ones. We cannot give good lives to animals who cannot be tamed, because they cannot be cured of an aggressiveness that is dangerous to us, and we are dangerous to them as a result. We cannot give many social animals a good life unless we have room for enough of them. Human life does not fit well with the lives of birds, who need to fly, cannot be house-broken, and often live in large flocks in their natural state. Life alone in a little cage is not good enough for birds and for some rodents. Some of these problems could be solved simply by paying more attention to the conditions in which we keep them, of course. Maybe it would be okay to keep birds if you have room for an aviary, or a room devoted to their use where a number of them could fly around.

12.6.4 What about our old friends, the dogs and the cats? Should we abolish them, and thus, at least in the case of dogs, perhaps condemn their species to extinction? I have to admit that I find the idea that we cannot give dogs a good life implausible. Dogs evolved to live with people and their dependence on us is not an unnatural condition that is contrary to their good. They give every appearance of liking to live with people. Some of them even seem to like to work. Although it would have to be done with great care, they are omnivores like we are and could proceed with us into a vegetarian or even a vegan future.

The fate of house cats in that ideal future is iffier. One reason is that there is genuine controversy over whether an indoor life is good enough for them, while letting them live outdoors can be dangerous to them in the city, and has a deleterious effect on wildlife. Another problem is that they are obligate carnivores. Unless it turns out to be possible to artificially concoct an adequate diet for them, we would have to supply them with meat ourselves, or let them hunt, again with deleterious effects on wildlife. Perhaps artificially cultured meat will eventually solve this problem.

12.6.5 Okay, I admit it, this is personal with me. The five fellow creatures to whom this book is dedicated are the cats I've lived with over the last thirty-five years. With them I have lived a morally compromised life, feeding them the meat that I will not eat myself. They have given me as much joy and sorrow as the people I love. I think *that thinking about them has made me a better philosopher (although no doubt some readers of this book will not be very impressed with that claim). After all, if you want to know what it means to be human, a good question to start with is, "Compared to what?" I could tell myself, like the abolitionists do, that it's okay for me to have them, because someone else brought these cats into existence, and now that they are here, they need people like me to take care of them. But I am not going to tell myself that, because if I told myself that (and I'm not speaking for anyone else here), I'd be in bad faith.*

12.6.6 I think the abolitionist proposal to eliminate pet-keeping is about as feasible as the creationist proposal to eliminate predation. Given how easy it is to breed cats and dogs, a law against people having pets would suffer the same fate as Prohibition. You only have to imagine how much money the last legal kittens would fetch at auction in order to see my point. But I do not think this is just because people are selfish.

Human beings stand in a very different relation to the other animals than the members of the other species stand in with respect to each other and to us. We are much more interested in them than they are in us. It is both funny and pathetic that human beings spend money on scientific studies designed to determine whether our cats and dogs really love us or not. Some of our earliest artworks are paintings of animals. Okay, the animals our ancestors painted were the kinds of animals that they hunted, so maybe this means no more than the fact that my cats love to watch the birds outside the window. But to me those paintings speak of a certain empathy, or at least an empathetic curiosity, as if the artists were trying to figure out what it feels like to move through the world with a body with that kind of heft and shape. Some scientists think our partnership with dogs may go back much further than we used to believe.[31] Many of us obviously crave the company of animals. Forming a relationship with an animal adds a whole new dimension to life. I always want to laugh when people say that we cannot know what animals feel because they cannot talk. One of the things that you learn from getting to know an animal is how little of what you know about *people* is based on what they say, as opposed to expressions, posture, gait, direction of gaze.

I do not know how to argue for this, but I think human beings, or many of us anyway, *need* the company of other animals. In Chapter 3, I laid out what I believe to be the important differences between human beings and animals.

---

[31] In *The Invaders*, Pat Shipman presents evidence that suggests a much earlier date for the domestication of dogs and argues for the possibility that it explains how modern humans were able to drive the Neanderthals to extinction.

I think that those differences, and what they have done to us, have created this need. Some thinkers, like Aristotle, think human beings are merely a rank above the other animals on the great chain of being. Others, like Freud and Nietzsche, think that we are a kind of deviation, something a little unnatural and twisted, that in becoming moral animals we also become animals that are doomed to inflict torments on ourselves. We certainly do inflict torments on ourselves, and the company of animals may bring us some relief. They love us for the asking, without judgment, and give us a rest from the demands of normative identity (3.3.3).

But need apart, I also think forming relationships with animals, and working with them, and trying to figure out how they think and what they feel, is part of the specific good of being human. The company of animals is good-for us. So I hope the people of the future—the children and elderly especially—will be able to have pets. There is something about the naked, unfiltered joy that animals take in little things—a food treat, an uninhibited romp, a patch of sunlight, a belly rub from a friendly human—that reawakens our sense of the all-important thing that we share with them: the sheer joy and terror of conscious existence.

Bibliography

Amis, Martin. *London Fields*. New York: Random House, 1991.

Anderson, Elizabeth. "Animal Rights and the Values of Nonhuman Life." In Cass Sunstein and Martha Nussbaum (eds), *Animal Rights: Current Debates and New Directions*. New York: Oxford University Press, 2004.

Aristotle. *The Complete Works of Aristotle: The Revised Oxford Translation*. Edited by Jonathan Barnes. Princeton, NJ: Princeton University Press, 1984. References to Aristotle's works are given by the standard Bekker page, column, and line numbers. *Note: In quoting from this edition I have deviated from the translation in two ways: I translate "ergon" as "function" rather than "work," and "arete" as virtue rather than "excellence."*

Augustine of Hippo. *Confessions*. Translated by R. S. Pine-Coffin. Harmondsworth: Penguin Books, 1961.

Balcombe, Jonathan. *What a Fish Knows: The Inner Lives of Our Underwater Cousins*. New York: Scientific American Books, 2016.

Beauchamp, Tom L. and Frey, R. G. (eds). *The Oxford Handbook of Animal Ethics*. Oxford: Oxford University Press, 2011.

Bekoff, Marc and Pierce, Jessica. *Wild Justice: The Moral Lives of Animals*. Chicago: University of Chicago Press, 2009.

Bentham, Jeremy. *A Fragment on Government; with An Introduction to the Principles of Morals and Legislation*. Edited by Wilfrid Harrison. Oxford: Basil Blackwell, 1948 [1776; 1789].

Blackburn, Simon. *Ruling Passions: A Theory of Practical Reason*. Oxford: Clarendon Press, 1998.

Bland, Alastair. "Is the Livestock Industry Destroying the Planet?" *Smithsonian Magazine* website, August 1, 2012. <http://www.smithsonianmag.com/travel/is-the-livestock-industry-destroying-the-planet-11308007/>.

Bliss, Michael. *The Discovery of Insulin*. Chicago: University of Chicago Press, 1982, 2007.

Bok, Hilary. "Keeping Pets." In A. Beauchamp and A. Frey (eds), *The Oxford Handbook of Animal Ethics*. Oxford: Oxford University Press, 2011.

Braithwaite, Victoria. *Do Fish Feel Pain?* Oxford: Oxford University Press, 2010.

Callicott, J. Baird. "Animal Liberation: A Triangular Affair." *Environmental Ethics* 2, 1980, 311–38.

Callicott, J. Baird. *In Defense of the Land Ethic: Essays in Environmental Philosophy*. Albany, NY: SUNY Press, 1989.

Callicott, J. Baird. "Intrinsic Value in Nature: A Metaethical Analysis." *Electronic Journal of Analytic Philosophy* 3, Spring 1995.

Capra, Frank, Director. *It's a Wonderful Life*. RKO, 1946.

Capra, Frank, Director. *You Can't Take It With You*. Columbia Pictures, 1938.

Chamovich, Daniel. *What a Plant Knows: A Field Guide to the Senses*. New York: Scientific American Books, 2012.

Coetzee, J. M. *The Lives of Animals*. Princeton, NJ: Princeton University Press, 1999.

Coppinger, Raymond and Coppinger, Lorna. *What Is a Dog?* Chicago: University of Chicago Press, 2016.

Darwall, Stephen. *The Second-Person Standpoint: Morality, Respect, and Accountability*. Cambridge, MA: Harvard University Press, 2006.

Darwall, Stephen. "Two Kinds of Respect." *Ethics* 88(1), October, 1977, 36–49.

Darwin, Charles. *The Descent of Man, and Selection in Relation to Sex*. Princeton, NJ: Princeton University Press, 1981.

De Chant, Tim. "Per Square Mile: If the World's Population Lived Like ... " as of August 8, 2012. <https://persquaremile.com/2012/08/08/if-the-worlds-population-lived-like/>.

De Waal, Frans. *Primates and Philosophers: How Morality Evolved*. Lectures by Frans De Waal with commentary by Robert Wright, Christine M. Korsgaard, Philip Kitcher, and Peter Singer. Edited by Stephen Macedo and Josiah Ober. Princeton, NJ: Princeton University Press, 2006.

Donaldson, Sue and Kymlicka, Will. *Zoopolis: A Political Theory of Animal Rights*. Oxford: Oxford University Press, 2011.

Eisner, Thomas. *For Love of Insects*. Cambridge, MA: Harvard University Press, 2003.

Eisner, Thomas and Camazine, Scott. "Spider Leg Autotomy Induced by Prey Venom Injection: An Adaptive Response to 'Pain'?" *Proceedings of the National Academy of Sciences USA*, 80, June 1983, 3382–5.

Eliot, George. *Middlemarch*. London: Penguin, 1994.

Epicurus. "Letter to Menoeceus." In *The Art of Happiness*. New York: Penguin Books, 2012.

Evans, Edmund P. *The Criminal Prosecution and Capital Punishment of Animals*. Clark, NJ: Lawbook Exchange. Reprint edition, 2009.

Foot, Philippa. "The Problem of Abortion and the Doctrine of Double Effect." In *Virtues and Vices and Other Essays in Moral Philosophy*. Oxford: Basil Blackwell, 1978.

Francione, Gary. "Animals: Property or Persons?" In Cass Sunstein and Martha Nussbaum (eds), *Animal Rights: Current Debates and New Directions*. Oxford: Oxford University Press, 2004.

Frankel, Rebecca. *War Dogs: Tales of Canine Heroism, History, and Love*. New York: St. Martin's Press, 2015.

Frankfurt, Harry G. *The Importance of What We Care About*. Cambridge: Cambridge University Press, 1998.

Frankfurt, Harry G. *Taking Ourselves Seriously and Getting It Right*. Stanford, CA: Stanford University Press, 2006.

Godfrey-Smith, Peter. *Philosophy of Biology*. Princeton, NJ: Princeton University Press, 2014.

Grahek, Nikola. *Feeling Pain and Being in Pain*. Cambridge, MA: Massachusetts Institute of Technology, 2001.

Grandin, Temple and Johnson, Catherine. *Animals Make Us Human: Creating the Best Life for Animals*. Boston, MA: Houghton Mifflin Harcourt, 2009.

Gruen, Lori (ed.). *Critical Terms for Animal Studies*. Chicago: University of Chicago Press, forthcoming.

Gruen, Lori. *Ethics and Animals: An Introduction*. Cambridge: Cambridge University Press, 2011.

Hobbes, Thomas. *Leviathan*. Edited by Edwin Curley. Indianapolis, IN: Hackett Publishing Company, 1994.

HouseDustMite.com. "Dust Mite Questions and Answers: How to Get Rid of Dust Mites." <http://housedustmite.com/questions/>.

Hume, David. *Dialogues Concerning Natural Religion*. Edited by Richard H. Popkin. Indianapolis, IN: Hackett Publishing Company, 1982.

Hume, David. *Enquiry Concerning the Principles of Morals*. In *David Hume: Enquiries Concerning Human Understanding and Concerning the Principles of Morals*. Third edition edited by L.A. Selby-Bigge and revised by P. H. Nidditch. Oxford: Oxford University Press, 1975.

Hume, David. *A Treatise of Human Nature*. Second edition edited by L. A. Selby-Bigge and revised by P. H. Nidditch. Oxford: Clarendon Press, 1978.

Hursthouse, Rosalind. "Virtue Ethics and the Treatment of Animals." In Tom Beauchamp and R. G. Frey (eds), *The Oxford Handbook of Animal Ethics*. Oxford: Oxford University Press, 2011.

Hyner, Christopher. "A Leading Cause of Everything: One Industry that Is Destroying Our Planet and Our Ability to Thrive on It." *Georgetown Environmental Law Review*, October 23, 2015.

Jamieson, Dale. *Morality's Progress: Essays on Humans, Other Animals, and the Rest of Nature*. Oxford: Oxford University Press, 2002.

Kant, Immanuel. "An Answer to the Question: What Is Enlightenment?" Translated by H. B. Nisbett in *Kant's Political Writings*, second edition. Edited by Hans Reiss. Cambridge, Cambridge University Press, 1991.

Kant, Immanuel. *Anthropology from a Pragmatic Point of View*. Translated by Mary Gregor. The Hague: Martinus Nijhoff, 1974.

Kant, Immanuel. "Conjectures on the Beginning of Human History." Translated by H. B. Nisbett in *Kant's Political Writings*, second edition. Edited by Hans Reiss. Cambridge: Cambridge University Press, 1991.

Kant, Immanuel. *Critique of Judgment*. Translated by Werner S. Pluhar. Indianapolis, IN: Hackett Publishing Company, 1987.

Kant, Immanuel. *Critique of Practical Reason*. Translated by Mary Gregor. Cambridge: Cambridge University Press, 1997.

Kant, Immanuel. *Critique of Pure Reason*. Translated by Norman Kemp Smith. New York: Macmillan, St Martin's Press, 1965.

Kant, Immanuel. *Groundwork of the Metaphysics of Morals*. Translated by Mary Gregor. Cambridge: Cambridge University Press, 1998.

Kant, Immanuel. "Idea for a Universal History with a Cosmopolitan Purpose," in *Kant's Political Writings*. Translated by H. B. Nisbett in *Kant's Political Writings*, second edition. Edited by Hans Reiss. Cambridge, Cambridge University Press, 1991.

Kant, Immanuel. *Lectures on Ethics*. Translated by Peter Heath. Cambridge: Cambridge University Press, 1997.

Kant, Immanuel. *The Metaphysics of Morals*. Translated by Mary Gregor. Cambridge: Cambridge University Press, 1996.

Kant, Immanuel. "On a Supposed Right to Lie from Philanthropy." Translated by Mary Gregor. In *Kant: Practical Philosophy*. Cambridge: Cambridge University Press, 1996.

Kant, Immanuel. *Perpetual Peace: A Philosophical Sketch*. Translated by H. B. Nisbett in *Kant's Political Writings*, second edition. Edited by Hans Reiss. Cambridge, Cambridge University Press, 1991.

Kant, Immanuel. *Practical Philosophy*. Cambridge: Cambridge University Press, 1996.

Kant, Immanuel. *Religion within the Boundaries of Mere Reason*. Translated by George di Giovanni. Cambridge: Cambridge University Press, 1998.

Korsgaard, Christine M. "Animal Selves and the Good." In *Oxford Studies in Normative Ethics*. Edited by Mark Timmons. Oxford: Oxford University Press, forthcoming.

Korsgaard, Christine M. "Aristotle and Kant on the Source of Value." In *Creating the Kingdom of Ends*. Cambridge: Cambridge University Press, 1996.

Korsgaard, Christine M. "The Claims of Animals and the Needs of Strangers: Two Cases of Imperfect Right," forthcoming in the *Journal of Practical Ethics*.

Korsgaard, Christine M. *The Constitution of Agency: Essays on Practical Reason and Moral Psychology*. Oxford: Oxford University Press, 2008.

Korsgaard, Christine M. *Creating the Kingdom of Ends*. New York: Cambridge University Press, 1996.

Korsgaard, Christine M. "Fellow Creatures: Kantian Ethics and Our Duties to Animals." In *The Tanner Lectures on Human Values*. Edited by Grethe B. Peterson, Volume 25/26. Salt Lake City, UT: University of Utah Press, 2004; and on the Tanner Lecture website at <www.TannerLectures.utah.edu>.

Korsgaard, Christine M. "Getting Animals in View." *Point* 6, Winter 2013. Also available at: <http://www.thepointmag.com/2012/metaphysics/getting-animals-view>.

Korsgaard, Christine M. "Interacting with Animals." In *The Oxford Handbook on Ethics and Animals*, edited by Tom Beauchamp and R. G. Frey. Oxford: Oxford University Press, 2011.

Korsgaard, Christine M. "Just Like All the Other Animals of the Earth." *Harvard Divinity Bulletin* 36(3), Autumn 2008.

Korsgaard, Christine M. "A Kantian Case for Animal Rights." In *Animal Law: Tier und Recht*. Edited by Julia Haenni, Margot Michel, and Daniela Kuehne. Zurich: Dike Verlag, in cooperation with Berliner Wissenschafts-Verlag, 2012. Reprinted in *The Ethics of Killing Animals*. Edited by Tatjana Višak and Robert Garner. Oxford: Oxford University Press, 2015.

Korsgaard, Christine M. "Kantian Ethics, Animals, and the Law." *Oxford Journal of Legal Studies* 33(4), Winter 2013, 1–20.

Korsgaard, Christine M. "Kant's Formula of Universal Law." In *Creating the Kingdom of Ends*. Cambridge: Cambridge University Press, 1996.

Korsgaard, Christine M. "Morality and the Distinctiveness of Human Action." In De Waal, *Primates and Philosophers: How Morality Evolved*. Edited by Stephen Macedo and Josiah Ober. Princeton, NJ: Princeton University Press, 2006.

Korsgaard, Christine M. "On Having a Good." *Philosophy*, Journal of the Royal Institute of Philosophy 89(3), July 2014, 405–29. Reprinted in *Philosophers of Our Times*. Edited by Ted Honderich. Oxford: Oxford University Press, 2015.

Korsgaard, Christine M. "Rationality." In Lori Gruen (ed.), *Critical Terms for Animal Studies*. Chicago: University of Chicago Press, 2018.

Korsgaard, Christine M. Reflections on the Evolution of Morality. *Amherst Lecture in Philosophy* 5, 2010, 1–29. <http://www.amherstlecture.org/korsgaard2010/>.

Korsgaard, Christine M. "The Relational Nature of the Good." In *Oxford Studies in Metaethics*. Edited by Russ Shafer-Landau. Oxford: Oxford University Press, 2013.

Korsgaard, Christine M. "The Right to Lie: Kant on Dealing with Evil." In *Creating the Kingdom of Ends*. Cambridge: Cambridge University Press, 1996.

Korsgaard, Christine M. *Self-Constitution: Agency, Identity, and Integrity*. Oxford: Oxford University Press, 2009.

Korsgaard, Christine M. *The Sources of Normativity*. Cambridge: Cambridge University Press, 1996.

Korsgaard, Christine M. "Two Distinctions in Goodness." In *Creating the Kingdom of Ends*. Cambridge: Cambridge University Press, 1996.

Korsgaard, Christine M. "Valuing Our Humanity." In Oliver Sensen and Richard Dean (eds), Respect for Persons. Oxford: Oxford University Press, forthcoming.

Leopold, Aldo. "The Land Ethic." In *A Sand County Almanac*. New York: Oxford University Press, 1949.

Loss, Scott R., Will, Tom, and Marra, Peter P. "The Impact of Free-Ranging Domestic Cats on the Wildlife of the United States." *Nature Communications* 4, Article Number 1396, 2013. <http://www.nature.com/articles/ncomms2380>.

Maldarelli, Claire. "Although Purebred Dogs Can Be Best in Show, Are They Worst in Health?" *Scientific American* website, February 21, 2014. <https://www.scientificamerican.com/article/although-purebred-dogs-can-be-best-in-show-are-they-worst-in-health/>.

Mancuso, Stefano and Viola, Alessandra. *Brilliant Green: The Surprising History and Science of Plant Intelligence*. Washington, DC: Island Press, 2015.

Marx, Karl. *Economic and Philosophic Manuscripts of 1844*. Translated by Martin Milligan. New York: Prometheus Books, 1988.

McMahan, Jeff. "The Comparative Badness for Animals of Suffering and Death." In Tatjana Višak and Robert Garner (eds), *The Ethics of Killing Animals*. Oxford: Oxford University Press, 2016.

McMahan, Jeff. *The Ethics of Killing: Problems at the Margins of Life*. Oxford: Oxford University Press, 2002.

McMahan, Jeff. "The Meat Eaters." Editorial, *New York Times*, September 19, 2010.

Mill, John Stuart. *Utilitarianism*. Edited by George Sher. Indianapolis, IN: Hackett Publishing Company, 1979.

Moore, G. E. "The Conception of Intrinsic Value." In *Philosophical Studies*. London: Kegan Paul, 1922.

Moore, G. E. *Principia Ethica*. Cambridge: Cambridge University Press, 1903.

Morelle, Rebecca. "Cats Killing Billions of Animals in the US. *BBC News: Science and Environment*, January 29, 2013. <http://www.bbc.com/news/science-environment-21236690>.

Nagel, Thomas. *The Possibility of Altruism*. Oxford: Clarendon Press, 1970.

Nagel, Thomas. *The View from Nowhere*. New York: Oxford University Press, 1986.

Nature (WGBH television program) website. "Dogs that Changed the World: Selective Breeding Problems." September 16, 2010. <http://www.pbs.org/wnet/nature/dogs-that-changed-the-world-selective-breeding-problems/1281/>.

Nozick, Robert. *Anarchy, State, and Utopia*. New York: Basic Books, 1974.

Nussbaum, Martha C. *Frontiers of Justice: Disability, Nationality, Species Membership*. Cambridge, MA: Harvard University Press, 2006.

Palmer, Clare. *Animal Ethics in Context*. New York: Columbia University Press, 2010.

Palmer, Clare. "The Moral Relevance of the Distinction between Domesticated and Wild Animals." In Tom Beauchamp and R. G. Frey (eds), *The Oxford Handbook of Animal Ethics*. Oxford: Oxford University Press, 2011.

Parfit, Derek. *Reasons and Persons*. Oxford: Clarendon Press, 1984.

People for the Ethical Treatment of Animals (PETA) website. "Factory Farming: Misery for Animals." <https://www.peta.org/issues/animals-used-for-food/factory-farming/>.

PETA website. "Animal Rights Uncompromised: 'Pets.'" <http://www.peta.org/about-peta/why-peta/pets/>.

PETA website. "Doing What's Best for Our Companion Animals." <https://www.peta.org/issues/companion-animal-issues/companion-animals-factsheets/whats-best-companion-animals/>.

Plato. *Plato: Complete Works*. Edited by John M. Cooper. Indianapolis, IN: Hackett Publishing Company, 1997. References to Plato's works are given using the standard Stephanus numbers inserted into the margins of most editions and translations of Plato's works.

Powell, Russell. "On the Nature of Species and the Moral Relevance of Their Extinction." In Tom Beauchamp and R. G. Frey (eds), *The Oxford Handbook of Animal Ethics*. Oxford: Oxford University Press, 2011.

Rawls, John. *A Theory of Justice*. Cambridge, MA: Harvard University Press, 1971; second edition, 1999.

Regan, Tom. *The Case for Animal Rights*. Berkeley, CA: University of California Press, 1983; second edition, 2004.

Regan, Tom. "The Case for Animal Rights." In *In Defense of Animals*. Edited by Peter Singer. Oxford: Basil Blackwell, 1985.

Regan, Tom and Singer, Peter. "The Dog in the Lifeboat: An Exchange." *New York Review of Books*. April 25, 1985.

Rolston, Holmes, III. *Environmental Ethics: Duties to and Values in the Natural World*. Philadelphia, PA: Temple University Press, 1988.

Sagan, Carl. *Cosmos: A Personal Voyage*. 1990 television series.

Scanlon, T. M. *What We Owe to Each Other*. Cambridge, MA: Harvard University Press, 1998.

Schapiro, Tamar. "What Is a Child?" *Ethics* 109, July 1999, 715–38.

Scheffler, Samuel. *Death and the Afterlife*. New York: Oxford University Press, 2013.

Sensen, Oliver and Dean, Richard (eds). *Respect for Persons*. Oxford: Oxford University Press, forthcoming.

Shipman, Pat. *The Invaders: How Humans and Their Dogs Drove Neanderthals to Extinction*. Cambridge, MA: Harvard University Press, 2015.

Singer, Peter. *Animal Liberation*. New York: Harper Collins, 2009 [1975].

Singer, Peter (ed.). *In Defense of Animals*. Oxford: Basil Blackwell, 1985.

Singer, Peter. "Killing Humans and Killing Animals." *Inquiry: An Interdisciplinary Journal of Philosophy* 22, 2008, 145–56.

Singer, Peter. *Practical Ethics*, third edition. Cambridge: Cambridge University Press, 2011.

Singer, Peter. "Ten Years of Animal Liberation." *New York Review of Books*, January 17, 1985.

Smith, Adam. *The Theory of Moral Sentiments*. Edited by D. D. Raphael and A. L. Macfie. Indianapolis, IN: Liberty Classics, 1982.

Sunstein, Cass R. and Nussbaum, Martha C. (eds). *Animal Rights: Current Debates and New Directions*. New York: Oxford University Press, 2004.

Thompson, Michael. *Life and Action: Elementary Structures of Practice and Practical Thought*. Cambridge, MA: Harvard University Press, 2008.

Thompson, Michael. "What Is It to Wrong Someone? A Puzzle about Justice." In *Reason and Value: Themes from the Moral Philosophy of Joseph Raz*. Edited by Michael Smith, Philip Pettit, R. Jay Wallace, and Samuel Scheffler. Oxford: Oxford University Press, 2004.

Thomson, Judith Jarvis. "A Defense of Abortion." *Philosophy and Public Affairs* 1(1), Autumn, 1971, 47–66.

Thomson, Judith Jarvis. "The Trolley Problem." *Yale Law Journal* 94(6), May 1985, 1409.

Tweti, Mira. *Of Parrots and People: The Sometimes Funny, Always Fascinating, and Often Catastrophic Collision of Two Intelligent Species*. New York: Penguin Books, 2009.

Višak, Tatjana and Garner, Robert (eds). *The Ethics of Killing Animals*. Oxford: Oxford University Press, 2016.

Wikipedia. Scarlett (cat). https://en.wikipedia.org/wiki/Scarlett_(cat)). Last edited July 19, 2017.

Williams, Bernard. *Ethics and the Limits of Philosophy*. Cambridge, MA: Harvard University Press, 1985.

Williams, Bernard. "The Human Prejudice." In *Philosophy as a Humanistic Discipline*. Princeton, NJ: Princeton University Press, 2009.

Williams, Bernard. *Problems of the Self*. Cambridge: Cambridge University Press, 1973.

Wilson, E. O. *Half-Earth: Our Planet's Fight for Life*. New York: W. W. Norton & Co., 2016.

Wolfson, David J. and Sullivan, Mariann. "Foxes in the Henhouse: Animals, Agribusiness, and the Law: A Modern American Fable." In *Animal Rights: Current Debates and New Directions*. Edited by Cass Sunstein and Martha Nussbaum. New York: Oxford University Press, 2004.

Index